Our Land of Israel

Written and Illustrated by
Chaya M. Burstein

UAHC Press
New York, New York

To my favorite Israelis—

Sam, Ben, Yoav, Noa,

and the other kids of Har Halutz

Library of Congress Cataloging-in-Publication Data
Burstein, Chaya M.
Our land of Israel/written and illustrated by Chaya M. Burstein.
p. cm.
ISBN 0-8074-0527-2
1. Israel—Juvenile literature. 2. Jewish religious education—
Textbooks for children. [1. Israel.] I. Title.
DS102.95.B88 1994
956.94—dc20 93-47096
CIP
AC

This book is printed on acid-free paper

Designed by Levavi & Levavi
Manufactured in China
10 9 8

Feldman Library

The Feldman Library Fund was created in 1974 through a gift from the Milton and Sally Feldman Foundation. The Feldman Library Fund, which provides for the publication by the UAHC of selected outstanding Jewish books and texts, memorializes Sally Feldman, who in her lifetime devoted herself to Jewish youth and Jewish learning. Herself an orphan and brought up in an orphanage, she dedicated her efforts to helping Jewish young people get the educational opportunities she had not enjoyed.

In loving memory of my beloved wife Sally
"She was my life, and she is gone;
She was my riches, and I am a pauper."

"Many daughters have done valiantly,
but thou excellest them all."

Milton E. Feldman

Acknowledgments

Warm thanks to the many people who have helped me think through this project. To the individuals featured in each chapter for sharing their experiences with me and for lending their bright personalities to the text; to Rabbis Bernard M. Zlotowitz, Ammiel Hirsch, and Naamah Kelman for reading the final draft of the book and to Steven Burnstein, Robin L. Eisenberg, Connie R. Reiter, Rabbi Eric Yoffie, Gail Teicher Fellus, Aron Hirt-Manheimer, Robert E. Tornberg, Dr. Zena W. Sulkes, Rabbi Jonathan A. Stein, Rabbi Daniel B. Syme, and Rabbi Gerald M. Kane for reading sample chapters; to Central Zionist Archives and to photographers Ed, Dov, and Arieh for sharing their photos with me; to thoughtful editor David P. Kasakove; to Kathy Parnass and Annette Abramson, copy editors who polished the text and checked facts; to photo editors Judith Goldman and Lori Stahl-Van Brackle for searching out apt images; and to Meryl Levavi for designing the book. Special thanks go to Stuart Benick and Seymour Rossel for guiding the book to final publication.

Photo Credits

Aron, Bill: p. 141
Bender, Jacob: pp. 20, 21, 41, 53, 86, 115, 118, 119, 125
Courtesy of Burstein, Chaya: pp. 43, 44, 48, 49, 55, 57, 58, 60, 65, 69, 76, 78, 85, 91, 94, 96, 98, 104, 105, 109, 115, 118, 126
Burstein, Dina: p. 137
Central Zionist Archives: pp. 15, 17, 21, 26, 69, 108, 128
Cooper, Debbi: p. 22
Eilav, Elana: p. 103
Courtesy of Geffen Records: p. 47
Goldman, Judith: p. 117
Gubitch, Dov: pp. 1, 3, 13, 27, 38, 41, 53, 77, 83, 86, 125
Grand, Dr. Samuel: p. 87
Hadassah: pp. 7, 8, 140
Hebrew Union College-Jewish Institute of Religion, Jerusalem: p. 97
Israel Action Center: p. 56
Israel Army: p. 120
Israel Government Press Office: pp. 61, 74, 75
Israel Information Services: pp. 77, 130
Israel Ministry of Tourism: pp. 3, 27, 32, 33, 34, 35, 36, 46, 49, 55, 59, 73, 83, 85, 87, 91, 93, 95, 97, 98, 103, 110, 137, 139
Israel Office of Information: p. 21
Israel Philatelic Agency in America: p. 149
Israel Press and Photo Agency: pp. 14, 127
The Jerusalem Post: p. 9
Jewish Theological Seminary of America, NY: p. 67
New Israel Fund: p. 121
Perlmutter, David: p. 127
Radovan, Zev: p. 107
Silver, Martin: p. 138
Stark, Arieh: p. 19
Toben, Ed: pp. 35, 55, 68, 77, 106, 107, 110, 118, 139
UAHC Press Archives: pp. 13, 18, 47, 65, 74, 129, 145, 147, 148
United Jewish Appeal Press Service: p. 22
United States Committee on Sports for Israel: pp. 45, 70
White House Photos: p. 131
Wide World Photos, Inc.: pp. 132, 133
Zionist Archives and Library: p. 109
Zlotowitz, Rabbi Bernard: pp. 92, 93

Contents

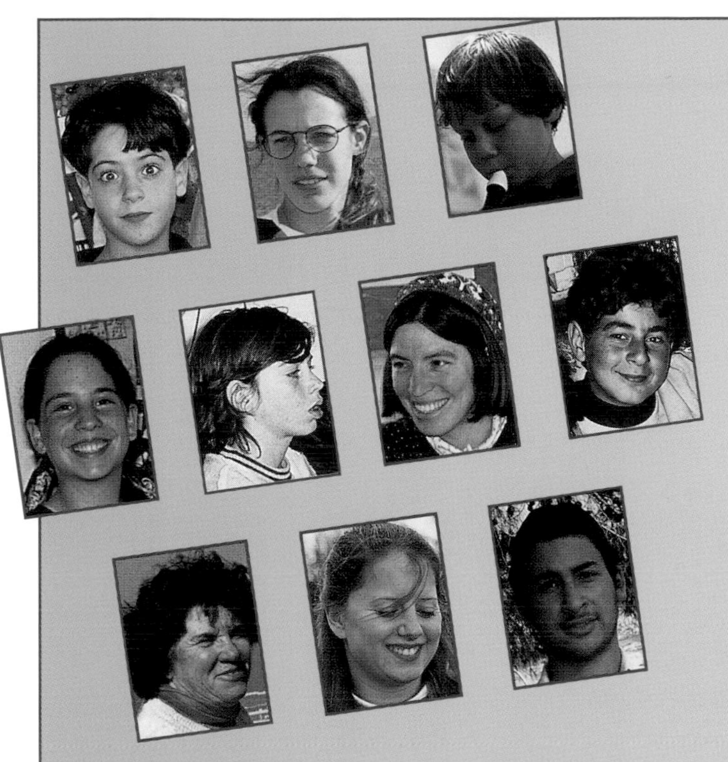

INTRODUCTION
Connections

Over five million people live in Israel. In this book you'll meet some of them. Among them are Sam, a twelve-year-old who lives on a mountaintop, Meirav, a scout who explores Israel's hills and valleys, Mohammed, an Arab boy from Jerusalem, and Uriah, a student.

To all of them, Israel is home. They belong there. But we American Jews live across a vast ocean. Do we have a connection to Israel?

We do! Here's the connection: We share a long history with Israeli Jews. It started many years ago when our people lived in the biblical Land of Israel. Today we share Jewish holidays and the Hebrew language. And we share the Jewish religion, with its strong ties to the Land of Israel.

One of our books of Jewish law, the Talmud, says that each Jew is responsible for every other Jew. That means that Jews of all countries need to care about and help one another. It's easier to care about people when we know them. So read on and meet some of the people (mostly kids) of Israel. Make the connection for yourself.

ISRAEL
LEBANON
SYRIA
MEDITERRANEAN SEA
GOLAN HEIGHTS
HULA VALLEY
Akko
Haifa
Safed
Tiberias
Lake Kinneret
Hadera
SAMARIA
(WEST BANK)
Jordan River
Tel Aviv
Yafo
JUDEA
Jericho
Jerusalem
Bethlehem
Ashkelon
DEAD SEA
GAZA STRIP
Masada
Beersheba
SINAI DESERT
NEGEV
KINGDOM OF JORDAN
ARAVAH
EGYPT
North
West
East
South
Eilat
RED SEA
SAUDI ARABIA

NAAMA AND THE LONG WALK From the Land of Israel to the State of Israel

Naama is a rabbi in Jerusalem. Born in New York, she attended rabbinical school at Hebrew Union College-Jewish Institute of Religion in Israel. She is the first woman to be ordained as a rabbi in that country.

Naama says: "My roots go deep into Jewish history. My father was a rabbi. My two grandfathers, their fathers, and their grandfathers were all rabbis. They loved the Jewish people. I also feel that love. That's why I want to work as a rabbi and a teacher.

"I teach third graders in an Israeli public school. We make puppets of Bible people like Abraham and Sarah to help us understand the Torah. And we use songs and dances to learn about holidays. I work with American kids, too. They're from synagogue youth groups. We travel around Israel together. We walk in ancient towns and synagogues. And we find connections between Jews of long ago and Jews of today.

"American Jews are a very important part of our people. They bring new ideas to Judaism. For example, the ordination of women rabbis first started in America.

"I could've been a rabbi in the United States, but I wanted to live in Israel. Here I feel as if I'm walking in the footsteps of our prophets and kings. King David walked here on Mount Zion, near my house. He looked out at these hills. They helped inspire him to write the poems that we say in our morning prayers.

"Our people have lived in many lands since the time of the prophets and kings. Now we're back in Israel, as we were in the days of the Bible. Israel is where the Jewish action is today!"

In the Land of Israel

Long before there was a State of Israel, there was a Land of Israel. Our ancestors lived there. Many of us are the great-great-great-grandchildren of the ancient Israelites. Come and meet a few of your ancestors. Then follow the long road that connects the ancient Land of Israel to the modern State of Israel.

Jews have always been great walkers. They started walking way back during the time of Abraham, the first Jew. Abraham and Sarah, his wife, were living in Haran when God called to him. God told Abraham to take his family to the land of Canaan, where they would become a great people. So Abraham and Sarah led their donkeys, camels, sheep, goats, children, and servants on the long walk to Canaan. When they arrived in Canaan, God made a promise to Abraham, saying, "I will give this land to your offspring."

Many years later there was a period when no rain fell in Canaan. The wells dried out, and the green plants dried up. Abraham and Sarah's great-grandchildren had to leave. They walked south to Egypt, where there was food and water. They settled down and began to do well—so well that the family

grew and grew until its members numbered in the thousands. The Egyptians became worried. These people are getting too strong, they thought. They set the Israelites to work as slaves. But God remembered the promise to Abraham. God spoke to Moses, saying, "I have seen the sufferings of my people in Egypt. I have come down to rescue them and to take them to a land flowing with milk and honey." With the help of God, Moses forced the pharaoh of Egypt to let the Israelites go free. Then Moses led the frightened people into the desert.

The Israelites were about to begin another long walk back to Canaan, a journey that would take forty years. Moses first led them to Mount Sinai, where he gave them an important gift from God—the Torah and the Ten Commandments. It was a gift that tied the Israelites to God and to one another. From that day until the present, Jews have studied Torah and tried to live according to its laws.

When the Israelites finally returned to the land that God had promised them, they lived in tribes. They called their land Israel. Years later the Israelites decided to form a kingdom. Solomon, the third king of Israel, built a Temple of marble and gold. It was a house for God in Israel's capital, Jerusalem. Happy and proud Israelites streamed to Jerusalem, bringing gifts to God's Temple.

But Israel was a small country. It wasn't very strong. Enemy armies attacked it again and again. They stole, burned houses, and took people away to be slaves. In 586 B.C.E. the Babylonians, a powerful neighbor, destroyed the Temple in Jerusalem. They forced many of the Israelites to leave their land and go to live in Babylonia.

That might have been the end of Israel. But its people would not give up. Many of them left Babylonia as soon as they could, walked back to Israel, and built the Second Temple. An even stronger enemy, the Romans, then attacked the country. They burned the Second Temple to the ground in the year 70 C.E. Again the Jews were forced to leave their land. This time it took them much longer to return.

A People without a Land

For nearly two thousand years the Jews had no land of their own. Often they went from country to country, looking for a place to settle down. In some lands life was good for a while. In other lands the Jews were robbed and beaten. They had to obey special, harsh laws because they were Jews. Stubbornly the Jews held on to their religion. Wherever they lived, they studied Torah. The Torah was like a homeland that the Jews carried with them wherever they went. They built schools and synagogues, learned Hebrew, and celebrated Jewish holidays. And each day they turned toward Jerusalem when they prayed.

The Land of Israel had become a sad, stony place, with no trees or green fields. The Romans had changed its name to Palestine. During these years Jews continued to live in the land. Jewish communities existed in Jerusalem, Safed, and Tiberias. But most Jews

Time Line of the Long Walk

Abraham	Moses	First Temple Built	Exile to Babylonia	Second Temple Built	Romans Drive Out Jews	Exile from the Land of Israel
1800 B.C.E	1350 B.C.E	950 B.C.E	586 B.C.E.	515 B.C.E.	70 C.E.	70 C.E. -1948 C.E.

remained in faraway lands. They were waiting for the Messiah, God's messenger, to come and take them back to Israel. They were sure that the Messiah would come someday. After all, God had promised that the Jewish people would return to their land.

The Zionists Go Home

A little more than one hundred years ago, some young Jews grew impatient. "Our people have waited long enough!" they said. "We're going home now!" They called themselves Zionists because they wanted to return to Zion. Zion was another name for the Land of Israel. A writer named Theodor Herzl became a Zionist. He led the movement to create a Jewish country. Many people were excited about the idea and became Zionists. Tens of thousands of Jews moved to Palestine. These pioneers started farms, built new villages, and founded Hebrew-language schools. Finally, after World War I, many countries asked Great Britain to help the Jews build a homeland in Palestine. It seemed as though the Jews' long walk was about to end at last.

But there was a problem with the idea of building a Jewish homeland in Palestine. Many Jews lived there, but Arab people lived there, too. Some of those Arabs were against the idea of a Jewish homeland. Some of the Arabs attacked the Jews and set fire to their fields and forests. When more Jews wanted to come settle in Palestine, the Arabs demanded that Great Britain keep them out.

Caught in the Holocaust

World War II began in 1939. Things got much worse for the Jews of Europe. The

Young immigrants aboard the Eliahu Golomb *entering the port of Haifa, May 19, 1946.*

Nazis in Germany began to put Jews into concentration camps. Some Jews escaped across the borders. But many countries would not let Jews in. Only their fellow Jews in Palestine wanted them. Some Palestinian Jews managed to enter Europe and lead European Jews on secret paths to escape the Nazis. "Let our brothers and sisters in!" cried the Jews of Palestine. But Great Britain refused. Most of the Jews of Europe were trapped.

By the end of World War II, six million Jews had been killed by the Nazis. Some of your relatives may have died. This killing of Jews was like a blazing fire that devoured one out of every three Jews in the world. It was called a holocaust—a great fire.

The Jewish people learned a lesson from the Holocaust. They learned that they had

Say It in Hebrew

English	Hebrew	How to Say the Hebrew
Land of Israel	אֶרֶץ יִשְׂרָאֵל	*E*-retz Yis-ra-*el*
State of Israel	מְדִינַת יִשְׂרָאֵל	Me-di-*nat* Yis-ra-*el*
Bible	תַּנַ״ךְ	Ta-*nach*
Holocaust	שׁוֹאָה	Sho-*ah*

to have their own country in which every Jew would have the right to live. And they learned that they had to be strong and always ready to fight. They could never allow themselves to be helpless again.

The End of the Long Road

Fighting between Palestinian Jews and Arabs increased after World War II. The United Nations tried to make peace. It divided Palestine into two parts. One part would be Jewish and the other would be Arab. The Jews agreed, but the Arabs did not. The fighting continued. At last the British gave up. They decided that they couldn't govern the country anymore. They couldn't stop the fighting. Slowly they began to pull out of the country. By 1948 the British had left. The Arabs of Palestine and the armies of five Arab countries

Hours after Prime Minister David Ben-Gurion read Israel's Declaration of Independence on May 14, 1948, Arab nations declared war on the Jewish state.

If you can't come to town, please telephone 4607

Lighting, Heating, Cooking, Refrigeration

CARL MARX

3 PRINCESS MARY AVE., JERUSALEM

THE PALESTINE POST

JERUSALEM
SUNDAY, MAY 16, 1948

PRICE: 25 MILS
VOL. XXIII. No. 6714

THE PALESTINE POST
THE SUBSCRIPTION DEPARTMENT has returned to The Palestine Post offices, Hassolel Street, Jerusalem, Tel. 4233.

STATE OF ISRAEL IS BORN

The first independent Jewish State in 19 centuries was born in Tel Aviv as the British Mandate over Palestine came to an end at midnight on Friday, and it was immediately subjected to the test of fire. As "Medinat Yisrael" (State of Israel) was proclaimed, the battle for Jerusalem raged, with most of the city falling to the Jews. At the same time, President Truman announced that the United States would accord recognition to the new State. A few hours later, Palestine was invaded by Moslem armies from the south, east and north, and Tel Aviv was raided from the air. On Friday the United Nations Special Assembly adjourned after adopting a resolution to appoint a mediator but without taking any action on the Partition Resolution of November 29.

Yesterday the battle for the Jerusalem-Tel Aviv road was still under way, and two Arab villages were taken. In the north, Acre town was captured, and the Jewish Army consolidated its positions in Western Galilee.

Most Crowded Hours in Palestine's History

Between Thursday night and this morning Palestine went through what by all standards must be among the most crowded hours in its history.

For the Jewish population there was the anguish over the fate of the few hundred Haganah men and women in the Kfar Etzion bloc of settlements near Hebron. Their surrender to a fully equipped superior foreign force desperately in need of a victory was a foregone conclusion. What could not be known, with no communications since Thursday morning, was whether and to what extent the Red Cross and the Truce Consuls would secure civilized conditions for prisoners and wounded, and proper respect for the dead. Doubts on some of these anxious questions have now been resolved.

On Friday afternoon, from Tel Aviv, came the expected announcement of the Jewish State,

...der of Jewish settlements in North-Eastern Galilee.

The Security Council met yes-

JEWS TAKE OVER SECURITY ZONES

The Battle for Jerusalem, which began when the British forces withdrew on Friday morning, continued all day Friday and yesterday. The crackle of small-arms fire and explosions of mortar shells were still being heard in the early hours of this morning as the battle entered its third day.

Repeated efforts on Friday evening and again on Saturday by the U.N. Truce Commission to bring about a "cease fire" were brought to nought when the Arab representatives failed to agree within the specified time limit.

On Friday morning, Jewish

Egyptian Air Force Spitfires Bomb Tel Aviv; One Shot Down

Kol Israel, the Tel Aviv broadcasting station, reported at 2 o'clock yesterday afternoon that Tel Aviv had been bombed three times in the previous evening and morning, and that one plane had been shot down and its Egyptian pilot taken prisoner.

In the first raid, four planes attacked from a height of 300 feet. Two dropped bombs, while the others strafed the city. Little damage was caused. In the second attack two hours later, the airport to the north of the city was bombed, and an Air France plane parked there was damaged. The third raid was launched shortly before midday, but the

A country-wide blackout was ordered by Air Raid Precaution Headquarters in Tel Aviv.

Mr. David Ben Gurion, the Prime Minister, broadcast from Tel Aviv to the people of America yesterday morning. As he spoke, Egyptian planes were bombing the city.

In the north, the settlements of Ein Gev and Shaar Hagolan and Dan had been shelled, but no further details were available.

Kalandia airfield was taken by the Jewish army on Friday morning, shortly after the High Commissioner had left there by plane for Haifa.

U.S. RECOGNIZES JEWISH STATE

WASHINGTON, Saturday. —Ten minutes after the termination of the British Mandate on Friday, the White House released a formal statement by President Truman that the U.S. Government intended to recognize the Provisional Jewish Government as the *de facto* authority representing the Jewish State.

The U.S. is also considering lifting the arms embargo but it is not known whether to Palestine only or the entire Middle East, and the establishment of diplomatic relations with the Jewish Provisional Government.

Proclamation by Head Of Government

The creation of "Medinat Yisrael", the State of Israel, was proclaimed at midnight on Friday by Mr. David Ben Gurion, until then Chairman of the Jewish Agency Executive and now head of the State's Provisional Council of Government.

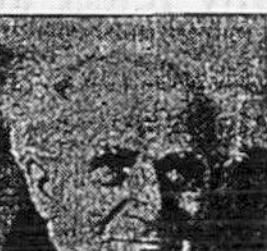

The first act of the Council of Government, as announced by its head, was to abolish all legislation of the 1939 White Paper of the late Mandatory Power, particularly the Ordinances and Orders relating to immigration and land transfer.

In the declaration of independence, Mr. Ben Gurion called on the Arabs of Palestine to restore peace, assuring them full civic rights and full representation in all governmental organs of the State.

The front page of The Palestine Post, *May 16, 1948.*

waited. Their guns, tanks, and planes were ready to destroy the new Jewish state.

What should the Jews have done? Should they have declared the birth of a new state? Or should they have waited? If you had been in charge in 1948, what would you have done?

The decision was quickly made. On the same day that the British left, May 14, 1948, David Ben-Gurion, the new prime minister, announced, "The State of Israel is born!" The Jewish people could finally stop walking. They had reached the end of the road that connects the ancient Land of Israel with the modern State of Israel.

And on the very next day the War of Independence began.

SUMMING UP

Many years ago the Jewish people lived in the Land of Israel. They built a Temple for God in their capital city, Jerusalem. Most of the time they tried to follow the laws of the Torah. But their enemies destroyed the Temple. Those enemies drove the Jews from their land. After that the Jews lived in many countries. But they did not forget their religion and the Land of Israel. Finally, about one hundred years ago, Jews began to return to Israel.

Not only Jews but many Arab people also lived in the land. These people called the land Palestine. Some of the Arabs tried to stop the Jews from returning. But more and more Jews wanted to live in Palestine. When the Nazis came to power in Germany, they began killing Jews. Most of the Jews of Europe could not escape. The doors of Palestine and other countries were closed to them. After a long war the Nazis were defeated. But it was too late to save most of the Jews of Europe. During the war years the Nazis had killed six million Jews.

In 1948 the nations of the world voted that the Jews should have their own country. Quickly the Jews announced the birth of the State of Israel. But the next day five Arab countries went to war against the new state.

ACTIVITIES

WHAT HAPPENED FIRST, SECOND, AND THIRD?

Put the following events in order by writing **1**, **2**, or **3** next to each group.

_____The State of Israel was born.

_____The Torah was given to the Jewish people at Mount Sinai.

_____Theodor Herzl worked to form a Jewish state.

_____One-third of the Jews in the world were killed in the Holocaust.

_____The War of Independence began.

_____The Second Temple was destroyed.

_____Abraham and Sarah went to Canaan.

_____The United Nations divided Palestine into two states.

_____The Israelites were slaves in Egypt.

_____Many Israelites were forced to go to Babylonia to live.

_____King Solomon built the Temple.

_____The Jews walked from country to country.

_____Moses led the Jews out of Egypt.

_____Great Britain was asked to help create a Jewish state in Palestine.

_____Babylonia destroyed the First Temple.

THE DREAMER

Almost one hundred years ago Theodor Herzl started the World Zionist Organization. Its members worked to build a Jewish state. Herzl said, "If you will it, it is no dream."

What do you think Herzl meant? ______________________________

____

____

The Long Walk

Tell the story again by filling in the blanks below.

1. A _ _ _ _ _ _ and _ A _ _ _ led their family to Canaan.
2. The Jews received the T _ _ _ _ at Mount Sinai.
3. The armies of B _ _ _ _ _ N _ _ and R _ _ _ destroyed the First and Second Temples.
4. Although they lived in faraway lands, the Jews did not forget the T _ _ _ _ and the city of _ E _ _ _ _ _ _ M.
5. They hoped that the M _ _ _ _ _ H would come and take them back to the L _ _ _ of _ S _ _ _ L.
6. The Z _ _ _ _ _ _ S couldn't wait. "We're going home now!" they said.
7. T _ _ _ _ _ R H _ _ _ _ asked people to help create a Jewish state.
8. Many A _ _ _ _ were against the idea of the creation of a Jewish state in Palestine.
9. The tragedy of the H _ _ _ _ _ _ _ T taught Jews that they had to be strong and have their own C _ _ _ T _ Y.
10. D _ _ _ _ B _ _ -G _ _ _ _ N was Israel's first prime minister. "The S _ _ _ _ of Israel is born!" he announced.

Jews have gone from country to country for two thousand years. Even in the last one hundred years Jews have moved around a lot. Do a survey. Ask three grown-ups about the birthplaces of their parents, grandparents, and great-grandparents. Write the results on the chart below. An example is given.

	Person's Name	Birthplace	Parent's Name	Birthplace	Grandparent's Name	Birthplace	Great-Grand-parent's Name	Birthplace
1.	Beth Burstein	Bethpage, New York	Chaya Burstein	Brooklyn, New York	Rivka Malamud	Savran, Russia	Chaya Zeile	Uman, Russia
2.								
3.								

Hatikvah

Hatikvah means "The Hope." It is the title of a Hebrew song that was written about one hundred years ago. The song expresses people's strong feelings. It became the anthem of Jews all over the world. Here are some of the words of "Hatikvah" translated into English.

As long as there is a Jewish spirit in our hearts,
Our eyes will turn to the East—to Zion.
Our hope is not lost, our two thousand-year-old hope,
To be a free nation in our own land, in Zion and Jerusalem.

Some questions about "Hatikvah":

What is a "Jewish spirit"?____

____

What is "Zion"?____

TAMAR REMEMBERS
How Israel Was Born and How It Grew

Tamar was born in Haifa, Israel. She was thirteen in November 1947, the year in which the United Nations voted to divide Palestine into two parts.

Tamar says: "I'll never forget the night when the United Nations voted. It was going to decide if we Jews could have our own country. My mother, father, big sister, and I sat around the radio. We were listening to the voting. It got late and I fell asleep. Suddenly my father was shaking me. 'Tamar, Tamar, we won! We have a state!' he was yelling. It was four or five o'clock in the morning. We all ran outside. The streets were full of people. Honking cars pushed through the crowds. People were sitting on the hoods of cars, waving flags and cheering. Others were dancing in circles, singing, kissing one another, and yelling, 'We have a state. Hurrah!'

"After that the shooting between the Jews and Arabs started. My sister Tova, who was nineteen, was in the middle of it. She carried messages and orders for the army, called the Haganah. Sometimes she wouldn't come home for several days. I was proud of her and of my father, too. He fought with the Haganah in Haifa. But my mother was very frightened. In one night her hair turned white.

"Arabs shot down on us from the roofs. They didn't want us to have a country of our own. They wanted all of Palestine for themselves. Cars and buses were attacked. Sometimes fires were set that made all of Haifa black with smoke. But I wasn't afraid. It was exciting. We Jews were all fighting together.

"Now I am a mother and a grandmother. My children act and feel as if there has always been a State of Israel. But I remember how it used to be. I remember how happy we were when the State of Israel was formed, even though we knew we'd have to fight to keep it."

The War of Independence

"We'll drive the Jews into the sea!" cried the leaders of the Arab countries that bordered Israel.

It was May 15, 1948. The State of Israel had just been formed. Five enemy armies marched across its borders. Guns hammered at its villages and farms. Bombs dropped onto Israel's largest city, Tel Aviv. The Jews were outnumbered. For each Jew in Israel, there were forty Arabs in the neighboring countries. The Jews knew that they couldn't run away. They had to stay and fight.

At first the Israelis had few weapons. They attached sheets of metal to the sides of taxis, buses, and trucks to stop the enemies' bullets. Then they drove these vehicles into battle. The Israelis made bombs out of pop bottles filled with gasoline. Little Piper Cub airplanes dropped the bottles on the enemy. The bottles didn't do much damage, but they did make a loud noise.

Israelis battle for Jerusalem during the War of Independence. The Arab forces shelled the Jewish Quarter of the old city until it was forced to surrender. Brave Jewish soldiers successfully defended the new city of Jerusalem.

Say It in Hebrew

English	Hebrew	How to Say the Hebrew
immigrants to Israel	עוֹלִים	o-*lim*
Hebrew (language)	עִבְרִית	Iv-*rit*
independence	עַצְמָאוּת	atz-ma-*ut*
old-timers	וְתִיקִים	ve-ti-*kim*

While the fighting was going on, ships were bringing more people to the new state. Jews from all over the world were coming home to Israel. And many of the Arabs were leaving. Tamar says, "Arab buses and trucks lined up in the streets. Our Arab neighbors left their food on the table. They quickly packed some clothing, boarded the buses, and drove out of Israel."

The War of Independence was a hard fight. Thirty thousand Israelis were killed or wounded. Most of them were young men and women in their teens and twenties. Tamar's sister Tova lost three of her best friends. For eight months the war went on. By the time it was over, the country had changed. A large number of Arabs had left the country. And an equal number of Jews

A homemade tank rattles through a village on its way to the war front.

had left Arab lands and had come to live in Israel. With desperate courage the young army had defended the borders of Israel. The country was finally safe. It was ready to grow.

New Israelis

More and more Jews arrived in the next few years. They were called *olim*. That's Hebrew for "those who go to Israel" or "those who go up." Jews who move to Israel make *aliyah* (a "going up"). The streets looked as if an unending Purim costume party were going on. Each newcomer wore the colorful skirts and robes of his or her old country. Jews came from many countries—India, Morocco, Poland, Yemen, and others. New Israelis spoke languages like Kirghiz, Armenian, and Portuguese. Old-time Israelis had never heard these languages before. American Jews came, too. "This is fantastic," said a woman from New Jersey. "After two thousand years we Jews have our own land again. We're making history here! I *have* to live here!" On the streets and buses people asked one another eagerly in broken Yiddish, Hebrew, or Arabic, "Where are you from? How did you get here? *Baruch haba leartzenu!*" ("Welcome to our homeland!")

All Jews were welcome. A law called the Law of Return was passed. It said that every Jew and his or her family had the right to come and live in Israel. No Jew would ever be homeless again.

How Many Jews Lived in Palestine and Israel from 1880 to 1995?

Key	
small figure	25,000
medium figure	100,000
large figure	1,000,000

In Palestine under Turkish rule 1880	25,000
In Palestine during World War I 1917	56,000
In Palestine under British Mandate 1923	80,000
In Palestine before World War II 1939	500,000
In Israel at birth of state 1948	650,000
In Israel at time of Six Day War 1967	2,000,000
In Israel in 1995	4,500,000

(above) ***New immigrants from North Africa are unpacking their suitcases and sacks. They'll live in tents in this immigrant camp for many months.***

(right) ***This family came from India to help build the new State of Israel.***

At first many families lived in tents and tin shacks. Some people had sent their furniture to Israel in big wooden boxes. They took out the furniture and lived in the boxes. Schools were filled with children who couldn't understand Hebrew. Imagine if your class at school suddenly had twenty new kids who couldn't read, write, or speak English and had never heard of baseball, hamburgers, or modern math. Israeli teachers worked hard to teach Hebrew to grown-ups and kids. Other Israelis who were nurses, doctors, and social workers also helped.

Old-Time Israelis and New Israelis Worked Together

Tamar was a nurse in the new village of Ein Yaakov. The people of the village had come from a mountainous country called

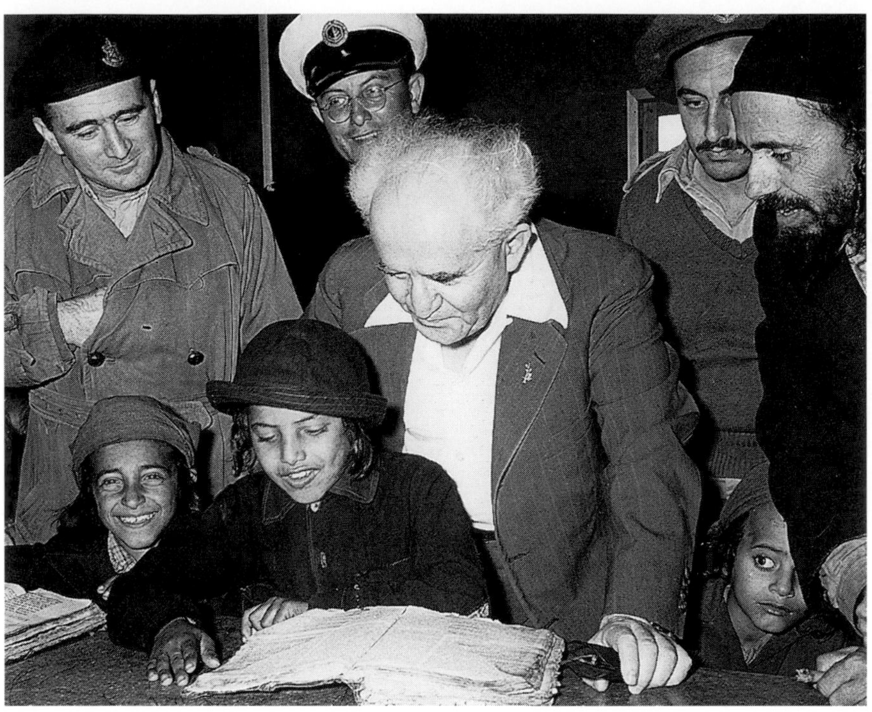

David Ben-Gurion looks on as young immigrants study Hebrew texts.

Kurdistan. They had never seen a toilet or a refrigerator. The children had not been vaccinated against smallpox or whooping cough. Many of them were sick. Tamar worked hard to teach the Kurds modern ways. Often they would laugh at her. "Such a young girl," they would say. "She doesn't even have a husband. What does she know?" But slowly they learned from her. And she learned from them. She watched the Kurdish healer gather certain grasses in the field. He chopped them up and used them as a medicine for skin diseases. The medicine worked! Tamar was surprised. Old-time Israelis and new Israelis could learn from one another, she thought.

How Israel Grew

The first prime minister of Israel was David Ben-Gurion. He was a short, roly-poly man with flyaway white hair and strong opinions. His government and the ones that followed built schools, towns, and electric plants. Giant machines growled and chewed at the mountainsides. They dug rock for cement to build more houses. A national airline called El Al began to fly. Ships of Israel's Zim Line carried oranges, cotton, and apples to Europe. They brought machinery, trucks, and other goods back to Israel.

More factories were built. Farmers learned to grow better crops with less work and water. Soon Israeli farmers were being sent to Africa and Asia to teach the farmers there more efficient ways to use their fields.

Today Israel has many modern factories. One company uses robots with dozens of arms to make plastic garden furniture. Other companies make gadgets that bounce messages off satellites. And Israel has its own satellite, which is like a giant computer floating in space.

Newcomers Become Old-Timers

Today Tamar's Ein Yaakov is a green, flower-filled village. The old people who used to laugh at Tamar all speak Hebrew now. And they know about microwave ovens, VCRs, and other modern things. Their families have cows, chickens, and groves of avocado and banana trees. And their grown grandchildren serve in the Israeli army. The people of Ein Yaakov are old-timers now.

Ein Yaakov and Israel have changed over the years. Only 650,000 Jews lived in Israel when it became a state. Today there are more than 4,000,000 Jews and more than 900,000 non-Jews. Each week new people land at Ben-Gurion Airport. They want to be Israeli citizens. They will have to work hard to find homes and jobs. "Israel is not the easiest place in which to live," says Tamar with a shrug, "but it's ours."

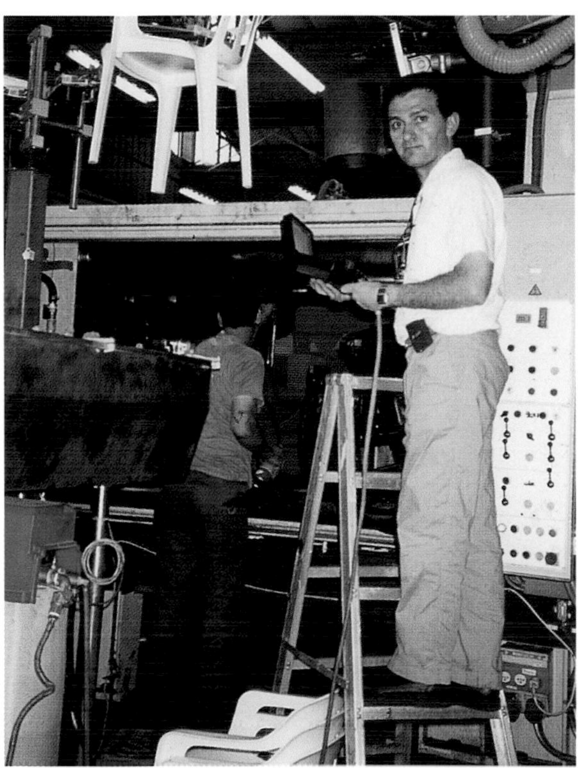

This man is checking lawn chairs that are moving along a track in a modern Israeli factory.

Two Sad Stories with Happy Endings

Some people have tried for years to make *aliyah* to Israel. The stories of the Jews of the former Soviet Union and Ethiopia are very sad. But both stories have happy endings.

For years some Soviet Jews had asked for permission to go to Israel. The Soviet government would not let them leave. The gates were closed to all Soviet citizens. But the Jews were determined. They studied Hebrew and the Jewish religion, which was against Soviet law. And they kept going to government offices, demanding to be allowed to leave. As a result, some Jews were fired from their jobs. Others were sent to prison.

All over the world, Jews protested against the Soviet government. The United States government put pressure on the Soviet Union. Finally the gates were opened a little. Soviet Jews began to leave for Israel. Today all the people living in the former Soviet Union are free to come and go. In the last few years, hundreds of thousands of Jews have moved to Israel from the lands of the former Soviet Union.

Ethiopia's Jews have a long history. King Solomon and the Queen of Sheba were their ancestors. For hundreds of years, Ethiopian Jews followed the Jewish religion and remembered Jerusalem. When they heard that there was a Jewish state again, they wanted to return to Jerusalem. But the Ethiopian government refused to let them leave. Families packed food and crept across the border secretly. They carried their babies on their backs and walked. Somehow, they thought, they would reach a port, and then, somehow,

Israel's Vegetable Soup Immigration

Morrocan Jews at a Maimuna festival.

The United States used to be called a melting pot because people from many countries immigrated there and became Americans. Israel is more like a vegetable soup. Jews poured into the land from all over the world after the state was created in 1948. But just like the peas, carrots, and noodles in a vegetable soup, these Jews didn't blend together. They became Israelis but kept many of their old customs. For example, at the end of Pesach, Moroccan Jews have a feast called Maimuna. They visit one another, have barbecues, sing and dance, and say good-bye to the holiday together. Ethiopian Jews observe a fast day called Sigd, which celebrates the giving of the Torah to the Jewish people at Mount Sinai. On Sigd, Ethiopian Jews climb to the top of a hill and recite the Ten Commandments and words of the prophets. Then they go down and have a big holiday meal.

A few of the kids whom you'll meet in this book were immigrants to Israel. But most of the boys and girls who appear in these chapters were born in Israel. They are Sabras. Many of their parents or grandparents were olim. Yotam's dad is from Holland, and Uriah's father came from Yemen. Meirav's grandparents are from the United States. Her uncle and his family came from Morocco. Tamar's parents arrived from Germany, Aviram's grandparents from Turkey, Sam's mom from Switzerland, Abigail from England. And these are just a few of Israel's immigrants.

The largest wave of immigrants came to Israel in the 1950s. More than one million people from seventy countries arrived within ten years. And they've been coming ever since. It took a while for all these people to learn to live together. Most of the Jews from Asia, Africa, and Southern Europe were Sephardim. They often spoke Arabic or Ladino (a mixture of Spanish and Hebrew). Most of the Jews from Central and Northern Europe, Canada, and the United States were Ashkenazim. Many of them spoke Yiddish (a mixture of German, Hebrew, and other languages). The foods of these two groups were new and strange to each other. Their clothing and customs were unfamiliar. Even their prayers had different melodies.

Over the years Ashkenazim and Sephardim began to understand each other better as everyone learned to speak Hebrew. Their children grew up and served together in Tzahal, the Israeli army. After Tzahal some of the Sephardic and Ashkenazic boys and girls got married. The vegetable soup began to mix and blend.

Plenty of steam still rises from the soup. There are disagreements and rivalries. It may be a long time before Ashkenazim, Sephardim, Ethiopians, and other groups blend together completely. In the meanwhile they learn from one another, argue with one another, and sample one another's foods and customs. Sigd and Maimuna are for everyone to enjoy.

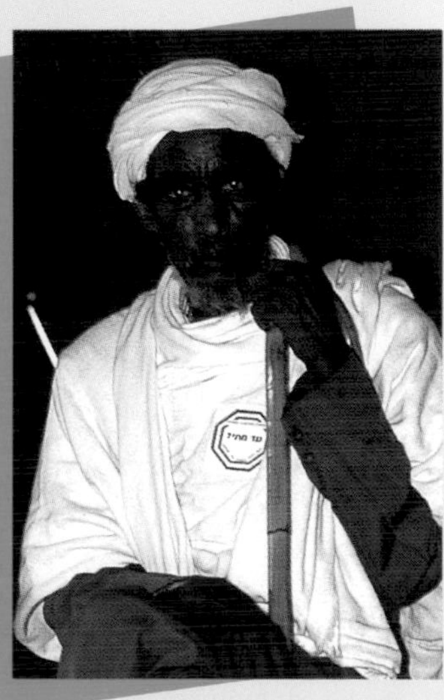

(above) *Four generations of a Bukharan family celebrate Chanukah.*

(right) *Russian* olim *arrive in Israel.*

(far right) *An elderly Ethiopian man.*

(above) *Ethiopian* olim *discuss their new life in Israel.*

(below) *A family of Russian Jews leave Russia by train. They look worried. They may be thinking, Will life in Israel be hard?*

they would reach Israel. Instead, many Jews were caught at the border. They were beaten and robbed. Some were imprisoned. Others crossed the border successfully only to die of hunger and exhaustion.

The governments of the United States and Israel pleaded with the rulers of Ethiopia. Groups of Jews worked to persuade them. At last the gates were opened. In 1991 two great airlifts, called Operation Moses and Operation Solomon, carried 14,000 Jews to Israel. El Al jets had brought them home.

The ingathering continues. No matter where Jews live, when they want to come home to Israel, they are welcome.

SUMMING UP

The Jews of Israel had to fight five Arab armies in the War of Independence. Many Palestinian Arabs ran away and many Jewish *olim* arrived during the war. Thousands of Israelis were hurt and killed.

"So many people died," Tamar says. "But it wasn't like being killed by a mugger. We were fighting together. We were fighting to keep our country."

In the years after the war ended, Israel's population grew quickly. Schools, houses, and jobs were found for the newcomers. They learned to speak Hebrew. And they, their children, and their grandchildren have become old-timers. Israeli industry and farming have also developed. Today Israel has a number of high-tech companies.

The newest *olim* are from the former Soviet Union and Ethiopia. They had to struggle and suffer before they were allowed to leave their country. The new *olim* were happy to reach Israel. But they face several problems. They must learn Hebrew and find work and a home. Then they will truly feel "at home" in Israel.

ACTIVITIES

WHAT A MIX-UP!

Here's a mixed-up story. Read it carefully. Put a **1** next to the event that happened first. Put a **2** next to the event that should come next. Then do **3**, **4**, **5**, **6**, and **7**.

_____After the war *olim* from all over the world went to Israel.

_____Many people were hurt and killed in the War of Independence.

_____They couldn't speak Hebrew.

_____Today new *olim* are arriving from Ethiopia and the former Soviet Union.

_____The Israelis had to fight against five enemy armies in the War of Independence.

_____Slowly the *olim* got homes and work.

_____They lived in tents.

CONNECTIONS

Write the number of each word or group of words from Column **A** in the box next to a connected word or group of words in Column **B**.

A		B
1. *Olim*	☐	It says that no Jew will ever be homeless again
2. Law of Return	☐	First prime minister
3. Ethiopian Jews	☐	It means "those who go to Israel"
4. Ben-Gurion	☐	The great-great-grandchildren of Solomon and Sheba
5. Haganah	☐	May 15, 1948
6. War of Independence	☐	A Jewish army
7. State of Israel	☐	*Olim*
8. Jews of Ethiopia and the former Soviet Union	☐	It was reborn after two thousand years
9. El Al	☐	To form a Jewish state and an Arab state
10. Plan of the United Nations	☐	Israel's national airline

WRITE A LETTER

Pretend that you have come to Israel during the War of Independence. Write a letter home, telling your family about three things that you have seen or are doing.

____

____

____

____

____

❄ SCRAMBLED OLIM ❄

The *olim* below are wearing the clothing of their former country. Unscramble the letters to find the name of each country.

Can You Read the Picture?

This photo was taken in 1949 when *olim* were first coming to Israel from many countries. Describe what you see. Who are the people in the picture? What are they doing?

Now read the upside-down caption. Did you guess right?

Young Israeli women are teaching *olim* from Yemen how to read and write modern Hebrew.

WHAT DO YOU THINK?

How do you feel about the State of Israel? Check the statements you agree with.

______I feel as if there has always been a Jewish state.

______I feel happy that the Jewish state was born again after two thousand years.

______I feel that we must help and try to protect Israel.

______Other ideas:____

____

Explain your answers.____

____

____

MEIRAV HIKES Up, Down, and All Around Israel

Meirav is fourteen and a half. She lives in Karmiel, in northern Israel.

Meirav says: "I love to hike. It feels good to be with my friends in the middle of nature. My favorite places are near streams. Once we climbed down a hill to the Kziv Stream. Suddenly it started raining. Everyone was slipping and sliding on the wet rocks. We helped one another climb back up the hill. We got soaked!

"Overnight hikes are fun. We sleep in sleeping bags and cook over a camp fire. Sometimes we dance around the fire, or we sing and tell jokes.

"My hiking group is part of the Society for the Protection of Nature in Israel. This is a group of people who work to solve the problem of pollution in our country. Once we went hiking with big plastic bags. We filled them with garbage that people had left on the trail, and we took the bags out of the park area. The Society for the Protection of Nature in Israel also tries to keep forest and parkland open. We want to have wild, natural places where we can go hiking and camping. Last Sukot my group explored Jerusalem. During

Chanukah vacation we're going to hike in a big crater called the Machtesh Ramon.

"At school I like biology and chemistry. After school I take ballet lessons. We do classical and jazz dancing. I also like to go walking with my friends and to play video games."

Israel's Neighborhood Is the Middle East

Meirav knows a lot about the mountains, rivers, and cities of Israel. In this chapter you'll find out about them, too. But first let's talk about Israel's neighborhood, which is called the Middle East. To get there, you fly east across the Atlantic Ocean, Europe, and the Mediterranean Sea. If you start in New York, the trip will take about ten hours. When you get to Israel, you'll have to move your watch forward. Five A.M. in Israel is ten P.M. of the night before in New York. Israeli kids are waking up for school at just about the time that New York kids are going to sleep. The kids in California are still doing their homework or watching TV at that time.

The Middle East is sunny and warm much of the year. There's no rain in the summer. But rain and even some snow do fall in the winter. Parts of the Middle East are dry desert, with lizards and scraggly trees. Because there's oil in some of those deserts, several Middle Eastern countries are very rich. Israel has little oil, but it does have some good soil for farming.

Two Borderlines

Israel has two sets of borderlines. One borderline was established after Israel's War of Independence in 1948. The second borderline was created after a war in 1967, which added much more land to the country. In this chapter you'll find out about the State of Israel that existed at the time that

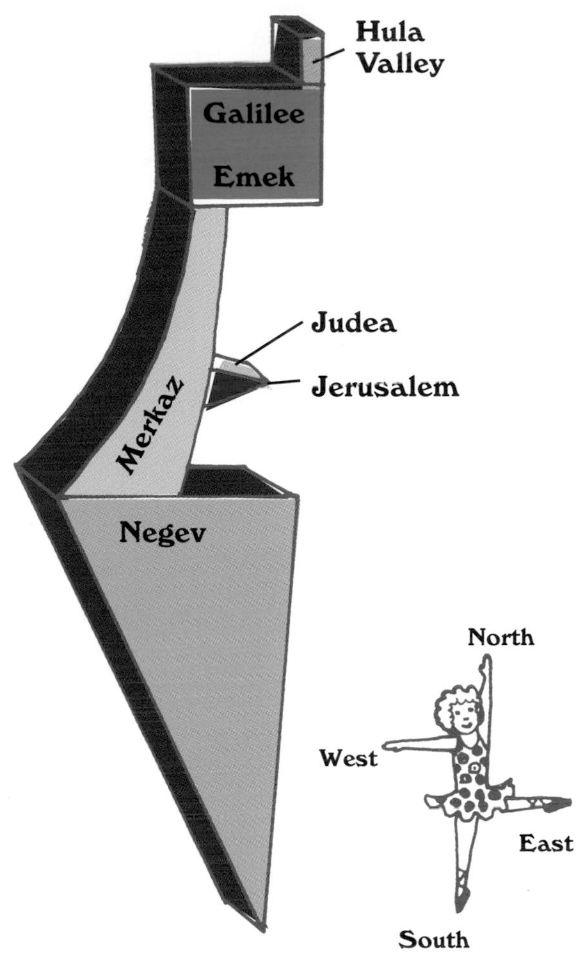

The country has long, twisting borders. The center of Israel is only nine-and-a-half miles wide. You can ride your bike straight across the country from east to west in an hour. But if your family wanted to travel from the northern tip to the southern tip, it would take longer. Allow time for a falafel sandwich and a few traffic jams. It may take you 8 hours to travel the 290-mile distance.

On the map Israel looks like a carrot that a rabbit has nibbled on in the middle. You can also imagine that the country is made of blocks. Southern Israel, the Negev, is a big block shaped like a triangle. The Merkaz, the middle of Israel and the Coastal Plain, is a long shape like a *shofar*. A small triangle pokes out of the middle block, pointing east. At the sharpest point of the triangle, you'll find Jerusalem, the capital of Israel. The northern part, the Galilee and the Emek, is a square. A small rectangle pokes up like a finger from the top of the square. It is the Hula Valley.

the 1948 borders were established. You will also learn about the countries on Israel's borders. In Chapter 12 you will read about the post-1967 lands.

The Tiny Land

Israel is about the size of New Jersey–8,000 square miles. That's small. But the country is full of surprises, like a grab bag at a birthday party. In just a short drive you can travel from snowy mountains to warm blue waters and from deserts to forests. For the full picture look at the map on pages 30–31.

The Hula Valley

Let's start with the green Hula Valley in northern Israel. The valley is filled with farms and fields and streams of cold, clear water. People like to float down the streams on rubber tubes or paddle down in kayaks. The streams feed the Jordan River, Israel's only big river. Bananas, apricots, cotton, and other crops grow in the Hula Valley.

The Galilee

Almost all of the top part of the square is filled with the Galilee mountains. Only a

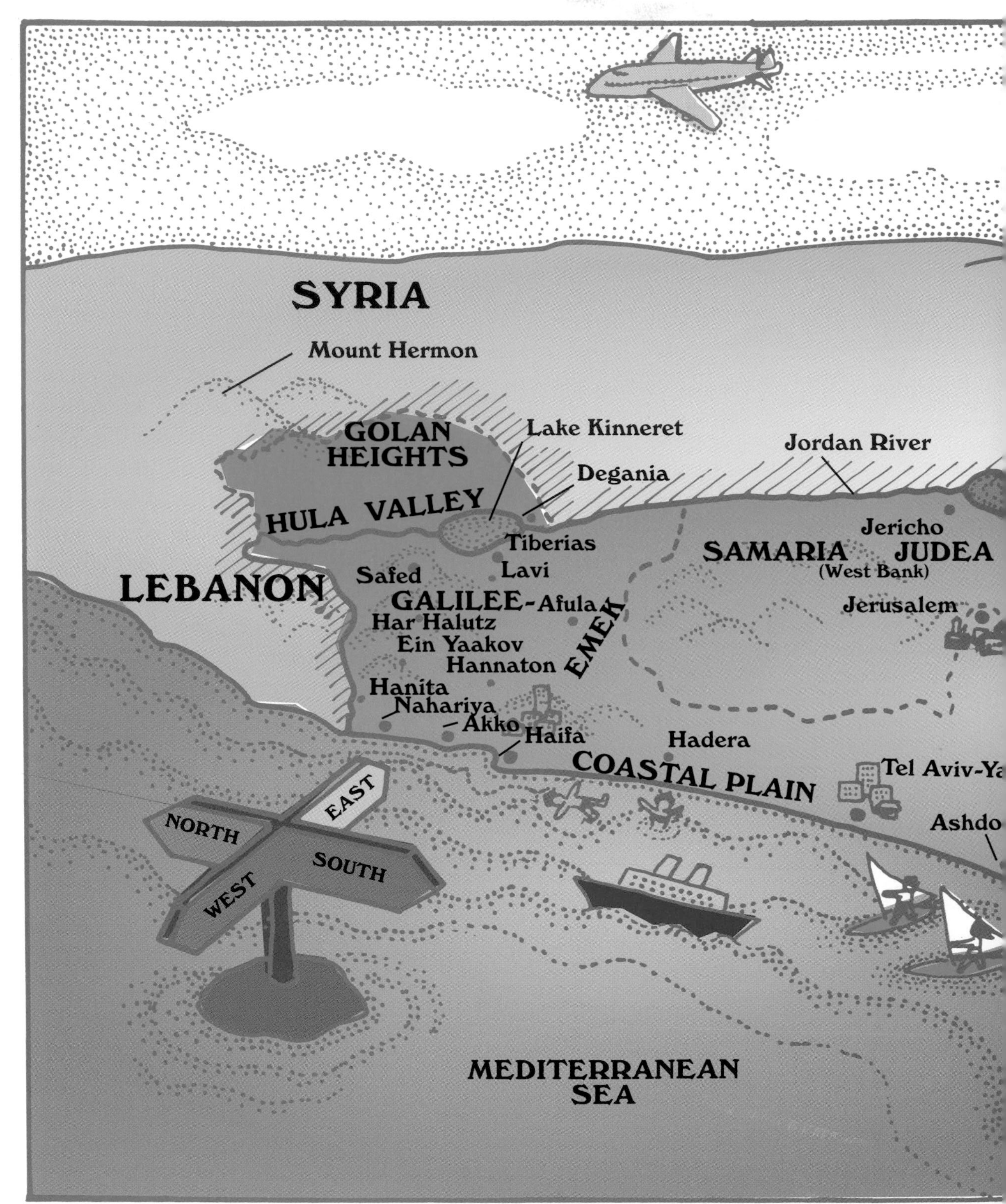
SYRIA
Mount Hermon
GOLAN HEIGHTS
Lake Kinneret
Jordan River
Degania
HULA VALLEY
Tiberias
Jericho
SAMARIA
JUDEA
(West Bank)
Lavi
LEBANON
Safed
GALILEE
Afula
Jerusalem
Har Halutz
Ein Yaakov
Hannaton
EMEK
Hanita
Nahariya
Akko
Haifa
Hadera
COASTAL PLAIN
Tel Aviv-Ya
Ashdo
NORTH
EAST
SOUTH
WEST
MEDITERRANEAN SEA

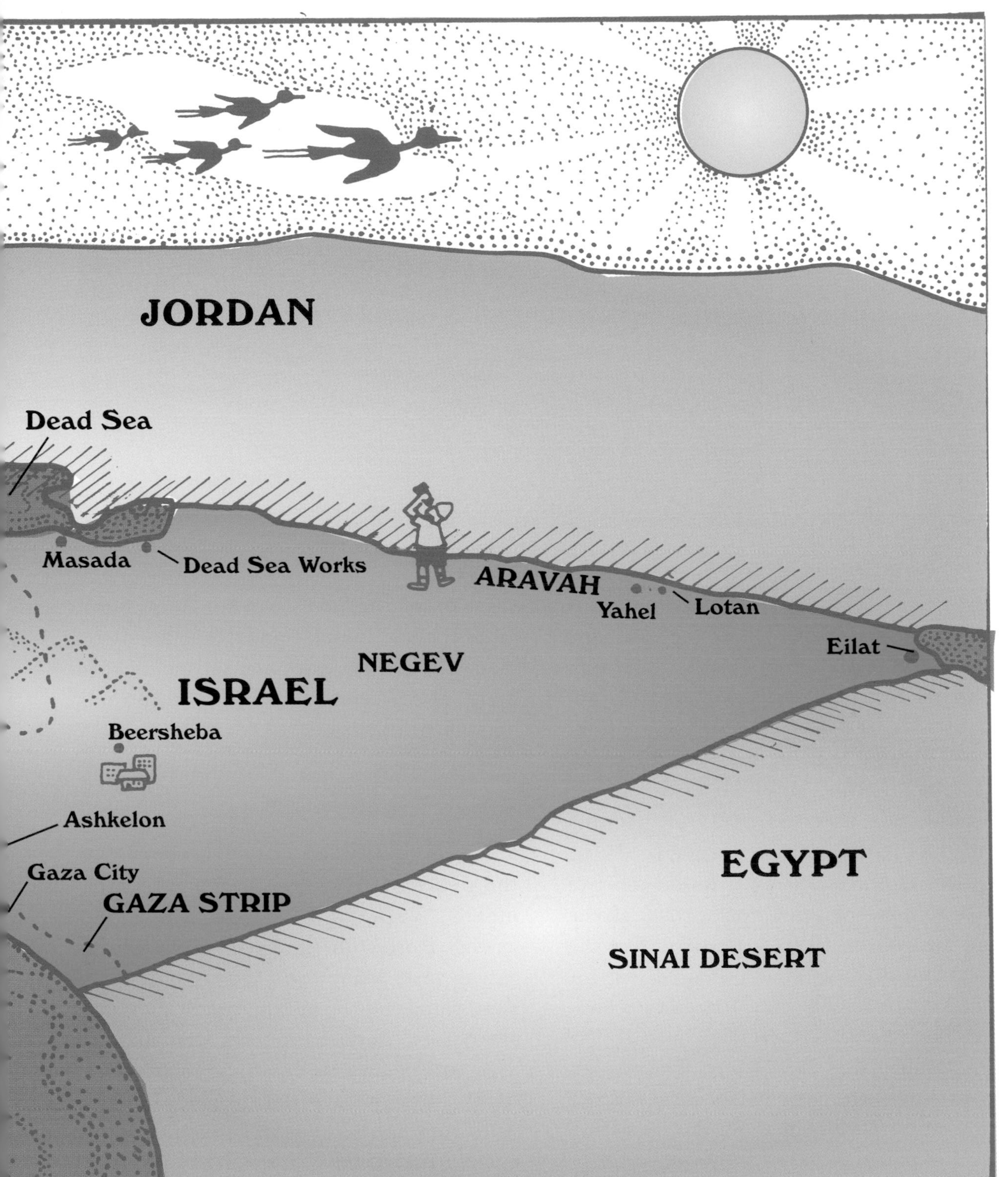
JORDAN
Dead Sea
Masada
Dead Sea Works
ARAVAH
Yahel
Lotan
Eilat
NEGEV
ISRAEL
Beersheba
Ashkelon
Gaza City
GAZA STRIP
EGYPT
SINAI DESERT

Fishermen on the Kinneret, Israel's largest freshwater lake.

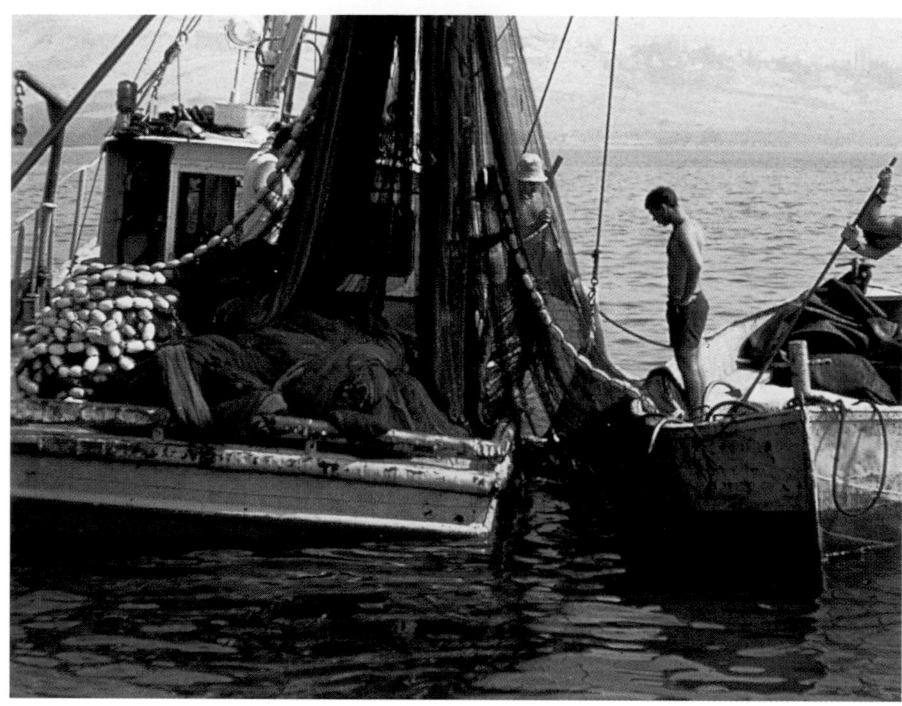

few years ago most of these mountains were bare gray stone. Now they are covered with shady green forests that were planted by the Jewish National Fund. Many villages dot the valleys and the hills. Olive, almond, and fig trees fill the fields. The city of Safed sits high in the mountains. It is a very old city with winding streets and small, dark synagogues.

Tiberias is a vacation city on the shore of Lake Kinneret. Fishing boats, water skiers, and swimmers all use the lake. But the sparkling blue water is not used just for fun. The Kinneret is Israel's largest freshwater lake. Water is carried from it to the thirsty farms of the Negev. The Jordan River leaves the lake below Tiberias and runs south. We'll read about this lake again in a few paragraphs.

The biggest city in the Galilee is Haifa. That's where Tamar lives. It is a port on the shore of the Mediterranean Sea. Ships bring automobiles, lumber, and other goods to Haifa's docks. Factories that surround Haifa make paint, cement, orange concentrate, and other products.

The Emek

A long, wide valley fills the lower part of the square. It is called the Emek, which means "Valley" in Hebrew. The Emek extends most of the way across Israel, from east to west. Many years ago the Emek was swampland, full of mosquitoes that carried sicknesses. Zionist pioneers went to this area to live and to dry out the swamps. Many of them got sick and died. But the work continued. The land became the richest farmland in the country. When you look down from the mountains, the Emek is a checkerboard of fields, orchards, and parks.

(left) *Some winters bring heavy snow to northern Israel. People drive up from the flatlands to ski on Mount Hermon.*

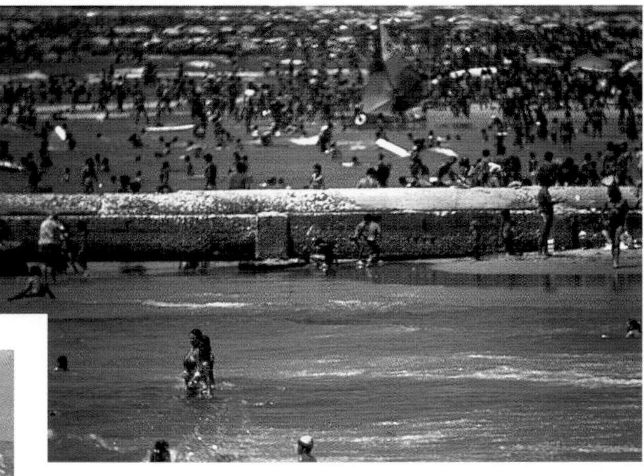

(above) *People come to Tel Aviv from all over to enjoy a leisurely day at the beach in the cool waters of the Mediterranean Sea.*

(left) *The Galilee.*

The Coastal Plain

The long *shofar* shape is the center of Israel—the Merkaz. It is flat land along the Mediterranean coast. This is the most crowded part of the country. People swim and surf off the white sand beaches. Kids scream as they go down giant slides at seaside amusement parks. Towns and farms with orange groves and fish ponds fill the Coastal Plain. The country's second-largest city, Tel Aviv, is located here, on the shore of the Mediterranean. Ashdod, an important port, is south of Tel Aviv.

Judea

The small triangle that pokes out of the *shofar* shape extends from the flat coast up into the hills of Judea. Israel's biggest airport was built on this flat land. Then the land rises until it reaches Jerusalem, Israel's largest city. Jerusalem was once the capital of the Land of Israel. Today it's the capital of the State of Israel.

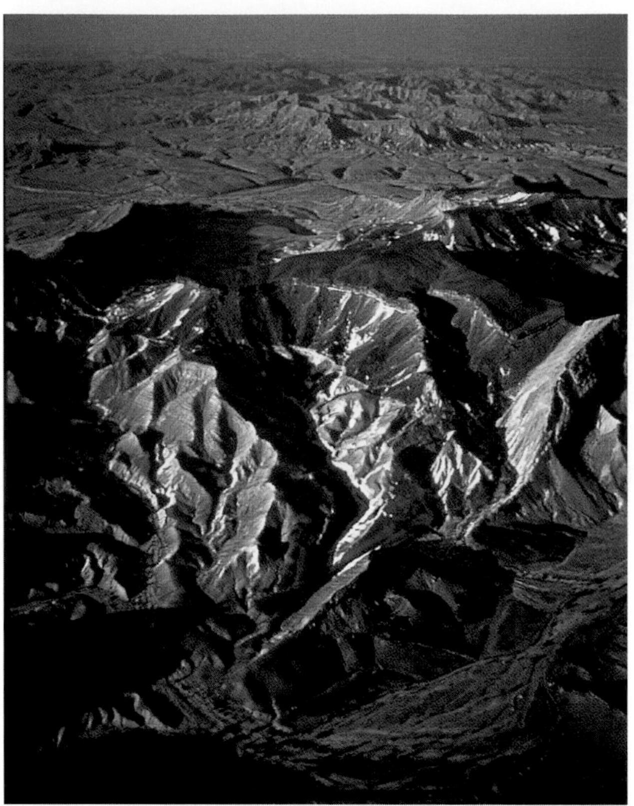

Parts of the Negev are like the badlands of Texas or Arizona. Some American filmmakers come here to make Westerns.

The Negev

The biggest block of all is the triangle in the South called the Negev. Meirav will be coming down here during the Chanukah vacation. Some of the Negev's land is stony desert, but some of it is good farmland. Fewer people live in this area than in other parts of Israel. There's not much rain in the Negev. Most of the water has to be brought from faraway Lake Kinneret. Black tents made of goatskin stand on the dry brown hills. They are the homes of Arab shepherds called Bedouin, who lead their herds of goats over the hills, looking for grass and shrubs to eat.

Beersheba, at the center-top of the triangle, is the Negev's biggest city. And far down at the southern tip is sunny Eilat, where swimmers splash in the warm water. Skin divers slip past underwater coral to follow the colorful fish. And big ships are anchored in the docks nearby.

Say It in Hebrew

English	Hebrew	How to Say the Hebrew
hike or trip	טִיּוּל	ti-*yul*
Galilee (northern Israel)	גָּלִיל	Ga-*lil*
Negev (southern Israel)	נֶגֶב	*Ne*-gev
Merkaz (center of Israel)	מֶרְכָּז	Mer-*kaz*

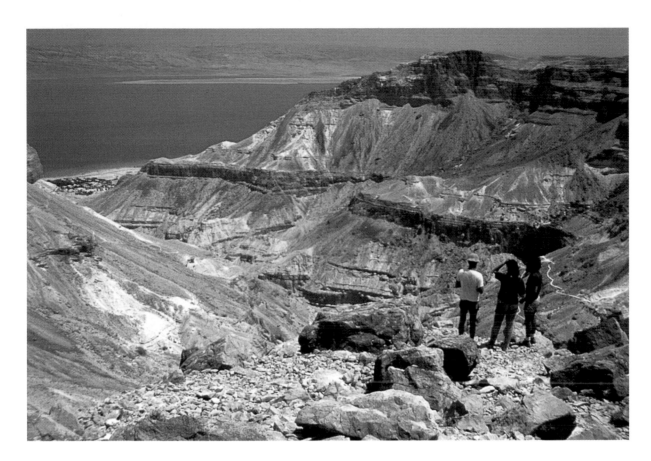

Tourists look out at the Dead Sea and the surrounding Judean Desert.

The Dead Sea, Israel's biggest lake, is the lowest point on earth. It lies on the eastern border of the country. It's so warm there that steam comes up from the water. The sweet water of the Jordan River pours into the salty Dead Sea. Factories remove useful salts and minerals from the sea. The water is so thick with minerals that swimmers can't sink in the sea. They just bob up and down. If you can't swim, you'll love it!

Two Bedouin kids and their camel are standing at the bottom tip of the Aravah at Eilat. It's hot there!

The Aravah

A dry valley runs from the Dead Sea down to Eilat. It is called the Aravah. No ships sail down the Jordan, the Dead Sea, or the Aravah. The valley isn't a waterway. But hot air rises from the valley and makes a fly-way in the sky. Storks, pelicans, and other birds fly south in the fall and north in the spring. When they get tired, they rest by floating on the hot air from the Jordan-Aravah Valley. From the Hula Valley to Eilat, bird-watchers wait with binoculars. They like to watch these feathered tourists pass over Israel. Farm settlements grow dates and other crops in the Aravah. Yahel and Lotan are two Aravah settlements that belong to the Reform movement.

Wild Animals

Would you believe that many wild animals live in a country as small as Israel? They do! Jackals howl in the hills. Porcupines bumble along, nibbling at soft grass in the meadows. Foxes scurry across the roads, chasing field mice. Families of boars grunt and dig up tender roots. Ratlike hyraxes lie on the rocks and sun themselves. There are water buffalo in the Hula Valley. In the Negev there are leopards and wild goats. And an elephant tusk that is taller than the ceiling of your house was found in the Jordan Valley. But it was a few hundred thousand years old. There haven't been any elephants around Israel lately.

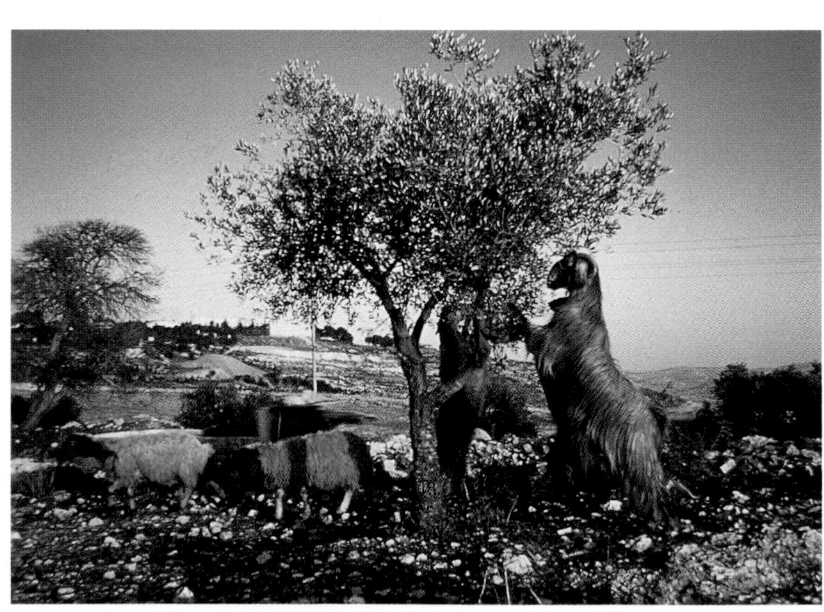

Goats chewing on a tree near a Bedouin camp in Bethlehem.

Israel's Five Neighbors

Most of the people in the Middle East are Arabs who are Muslim. Muslims follow a religion called Islam. Allah is the Muslim name for God. And Mohammed is Allah's prophet. Mohammed founded the religion of Islam in the Middle East about thirteen hundred years ago. His words and beliefs are recorded in the Muslim Bible, the Koran, which borrows many stories and ideas from the Hebrew and Christian Bibles. Christians, Druse, and people of other religions also live in the Middle East. Israel has many Arab citizens. We'll learn more about the Arabs of Israel in Chapter 11.

Israel's largest neighbor, Egypt, is on its southern border. Egypt is almost forty times as large as Israel. Many of Egypt's fifty-five

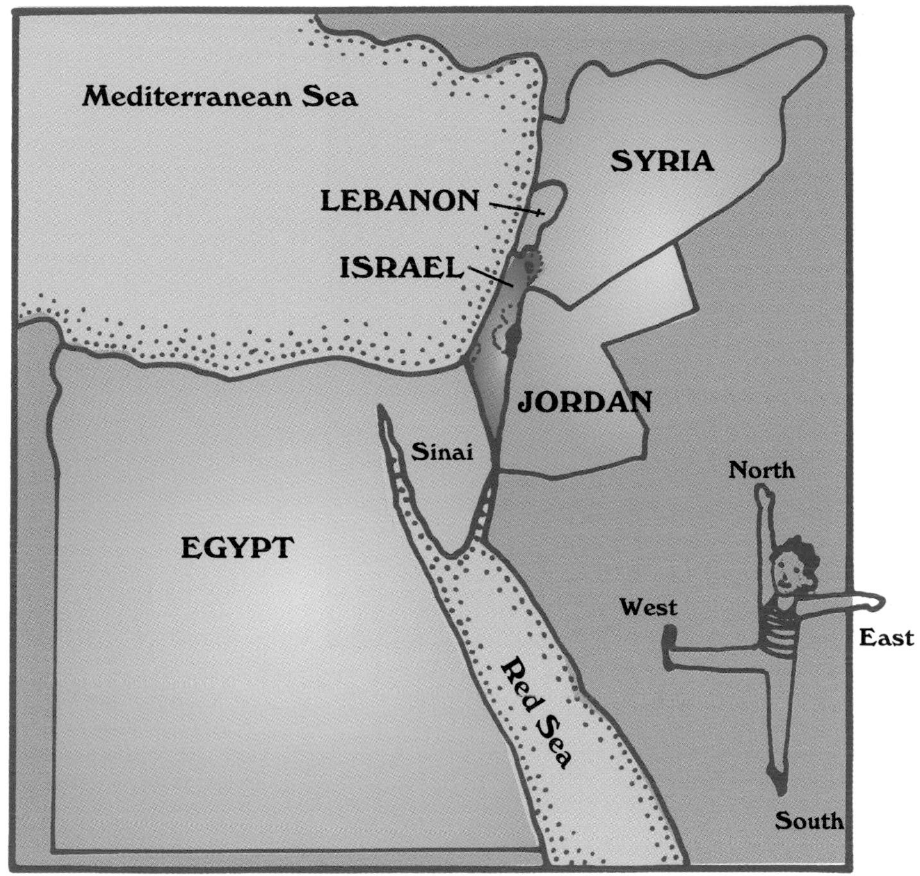

million people are farmers. They grow cotton and vegetables on the land around the Nile River. The rest of Egypt is desert. But the Egyptians are pumping oil from the desert. Today there is peace between Israel and Egypt. Israeli tourists travel to Egypt to climb the pyramids and enjoy other sights.

Jordan is Israel's neighbor on the East. Jordan is almost four times as big as Israel. But much of Jordan's land is desert. Four million people live in Jordan. Israel and Jordan share the fresh water of the Jordan River. They also share the chemicals of the Dead Sea. Today there is peace between Israel and Jordan.

Syria is Israel's neighbor on the North and East. Syria is ten times the size of Israel and has twelve and one-half million people. Syria has oil and some good farmland.

Lebanon is Israel's neighbor on the North. It is even smaller than Israel and has three and one-third million people. Lebanon has good farmland and plenty of water. But many of its cities and towns were damaged in fighting during its recent civil war.

Israel's biggest and most peaceful neighbor is the Mediterranean Sea. The sea forms Israel's western border. Haifa and Ashdod, ports on the Mediterranean, are Israel's gateway to the world. Fishermen and swimmers love the warm, friendly water of the Mediterranean.

The peaceful Mediterranean.

SUMMING UP

Israel is in the Middle East, a sunny part of the world that has rain and a little snow in the winter. Most of the people who live in the Middle East are Arabs who are Muslim. Parts of the Middle East are desert. But some of the Middle Eastern countries are rich because they have a lot of oil.

Israel is a tiny country. It can be divided into five sections. In the Far North is the green Hula Valley. Also in the North are the mountains of the Galilee and the farmlands of the Emek. The center is a flat coastal plain. It is Israel's most crowded area. A finger of land extends across to Jerusalem, the country's capital. In the South is the dry Negev. The Jordan is Israel's only big river. It brings sweet water to Lake Kinneret and the Dead Sea. Kinneret water is also piped to the Negev. The three biggest cities in Israel are Jerusalem, Tel Aviv, and Haifa.

On Israel's western border is the Mediterranean Sea. Israel's other neighbors are Egypt, Jordan, Syria, and Lebanon.

ACTIVITIES

MAP HUNT

Find the number on the map for each place on the list below. Write the number in the box.

- ☐ Hula Valley
- ☐ Galilee
- ☐ Mediterranean Sea
- ☐ Lake Kinneret
- ☐ Jordan River
- ☐ Dead Sea
- ☐ Emek
- ☐ Negev
- ☐ Aravah
- ☐ Coastal Plain
- ☐ Jerusalem
- ☐ Haifa
- ☐ Tel Aviv

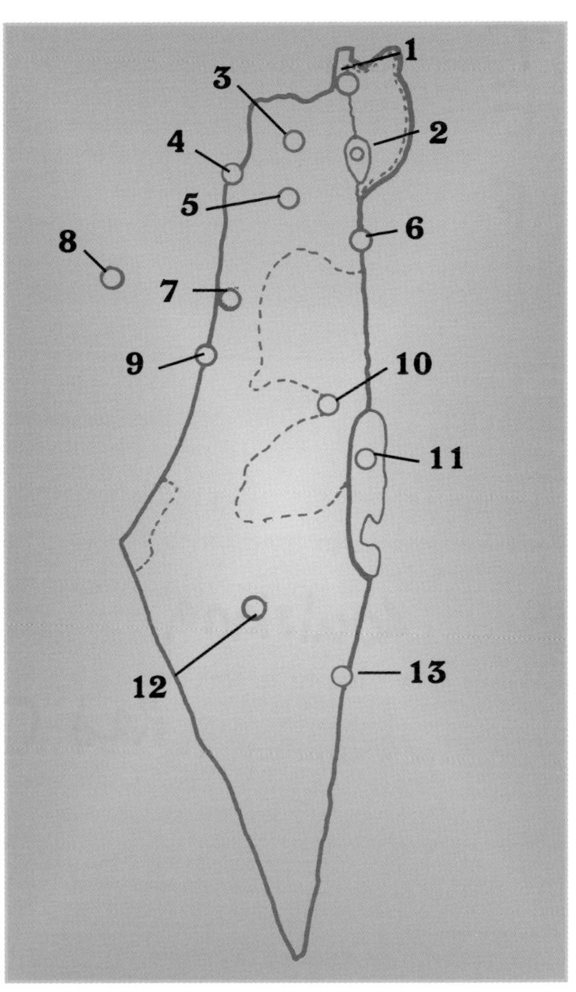

❄ SCRAMBLED NEIGHBORS ❄

Can you unscramble the names of Israel's neighbors?

On the North	N A L O N E B
On the Northeast	I S A Y R
On the East	N O J A R D
On the South	T Y P E G
On the West	M I T N E E R D R A E N A A S E

TRUE OR FALSE

Put a **T** in front of each true statement. Put an **F** in front of each false statement.

F The Dead Sea is Israel's biggest fresh-water lake.

T The Koran is the Muslim Bible.

F Some of Israel's neighbors are rich because there's gold in their deserts.

F Eilat is the biggest city in the Galilee.

F The Aravah is a flyway in the sky.

T Israel and its neighbors are in the Middle East.

T You can ride your bike across Israel in one hour.

F Israel is about the size of Texas.

Saving Nature

Meirav says that she and her friends want to save the wild, natural places in Israel. Many Americans are also trying to save their country's natural areas. Think about an area in the United States that you would like to save. What is the name of the area?

Louisiana

What is the name of an American organization that is like the Nature Protection Society in Israel?

Red Cross.

BE A TRAVEL AGENT

Write a jingle or a TV commercial or draw a poster that would interest people in visiting Israel.

If you go to Tel Aviv we promise you won't want to leave.

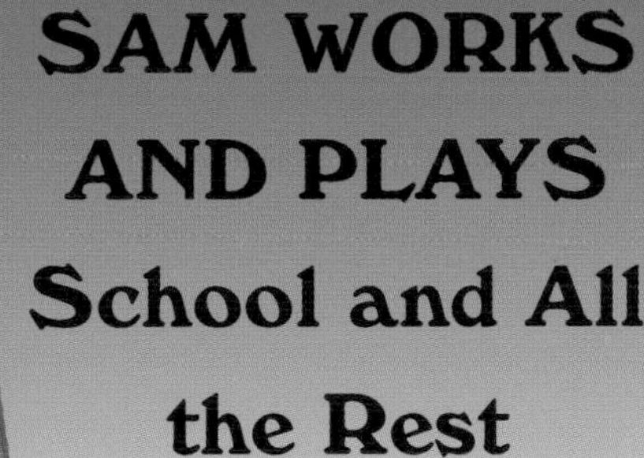

4 SAM WORKS AND PLAYS

School and All the Rest

Sam came to Israel from the United States when he was five. Now he is twelve and in the seventh grade. He lives in a small town on a mountain in the Galilee. Sam is playing a computer game with his brother Ben and his friend Ari.

Sam says: "What I like most is to play Dungeons and Dragons. We play it in Hebrew. It's educational because you have to read and write a lot in order to play. I wash cars to earn money for the games. The prophet Elijah is my favorite character in the Bible. He's mysterious because he never died. In Dungeons and Dragons he is an immortal.

"A school bus takes us to school. School is okay. I like math and Bible. There's no dress code at our school. You can't go barefoot, but everything else is alright. After school there are all kinds of clubs. You can build model airplanes, learn to play the recorder or the accordion, play tennis, swim, or go camping.

"After school I play soccer and basketball with my friends. Sometimes we have parties and listen to rock music.

"My father, my brother Ben, and I like to hike. We look for very old ruins from the time of the Bible. My parents came to Israel because they thought that it was the best place for Ben and me to grow up."

Sam's brother Ben is nine. He says: "We take a lot of trips. Last Pesach we went to the Negev. We found a museum that has weird rocks and snakes. It's built over a deep crater called the Machtesh. You feel as if you're going to drop right into it! We slept in a pine grove. It was so cold that we had to build a fire and sit around it all night. There's interesting stuff right around our village, too. I found an ancient well, all paved, with a tunnel leading to it. I wonder who built it."

The Same As You but Different

If you were a kid in Israel, here are some of the things that you might do:

- Eat tomatoes, cucumbers, and cottage cheese for breakfast
- Be at school from 7:30 A.M. to 12:30 P.M. every day except Saturday
- Wear shorts and sandals half the year
- Get all the Jewish holidays off from school without having to bring in a note
- Hang out in shopping centers and eat pita or pizza
- Call your teacher by his or her first name
- Eat tomatoes, cucumbers, and cottage cheese for supper
- Watch American TV programs with Hebrew subtitles
- Call the police if you see a package left on the street or on a bus

And here are some of the things that you wouldn't do:

- Have to learn Hebrew for your bar or bat mitzvah (Guess why not)
- Hear Christmas carols on the radio and TV at Christmastime
- Wear a raincoat and rubber boots from spring until fall

Does this list seem strange to you? Are the activities it lists different from those in your life? Now read about schools in Israel. See how they are like your school and how they are different.

All Kinds of Schools

There are many kinds of schools in Israel. The biggest differences between them are the ways in which religion is taught.

Most Jewish Israeli kids attend "regular" schools, where they learn math, social studies, science, etc., just as you do. But they also study Bible and Jewish history. The TALI schools are also part of the regular school system. But more time is spent on Bible, Jewish history, holidays, and religion

Many preschool-aged kids go to nursery schools because their mothers and fathers work full-time. These preschoolers are at the playground in the village of Har Halutz.

in a TALI school than in a regular school. Then there are modern Orthodox schools that teach all the regular subjects. But kids who attend these schools also spend a lot of time learning Bible and religious laws and customs. There are also ultra-Orthodox schools in which Bible and religious laws and customs are the most important subjects. Ultra-Orthodox boys and girls go to separate schools.

And there are schools that teach in Arabic for Arab students. Students in these schools learn most of the same subjects that students in Hebrew-speaking schools do. In some Arab schools kids also study the Koran.

In the big cities some Jewish and Arab kids go to the same schools.

School is expensive. Families have to pay for textbooks, crayons, drawing paper, and other supplies. And families also pay for school trips and after-school clubs. Israeli kids make money by collecting their old textbooks and taking them to the town square or the shopping center in the fall before school starts. Everyone spreads his or her books on the ground. Then everyone shops around, buying and selling books for the new year.

A Day at School

Sam's brother Ben is in the fourth grade. Here's what he does in the course of a day at a regular school:

- Gets to school at 7:30 A.M.
- Math
- Bible study (Ben is studying about Joshua)
- Morning discussion: The class talks about the news of the world or Israel; the teacher might read a news story and have the class discuss it
- Snack and run around the schoolyard
- Nature study

- Language—reading, grammar, and spelling (in Hebrew, of course)
- Special projects: Each student chooses a topic in math, science, or history and learns more about it on his or her own
- Returns home at 12:45 P.M. three days a week and at 2:30 P.M three days a week

Each week Ben also has a computer class, an art class, and library. Three times a week he has an English language class.

You'll meet Uriah in Chapter 5. His brother Shalom is in the sixth grade at an ultra-Orthodox school. Here's what Shalom does during a school day:

- Gets to school at 8 A.M. and says morning prayers
- *Gemara* study (*Gemara* is part of the Talmud, an important book of religious law)
- Studies religious law in daily life, learning about holidays, keeping kosher, and the Bible (Shalom is studying the Book of Prophets)
- Home for lunch
- *Mishnah* study (*Mishnah* is the first part of the Talmud)
- Math
- Language—reading, grammar, and spelling
- Reads Bible stories (the activity that Shalom likes the best)
- Returns home at 5:30 P.M.

Starting in the sixth grade, students go on a long trip called a *tiyul*. Each spring they explore a different part of the country. Some take the bus to Eilat and study tropical fish. Others hike in the desert. Still others explore Jerusalem. It's a fun way to learn.

(above) ***High school students from Karmiel take a break from their studies.***

(below) ***Uriah studies in a* yeshivah.**

Soccer is Israel's most popular sport.

After-School Sports

Soccer is the most popular sport in Israel. Sam and his friends kick soccer balls in the playground. Small towns build stadiums and play against other small-town teams. The major teams have big stadiums in the cities. Fans yell, stamp, and wave banners at the games. Sometimes they get angry and throw food at the players. When an important game is on TV, half the country stays home to watch.

Kids and grown-ups enjoy basketball, too. Some very tall American players like Winfred King play on Israeli teams.

Tennis is a new sport in Israel. Stars like Amos Mansdorf and Gilad Bloom play all over the world. Anna Smashnova is a tennis player who came from Russia. She has a smashing serve! Yael Arad is a judo champion who won a silver medal in the 1992 Olympics. Israelis were very excited and are proud of her.

Say It in Hebrew

English	Hebrew	How to Say the Hebrew
school	בֵּית סֵפֶר	bet *se*-fer
books	סְפָרִים	se-fa-*rim*
TV	טֵלֶוִיזְיָה	te-le-*viz*-yah
soccer	כַּדּוּר רֶגֶל	ka-*dur re*-gel

FOCUS

Screamers, Wailers, and Rockers

At the Sultan's Pool, an open-air theater just outside the walls of Jerusalem's old city, the audience asks for an encore.

Smoke drifts across the stage. Red, green, and blue strobe lights poke through the smoke. The musicians are shadows in the smoke. They huddle over their drums, pianos, and guitars, bobbing up and down. In the spotlight the singer wiggles, sways, and wails into the mike. And the audience sings along, rocks, and claps to the rhythm of the music.

That's how music looks and sounds at a club or an outdoor park in Tel Aviv or Jerusalem, or on a TV variety show. Israeli popular music today doesn't sound like "Hatikvah" or "Artza Alinu." It rocks and rolls, and sometimes it howls and screams. The wailing music of the Middle East and Greece has influenced Israeli composers and singers. Many of the

The singer Noa (Achinoam Nini) was born in Israel and raised in the United States. When she was seventeen, she returned to Israel. Her music combines Israeli folk, traditional Yemenite songs, and jazz.

Israel is also a center for classical music. The Israel Philharmonic, one of the world's great orchestras, is shown playing at the open-air theater in Caesarea.

most successful singers are of Sephardic background. Shoshana Damari and Ophrah Haza, two flashing-eyed, black-haired Yemenite women, are the past and present queens of Israeli popular music. Yehuda Poliker sings verse after verse of nasal Greek melodies. And wearing worn blue jeans, Arik Einshtein talks and growls through his songs.

Western music is also very popular in Israel. Eric Clapton, Michael Jackson, and other performers have played there to packed audiences.

Love, friendship, war, and hopes for peace are themes that Israeli songwriters like Naomi Shemer and Ehud Manor write about. Shemer's most popular song is the joyous "Jerusalem of Gold." It was written just before Israel united the old and new cities of Jerusalem in 1967. Manor composed a wistful song called "Next Year." He wrote:

> You'll see yet, oh, you'll see
> Just how good it will be
> In the new, in the coming year.

In a thoughtful mood Shemer wrote another song called "Over All These":

> Watch, Lord, over this house,
> Over the garden and the wall,
> Protect them from sorrow, fear,
> And war.

Israel's music can be sad and thoughtful or wild and playful. It mirrors the country's many moods.

Meirav belongs to a folk dance group at her community center. Her group is so good that they were invited to dance at the Karmiel Dance Festival.

TV and Toys

You would feel right at home watching TV in Israel. You could see "Star Trek," "Murder She Wrote," and old Lassie movies. There are also cartoons in Hebrew. One program looks and sounds a little like "Sesame Street." It is "Rehov Sum Sum." Instead of Bert and Ernie, there are Benz and Arik. Big Bird becomes Kippy, a big prickly porcupine who wears house slippers. And everybody on "Rehov Sum Sum" speaks Hebrew or Arabic.

You would also feel right at home in an Israeli toy store. There are Barbie dolls, Ninja Turtles, Lego blocks, and more. In a computer store you'd find games like Ninja and Batman.

Clubs and Youth Groups

Most towns have a big community center. Rahely and Ruthy (you'll meet them in Chapter 9) do jazz dancing at their community center. Other groups participate in activities like pottery, yoga, and music.

Many kids belong to youth groups. There are religious youth groups like those run by the Reform, Conservative, and Orthodox movements. There are also Boy and Girl Scouts. In Chapter 8 you'll meet a scout named Aviram. Even political parties have youth groups.

Trips

When the weekend comes, kids beg their parents, "Let's go on a *tiyul,* please, please!"

(right) *Ein Gedi, near the Dead Sea, is a favorite place to hike. Up in one of the mountains is a stream that's fun to swim in.*

(left) *The grown-ups are dragging a little, but the kids are racing up the hill at Zippori. They'll see ancient ruins that are 1800 years old.*

Israeli families love to explore their country. During Passover week, Sam, Ben, and their father camped out in the Negev Desert. Yotam and Shai (you'll meet them in Chapter 6) drove through a wildlife preserve. They worried when the ostriches poked their head through the car window to grab their lunch. And Uriah and Shalom often picnic on the beach by the Mediterranean Sea with their family.

SUMMING UP

The lives of American and Israeli kids are alike but they are also different. Israel has several kinds of schools. There are "regular" schools, modern Orthodox schools, and ultra-Orthodox schools. Most Arab kids in Israel study in Arabic-speaking schools.

Israeli kids and adults like to play soccer, basketball, and tennis. Soccer is the most popular game. People go to games in stadiums and watch them on TV. Many American programs are shown on Israeli TV. There are also good Israeli programs. Toys and computer games are like those in the United States.

Israeli families enjoy exploring their country. Hikes and trips are favorite weekend and vacation activities. But Ben warns, "Take a map and be careful because Israel is small. One night we nearly drove out of Israel and into Egypt by mistake."

STARS AND X'S

Make a list of 10 things that you'd find different if you lived in Israel. Put a star next to the things that you'd like. Put an X next to the things that you wouldn't like.

____	1. ______________	____	6. ______________
____	2. ______________	____	7. ______________
____	3. ______________	____	8. ______________
____	4. ______________	____	9. ______________
____	5. ______________	____	10. ______________

WRITE A LETTER

Most Israeli kids want to know about the United States.

Write a letter to Sam, Meirav, or any of the other kids mentioned in this book. Tell about your life—your pets, religious school, hobbies, holidays, etc. Send your letter to the UAHC Press. They will forward it to me. And I will send it to the person to whom you've written.

____

____

____

____

____

____

❄ DISCOVER A PICTURE ❄

To find a favorite sport in Israel, copy each drawing below in the empty box that has the same number.

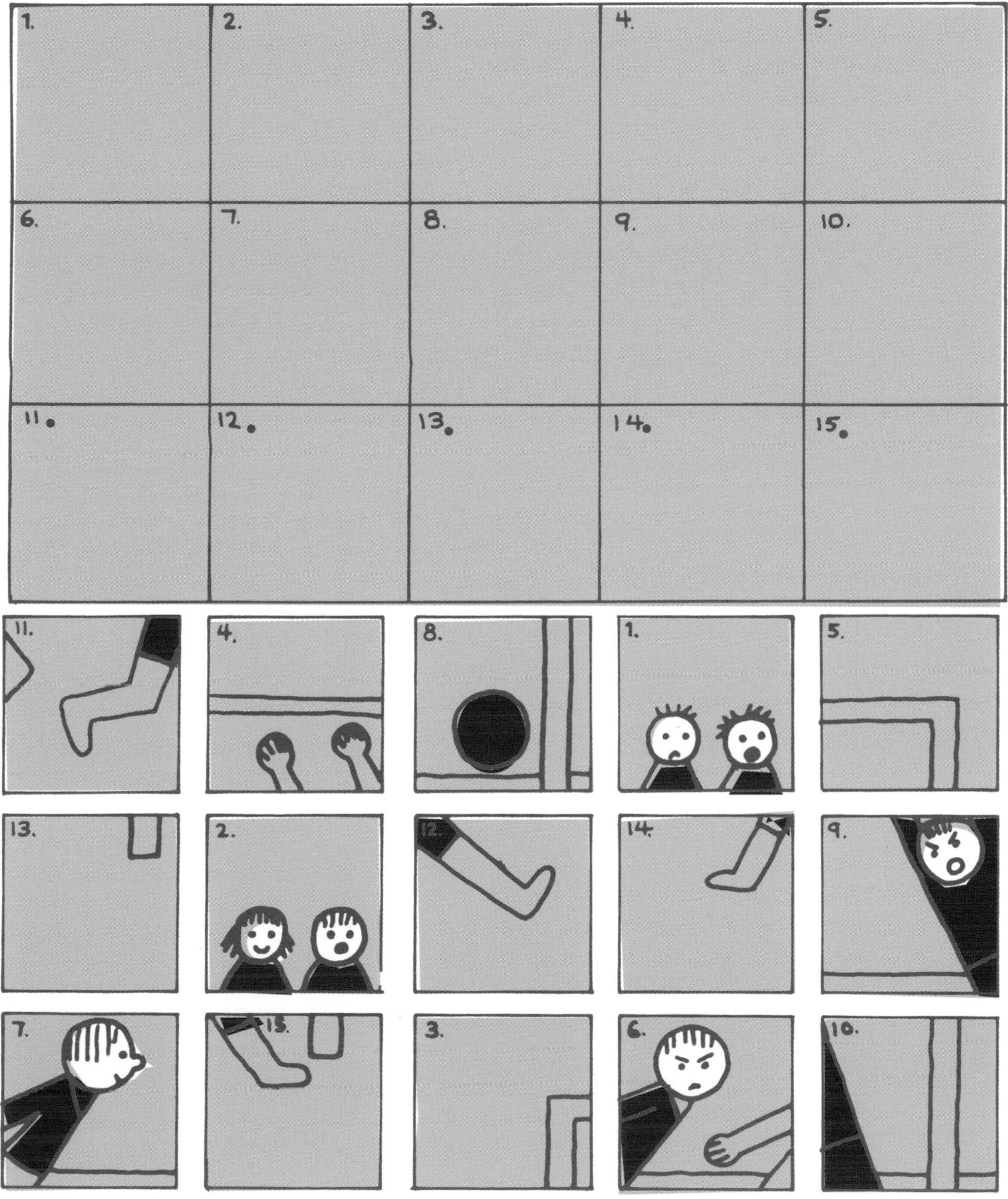

WHAT DO YOU THINK?

Choose one of the following words or set of words to fill in the blank in each sentence below.

ultra-Orthodox	Elijah	Orthodox
"Rehov Sum Sum"	"regular"	soccer
Hebrew	Arabic	*tiyul*
expensive		

1. After school, kids play ____________________ in the playground.
2. Kids sell their old textbooks because school is ____________________.
3. ____________________ boys and girls go to separate schools.
4. Sam's favorite Bible character is ____________________.
5. In Arab schools kids speak and study in the ____________________ language.
6. ____________________ is a Hebrew program like "Sesame Street."
7. A class trip is called a ____________________.
8. A lot of study time is devoted to the Bible and religious laws and customs in ____________________schools.
9. Israeli kids don't have to learn ____________________ for their bar or bat mitzvah.
10. ____________________schools in Israel are like public schools in the United States.

URIAH STUDIES TORAH

Being Jewish in the Holy Land

Uriah is thirteen. Uriah and his family are ultra-Orthodox Jews. They live according to Judaism's traditional laws and customs.

Uriah says: "First thing after breakfast, I go to the synagogue for morning prayers. School starts at eight in the morning. We study *Gemara* all morning. It's part of the Talmud, one of the most important books of Judaism. In the middle of the morning, we have a recess when we run around and play soccer or tag. At one o'clock we go home for lunch. That's when I play chess with my ten-year-old brother, Shalom. We just learned how to play.

"After lunch we study the Torah section of the week. And we learn the religious laws about food, clothing, holidays, and other things that a Jew needs to know. We don't study math, language, or science after the seventh grade. We only have religious studies. I get home from school at six-fifteen.

"I don't find school boring. I think that studying stretches my mind. Each day is new and exciting. I don't know what I want to do when I grow up. Right now I try to learn. Learning is what a Jew does."

All Kinds of Religions

People in Israel are Jewish, Muslim, Christian, Druse, Bahai, or something else. There's a mosaic of religions. Most Israelis are Jews. Then come Muslims, followed by Christians, Druse, and other smaller groups. Most of the non-Jews are Arabs who have lived in the Middle East for many years. There are also Jews from Arab countries. Their families have lived in the Middle East region for many years, too. So Israel is the home of many religions. In this chapter you'll find out about all kinds of Jews. In Chapter 11 you'll read about many kinds of Arabs.

RELIGIOUS GROUPS IN ISRAEL

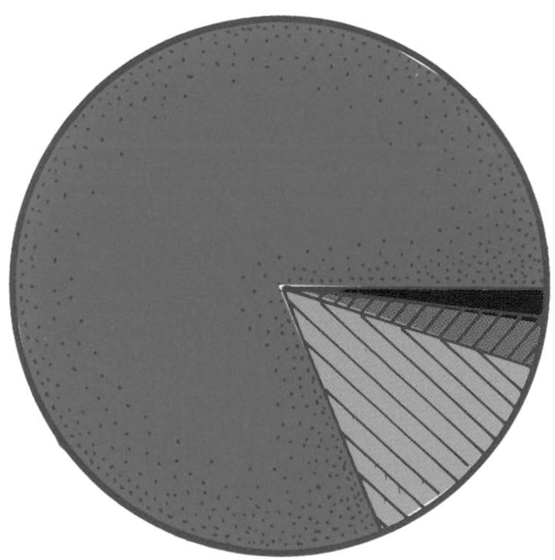

Jews–81.6% of population
Muslims–14% of population
Christians–2.7% of population
Druse and Others–1.7% of population

All Kinds of Jews

Israeli Jews observe Judaism in many different ways. There are Orthodox, Reform, and Conservative Jews. Most Israeli Jews celebrate the Jewish holidays. Yet many Israeli Jews do not attend synagogue regularly. If you asked them, many would say that they aren't "religious" at all. So are they Jewish? "Am I Jewish?" laughs a cabdriver as he picks up passengers on Shabbat. "What kind of question is that? I live in Israel. I speak Hebrew. I serve in the army. I feel like a Jew. Of course, I'm Jewish!"

Whether a Jew is observant or not, he or she can feel the spirit of Jewish life. On Shabbat and holiday mornings the streets are very quiet—so quiet that you can hear the cats chasing one another across the roofs. Buses don't run, stores are closed, and you just have to relax. Another special thing about Israel is that the Bible is all around you. Sam, who likes to read about

A chasidic Jew shops for books in Mea Shearim, an ultra-Orthodox community in Jerusalem.

Yiska and Shmaya, one of her younger brothers.

the prophet Elijah, can climb Mount Carmel near Haifa and see the cave where Elijah hid. And Uriah can visit the graves of the wise men who wrote part of the book that he studies, the Talmud.

Jewishness is all around.

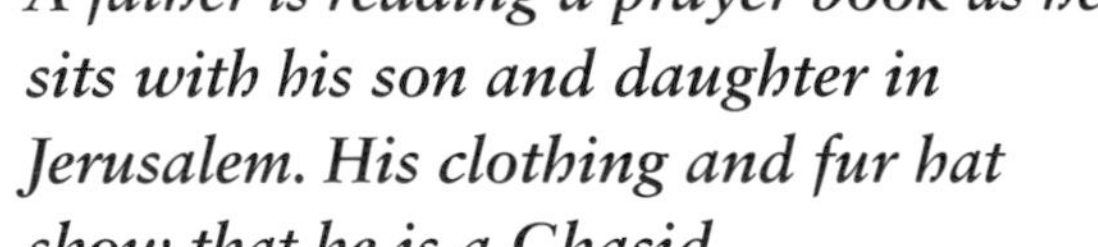

A father is reading a prayer book as he sits with his son and daughter in Jerusalem. His clothing and fur hat show that he is a Chasid.

Orthodox Jews

Orthodox Jews follow the traditional laws of Judaism. They believe that these laws, called *halachah,* were given by God to the Jewish people. Orthodox Jews cover their head with a hat, kerchief, or *kipah.* Some of the men have beards, and many Orthodox girls wear long skirts. It's easier to be Orthodox in Israel than in other countries. Schools and workplaces are closed on Shabbat and many other holidays. Nobody has to explain to the boss or teacher that he or she stayed home to observe a Jewish holiday.

Ultra-Orthodox Jews like Uriah are easy to recognize. The boys wear a black *kipah* on their head and a small *talit* under their shirt. Long curls called *peot* bob in front of their ears. Uriah's father has a beard, like most ultra-Orthodox men. Yiska, Uriah's sister, wears stockings and a long-sleeved blouse. It's important to Yiska and to other ultra-Orthodox girls to be modest. They wear clothing that covers most of their body. Yiska's skirt reaches below her knees, making it hard for her to turn her leg over a bouncing ball. But she's still a good ball bouncer.

Each day Uriah, the older boys, and the men pray in the synagogue. In an Orthodox synagogue only men can be counted for a *minyan* (a group of ten needed for public prayer). When women come to the synagogue, they sit in a separate section. Many ultra-Orthodox boys go to a *yeshivah* (religious high school and college) after finishing primary school. They usually do not serve in the army after high school. Instead, they keep on studying. Most other young men and women in Israel do army service.

Ultra-Orthodox girls have a shorter school day than the boys. But Yiska doesn't watch TV when she gets home. "There's nothing good or useful to learn from TV," say her parents. The family doesn't even have a TV set. Yiska and her girlfriends might go on to college. But they won't go into the army. Some of the girls will marry *yeshivah* boys. Then they'll cover their hair with a kerchief or a wig. And they'll probably have many children. Yiska has seven brothers and sisters, who all take turns playing with Shmuel Yosef, the baby.

Reform Jews

Other Jews are Reform or Conservative. Reform Jews believe that Judaism must change with the times. Reform Jews try to take an active part in creating new ways to celebrate Jewish life.

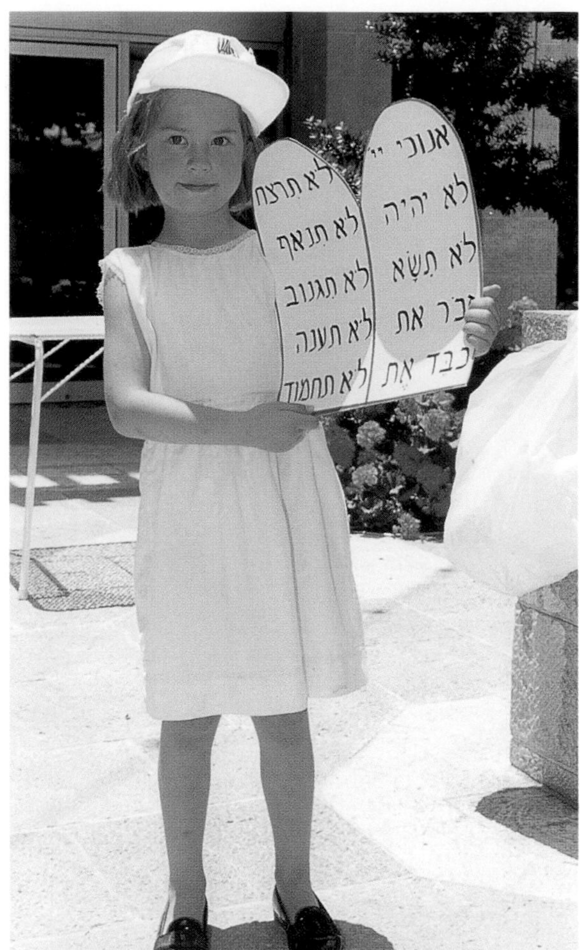

A girl holds the Ten Commandments as part of a Shavuot program at school.

Yoav's family belongs to a Reform congregation. On Friday evening Yoav's family welcomes Shabbat at the small temple in the village. The village is called Har Halutz. Men and women sit together. They're all part of the *minyan*. The people in Yoav's temple sing as they pray. Yoav's little sister Noa knows all the words to *Lechah Dodi*. Yael, the rabbi, sometimes talks about the Torah portion of the week. And sometimes she invites all the kids to sit on the rug beside her. Then she tells them a story or teaches them a prayer or a song.

One Shabbat morning the whole congregation went deep into a forest to an ancient ruined synagogue. Yoav thought, Jews haven't prayed here for one hundred and perhaps even one thousand years. Everyone sat on the crumbled stone walls and recited *Shacharit,* the morning prayer. Yoav looked into the shady, quiet woods. He whispered to his mother, "If those long-ago Jews were watching us now, I think they would be glad we're here."

(above) ***On Masada a bar mitzvah reads from the Torah.***

(below) ***Rabbi Yael leads morning prayer at the ruins of an 1800-year-old synagogue in northern Israel.***

FOCUS

Building the House of Judaism

Jewish religious law is like a house under construction. The Bible is the foundation of the house. Books that were written later are its walls. The roof is still on the drawing board.

The first five books of the Bible tell the story of the Jewish people, from the creation of the world until Moses led the Israelites to the Land of Israel. The Torah contains laws for Jews to follow. Every Shabbat, Monday, and Thursday, Jews unroll the Torah scroll and read a section. They read a new section each week until they have read the entire scroll. On Simchat Torah they start again from the beginning.

The Bible is composed of the Torah, Prophets, and Writings. Prophets tells about Israel's moral leaders who warned the people and the kings to live according to God's law and scolded them when they did not. Writings tells how the Jewish people built their kingdom and the Temple.

That's the foundation of our house. Now this is how the walls were built.

When the Jews were forced to leave their land, they took the Torah with them. In the countries they went to, many new problems arose. Rabbis and teachers looked for answers in the Torah. To make the answers clearer, they added their own comments. These comments were gathered into a huge new book called the Talmud. The Talmud became the first layer of bricks in the wall.

Many years passed. Each year Jews discovered new problems and questions that needed answers.

The Bar Am Synagogue was discovered high in the Galilee mountains. Two thousand years ago it was filled with worshipers and holiday celebrations. Today tourists wander around the ancient walls.

Rabbis and scholars continued to search the Torah and Talmud for the answers. Their ideas and comments were gathered into new books. For instance, a guide to Jewish daily life called the Shulchan Aruch was written about five hundred years ago. New sections were slowly added to the siddur and the Pesach haggadah. The way of life that Jews followed with the guidance of their holy books was called halachah. The wall was getting higher.

Today many books and customs guide Jews through their lives. Each Jew understands them in his or her own way. Uriah believes that God wrote every word of the Torah. Therefore, he thinks that the Torah and Talmud must be obeyed carefully and closely. Sam believes that Jewish laws came both from God and from rabbis and scholars. He thinks that we should accept many of them but we can also add our own ideas. Dafna (whom you will meet in Chapter 10) doesn't think about the Torah very much, but the cooperative way of life on her kibbutz is based on the teachings of the prophets.

Jews have been building the house of Judaism for many centuries. The work never ends. Today, as Jews search for answers in Israel and elsewhere, they continue to add new bricks to the walls.

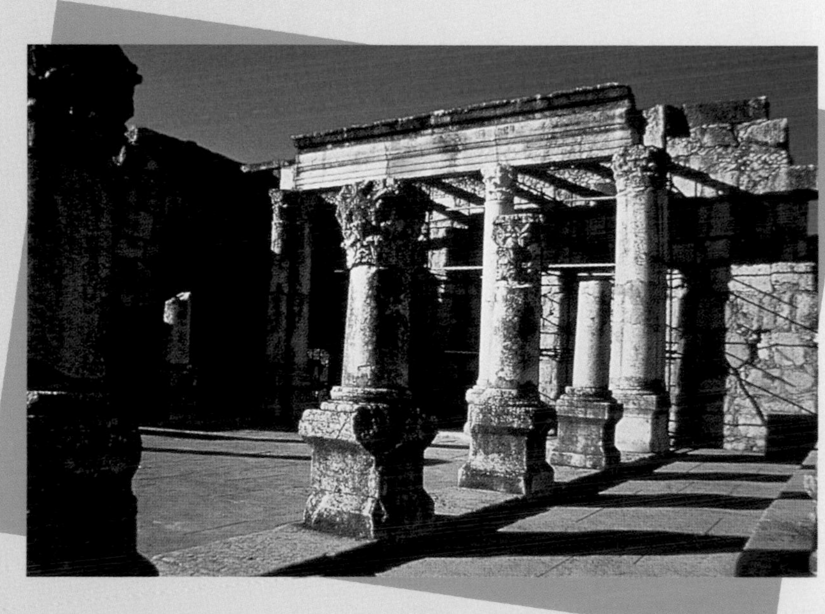

Columns line the remnants of a second-century synagogue in Kefar Nahum (Capernaum), located on the northern tip of Lake Kinneret.

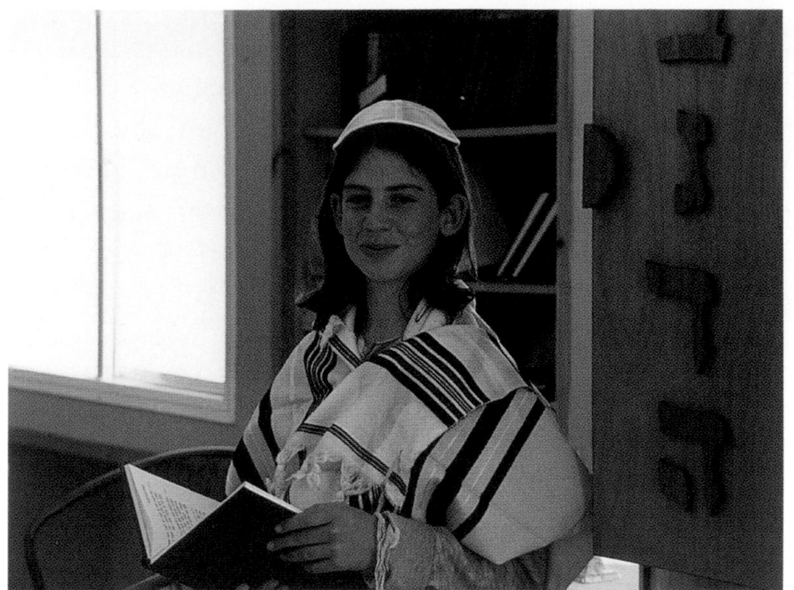

Sam is studying, preparing to become a bar mitzvah.

Conservative Jews

Sam belongs to a Conservative congregation. Conservative Jews also follow *halachah*. Although they agree that Jewish laws can be changed over time, these changes must first be approved by a committee of legal scholars and rabbis. Sam is studying his *haftarah* now, preparing to become a bar mitzvah. He'll learn to lead some of the morning services, too. If you go to Sam's synagogue, you may find that you know many of the melodies. The prayer book is very much like the Conservative prayer books used in the United States, although all the text is printed in Hebrew. Sam's mother and father attend a study group at the synagogue each week. They are learning to read and understand the Talmud.

Say It in Hebrew

English	Hebrew	How to Say the Hebrew
Judaism	יַהֲדוּת	Ya-ha-*dut*
morning prayer	שַׁחֲרִית	*Sha*-cha-rit
synagogue	בֵּית כְּנֶסֶת	bet *ke*-ne-set
yeshivah (religious high school and college)	יְשִׁיבָה	ye-*shi*-vah

The Ari Synagogue in Safed is named after Rabbi Isaac Luria, who is known as Ha-Ari ("The Lion").

Synagogues

The synagogues that Uriah, Yoav, and Sam attend all have ritual objects, just as your synagogue does. For example, there's a *bimah*, or a reading platform, an ark with Torahs, called an *aron hakodesh*, and a *ner tamid*, a light above the ark that is always lit. Most synagogues in Israel are simple. They don't have big Jewish stars or brightly colored glass windows. You might walk past a neighborhood synagogue without even noticing it. But there is a handsome synagogue in Jerusalem that you can't miss. It is Heichal Shlomo, the headquarters of Israel's chief rabbis. The sparkling white building of the Reform movement in Jerusalem, called Bet Shmuel, stands near the walls of the old city. It contains a synagogue. The building also has a museum of archaeology, which occupies part of the campus of the Hebrew Union College-Jewish Institute of Religion, a college for students who want to be rabbis, cantors, and teachers.

SUMMING UP

There's a mosaic of religions in Israel. Most Israelis are Jewish. They might be Orthodox, Conservative, Reform, or not religious at all. Ultra-Orthodox Jews spend a lot of time praying and studying Jewish holy books. They are easy to recognize because of the special way in which they dress.

Other Israeli Jews dress like you and your family. They attend synagogues that have Torahs and ritual objects, like those in your synagogue in the United States. One of Israel's largest synagogues is in Jerusalem. It is Heichal Shlomo, the headquarters of the chief rabbis of Israel. Bet Shmuel, the center of the Israeli Reform movement, is also located in Jerusalem.

Jewish holidays are a special time for most Jews in Israel. And everywhere there are places we read about in the Bible. Israelis are surrounded by Jewish history and customs.

WHAT DO WE ALL SHARE?

Jews live in many countries. In each country Jews have different ideas and customs. But some customs and ideas are shared by all Jews. Draw a circle around the customs and ideas listed below that you think all Jews share.

Torah study	A *mezuzah* on the doorpost
A Thanksgiving holiday	A *minyan* of ten men for prayer
Bar mitzvah	Eating matzah at Pesach
Bat mitzvah	A Halloween holiday
Jewish history	A *minyan* of ten men and women for prayer
A *brit* for baby boys	Eating kosher food
The State of Israel	Bagels and cream cheese

Can you think of any other customs and ideas that all Jews share? List them in the space below.

____

____

____

____

____

____

____

❄ WHAT DO YOU THINK? ❄

The cabdriver says, "Of course, I'm Jewish" even though he doesn't go to synagogue. Do you agree?________________________________

List three things that you think make a person Jewish.

1. ________________________________

2. ________________________________

3 .________________________________

WHICH WORDS ARE CORRECT?

Circle the correct words that complete each sentence.

1. Most Israelis belong to one of these four religions:

voodoo
Christianity
Bahaism
Judaism
Buddhism
Druse
Islam

2. A *yeshivah* is

an Israeli snack food
a religious school
an ancient mosque

3. Bet Shmuel is

the prophet Shmuel's birthplace
the headquarters of Israel's chief rabbis
a synagogue and college for Reform rabbinic students

4. It's important for Orthodox girls to be

good dancers
good soldiers
modest

5. A *minyan* is

a group of ten people for prayer
a Middle Eastern vegetable
a ritual bath

What Belongs to What?

Match the words in Column **A** with those in Column **B**. Write the number in Column **A** next to the correct word or words in Column **B**.

A	B
1. The headquarters of Israel's chief rabbis	_____ A synagogue platform
2. The religion of most Israeli Arabs	_____ Ultra-Orthodox women
3. A *yeshivah*	_____ Reform Judaism
4. A wig or kerchief	_____ Heichal Shlomo
5. Men and women count for a *minyan*	_____ Islam
6. *Bimah*	_____ Beards and *peot*
7. Shabbat and holidays	_____ *Aron hakodesh*
8. An ark for the Torah	_____ Prayer
9. Ultra-Orthodox men	_____ A Jewish religious high school and college
10. Words addressed to God in the synagogue	_____ Buses don't run in most of Israel

6

YOTAM CELEBRATES A Full Circle of Holidays

Yotam is nine. He lives in Nahariya, a town in northern Israel. He is in the third grade. Yotam's brother Shai is six and a half.

Yotam says: "On Purim my friends and I wear funny costumes. We go walking on the main street of town. Everyone laughs at everyone else. Once I was a frog and once I was an elephant. This Purim I'll be Captain Planet. My favorite holiday is Israel Independence Day. There are games, balloons, noisemakers, and things to eat in the town square. When it gets dark, fireworks are shot from the roof of City Hall. In Tel Aviv the fireworks are shaped like a giant Jewish star.

"I go to school from eight in the morning to about one o'clock most days. My favorite day is Monday. We do sports, tumbling, crafts and art—fun things all day. Bible is interesting. We read the Torah and talk about it. In fourth grade I'll start learning English. In junior high we choose another language to study, either French or Arabic."

Shai: "I'll choose Arabic because so many Israelis are Arabs. Who needs French?"

Yotam: "I play the recorder. I like to listen to rock music and to read. For my birthday I got a set of encyclopedias. In one of the books, there's a picture of the Statue of Liberty. It's gigantic. Some day I'll go to the United States and climb way up to the top of the statue."

Shai: "Me, too!"

Specialness

It's impossible to forget about Jewish holidays in Israel. Some people follow the holiday customs carefully. Others don't. But everyone feels that holiday time is special.

On the afternoon before a holiday, the smells of holiday foods float out of kitchen windows. Buses are crowded. Everyone is rushing to get home from work early. Families dragging kids and diaper bags are hurrying to Grandma and Grandpa's house.

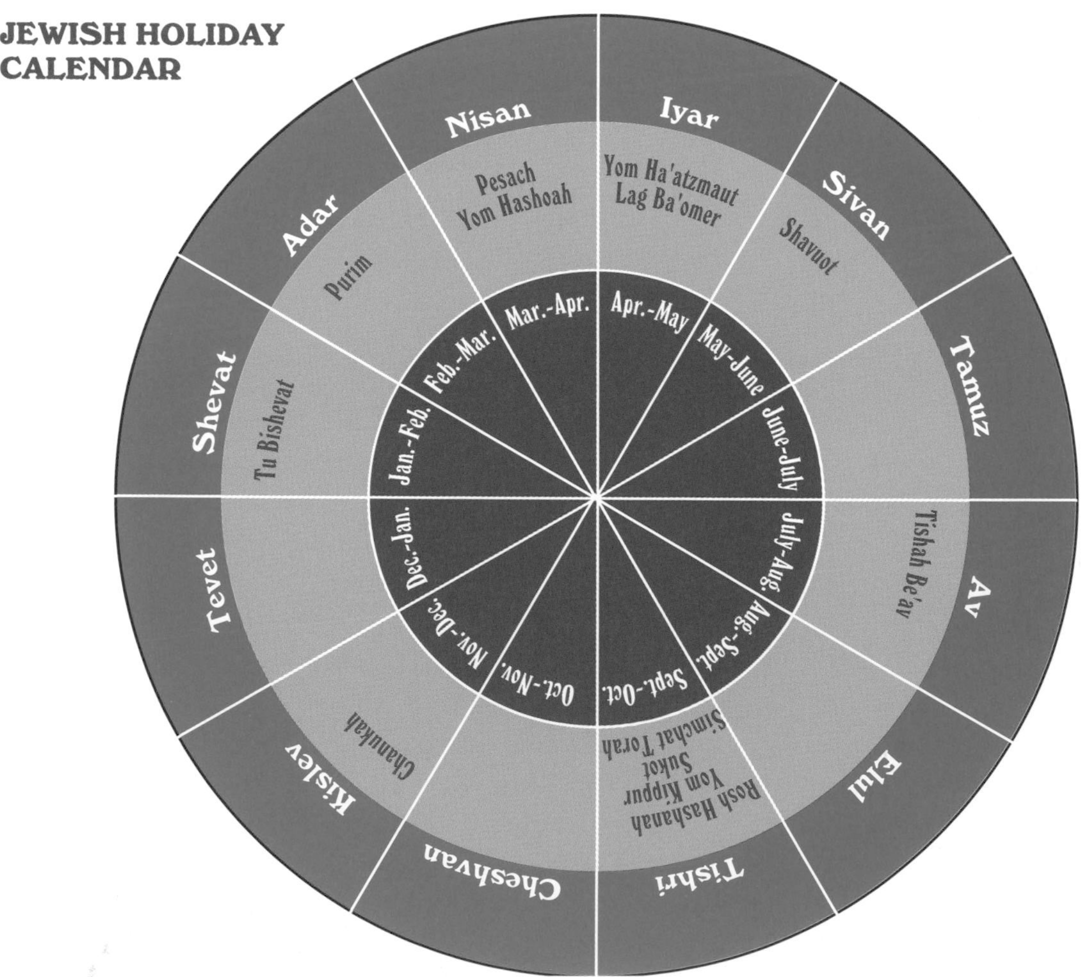

JEWISH HOLIDAY CALENDAR

And flower stands are busy selling bouquets. As evening comes, the streets begin to empty. Windows light up, and candles twinkle on kitchen tables. It's time to greet the holiday.

Shabbat

The best holiday of all comes every week. The Torah tells us to rest each Friday evening and Saturday. Most buses in Israel stop running on Friday afternoon. They start running again on Saturday evening. Shopping centers and stores are closed. Even El Al, the national airline, doesn't land in Israel on Shabbat.

Most people have a five-and-a-half or six-day workweek. And kids go to school six days a week. So when Shabbat comes, it's very welcome. Israelis enjoy the holiday in different ways. Shabbat is a friendly time. Dinner is often eaten at Grandma and Grandpa's house with uncles, aunts, and cousins. Grandma may complain about all the cooking that she does. But heaven help you if you don't come! Shabbat afternoon is a time for visiting friends or going on a *tiyul*. Some people take the suntan lotion and go to the beach. Soccer fans fill their pockets with sunflower seeds and head for the stadium.

In Chapter 5 you met Uriah. Here is how his family spends Shabbat. Uriah, his father, and his brothers go to the synagogue on Friday evening. By the time they return home, Uriah's mother has already lit the Shabbat candles. They say a blessing over the wine and challah. They sit down to a big Shabbat dinner. Between each course they sing Shabbat songs. After awhile the baby falls asleep in his high chair. The next oldest child is yawning. Even the candles are burning low. But the happy singing goes on.

Next morning the family attends Shabbat services in the synagogue. Then the kids have time for reading, playing hopscotch, dolls—doing lazy things. In the mid-afternoon Uriah's father sits down with each older child. Together they go over the Torah lesson of the week. After the sun has set, the family lights a fat twisted candle. It's called a *havdalah* candle. Shabbat is over. The workweek is about to begin again.

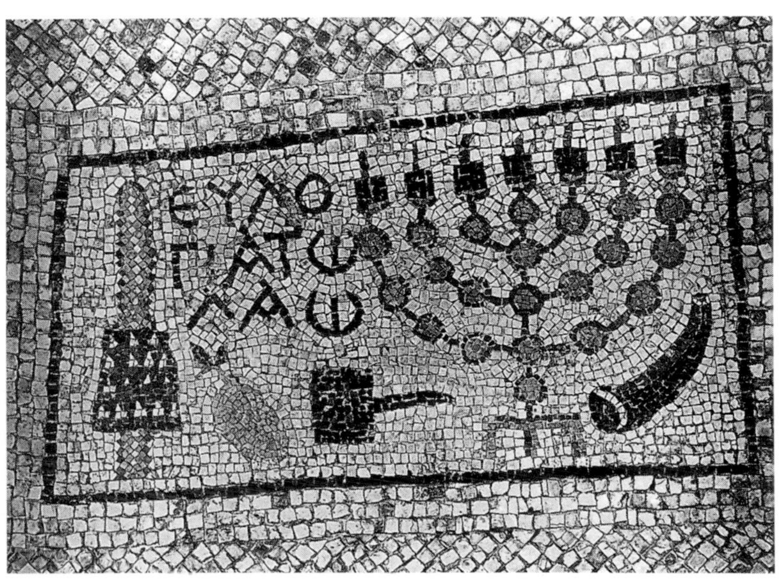

This mosaic from the sixth century, found at Huldah, depicts many Jewish holiday symbols.

Rosh Hashanah and Yom Kippur

School has just started after the long summer vacation. But before kids can even doodle in their new notebooks, school is out again. The autumn holidays are here. First comes Rosh Hashanah, the Jewish new year. Nine days later comes Yom Kippur.

Before the holiday the person who blows the *shofar* practices. The food stores sell honey cake and wine. On Rosh Hashanah apples are dipped in honey in each home. People hope that eating sweet food will bring them a good, sweet new year. Nobody goes to work. Some people go to the synagogue. Others drive off on an autumn vacation. Many people in Jerusalem hurry through the narrow streets to the Western Wall, the *Kotel*. The setting sun warms their backs. Slowly the sky grows dark. All over Israel men and women begin their Rosh Hashanah prayers.

Yom Kippur is a serious holiday. Many Jews don't eat on that day. They pray all day and think about how to live as good Jews and good people. And the roads in Israel are empty. Nobody is driving. As the sun goes down, the people in the synagogues wait for three stars to appear in the sky. Then the *shofar* is blown one last time. "*Gemar chatimah tovah*," people say to one another. "May it be a good year."

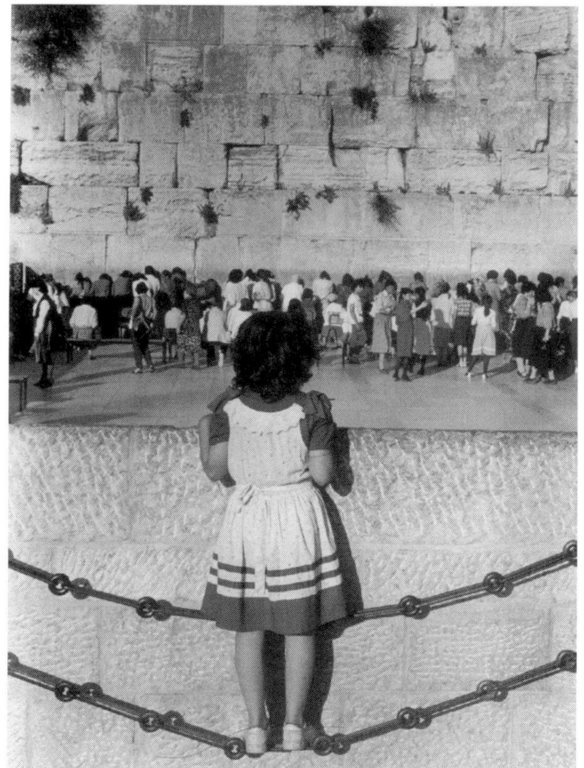

The space in front of the Kotel *in Jerusalem is divided into a women's section and a men's section. A little girl is looking into the women's side.*

Sukot

The fields are full of ripe tomatoes, squash, and cucumbers on Sukot. Many Israelis build a *sukah* on their porch or in their yard. Yotam and his family build a *sukah* on their balcony. They crisscross branches for the roof. They hang apples, grapes, and other good things from the branches. At mealtime in the *sukah*, everyone smells the sweet harvest smell. But people who sleep in the *sukah* need to keep a towel handy. Their faces may get washed by the first fall rain.

The *sukah* is a reminder that the Jews wandered through the desert. Each night those Israelites would put up a tent or *sukah* to sleep in. Synagogue-goers bring with them an *etrog* (a fruit like a lemon) and a *lulav* (branches of palm, myrtle, and willow tied together). During the services they wave the *etrog* and *lulav* in the air. The

A Jew from Bukhara in Asia is getting ready to shake his **lulav** *and* **etrog** *during Sukot.*

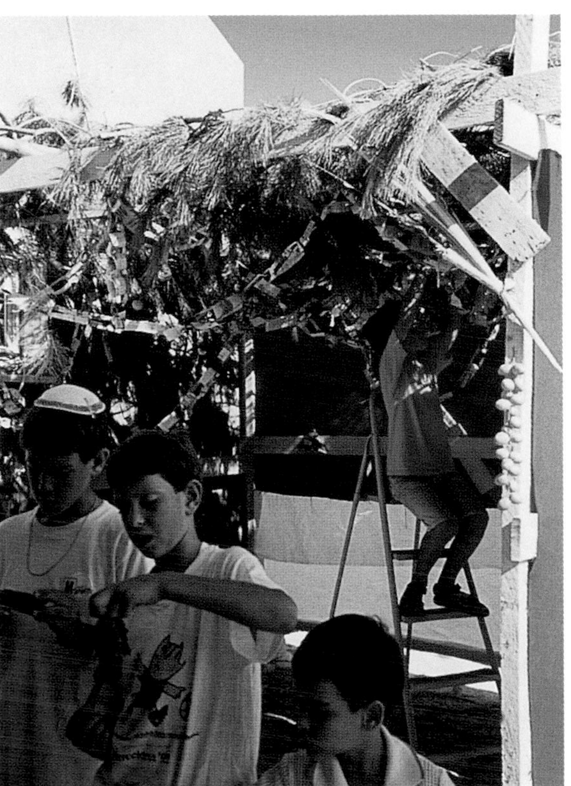

Ari, Matan, and Joel are decorating their **sukah.**

"shushing" sound reminds Jews of the harvest holiday that was celebrated in the Temple long ago.

There's no school during the week between Sukot and Simchat Torah. Many offices and factories also close. People go off on trips. Bright-colored tents dot the beaches around Lake Kinneret. The water is still warm from the summer sun. Swimmers, kayakers, and builders of sand castles play all day.

Simchat Torah

Dancing and singing with the Torah is a happy way to end Sukot. Jews have read the Torah in the synagogue all year. On Simchat Torah they finish the last chapter. The Torah scrolls of each synagogue are carried in a dancing, singing parade. In an Orthodox synagogue every man gets a turn to carry the Torah. In Reform and some Conservative synagogues, both men and women carry the Torah. Kids also join the parade. They wave Simchat Torah flags and sing and shout. Nobody shuts them up. It's a party!

At last all the Torahs are put back into the ark. Only one is left out. It is unrolled to the very beginning. Everybody becomes quiet, even the kids. The reader begins to chant, "In the beginning God created the heaven and the earth ..." And a new year of Torah study begins.

Say It in Hebrew

English	Hebrew	How to Say the Hebrew
holidays	חֲגִים	cha-*gim*
candles	נֵרוֹת	ne-*rot*
shofar (ram's horn)	שׁוֹפָר	sho-*far*
autumn	סְתָו	stav

Chanukah

When the kids go to school at this time of year, it's dark. And when some of them come home, it's dark again. Chanukah comes in mid-winter, when the days are the shortest. So it's a good thing that Chanukah is a holiday of lights. There are eight nights of lighting the candles of the *chanukiah*. There's no school all week. That leaves plenty of time to spin a *sevivon* (top) and eat jelly doughnuts.

Even with a mouthful of jelly doughnut, any Israeli kid can tell you about Judah Maccabee. He led the Jews in a war against the powerful Syrians. The Syrians had put idols in the Holy Temple. They had forced the Jews to pray to idols instead of God. But Judah's small, brave army drove out the Syrians and freed the Temple.

At Chanukah time young people climb up to Modin. That's the place where Judah Maccabee lived more than two thousand years ago. They light a torch and race with it to Jerusalem. The torch is a symbol of Jewish faith and courage.

Yael Arad, Israel's Olympic champion, holds a torch during a Chanukah celebration.

SUMMING UP

In Israel everyone knows when a Jewish holiday arrives. On most holidays there's no school. On some holidays buses don't run, and stores and workplaces are closed. Holidays are for everyone, and Israelis enjoy them in different ways. Some people follow religious customs carefully. They spend many hours in the synagogue. Other people go on trips, visit friends, or just relax.

Special holiday customs are followed in Israel. Here are a few examples. On Rosh Hashanah, Yom Kippur, and other holidays, many people pray at the *Kotel*, the Western Wall, in Jerusalem. Between Sukot and Simchat Torah, there's a long school recess. Sam and Ben's family and many others take vacation trips. And on Chanukah young runners carry the torch of the Maccabees to Jerusalem.

This chapter discussed the holidays in the first half of the year. In the next chapter you'll complete the full circle of holidays. You'll go all the way back to Rosh Hashanah.

ACTIVITIES

HIDDEN HOLIDAY WORDS

Find the following thirteen hidden holiday words. Look across and down. Circle each word that you find.

SHOFAR
CHANUKIAH
HONEY
SIMCHAT TORAH
HAVDALAH
TORAH
SUKAH
MODIN
SUKOT
CHANUKAH
ROSH HASHANAH
YOM KIPPUR
CHALLAH

```
R O S H H A S H A N A H O H
S U K A H S U T O R A H C O
Y W A V E S K S H O F O H L
O M O D I N O S A U R N A I
M O I A L A T K E S E E N D
K O L L C A N D L E S Y U A
I C H A L L A H O R C A K E
P H C H A N U K I A H O A E
P S I M C H A T T O R A H O
U P S H O F A R B L O W E R
R L A T K E S A R E G O O D
N E S G A D O L H A Y A P O
```

Here's a tough extra question. Can you find the Hebrew words for "A great miracle happened here"?

Which Words Are Correct?

Circle the correct word or words that complete each sentence.

1. The roof of a *sukah* is made of (tiles, branches, air).
2. Between (Yom Kippur and Chanukah, Sukot and Simchat Torah, Christmas and New Year) many Israelis take a vacation.
3. At the end of Shabbat, people light a (torch, *havdalah* candle, *chanukiah*).
4. In Israel during Shabbat, most (joggers, buses, water faucets) stop running.
5. Judah Maccabee lived in (Jerusalem, Modin, Brooklyn).
6. The *lulav* and *etrog* are (eaten, waved, hung from the roof) during Sukot.
7. Many Jews eat no food on (Halloween, Pesach, Yom Kippur).
8. Jews dance with a (Torah, *lulav*, *chanukiah*) on Simchat Torah.
9. In Israel a favorite Chanukah treat is (a hot-fudge sundae, jelly doughnuts, chocolate-covered matzah).
10. On Chanukah young Israelis carry a lighted torch to (Lake Kinneret, Jerusalem, Modin).

Connect the Dots

Name the holiday on which the activity pictured below is done.

____

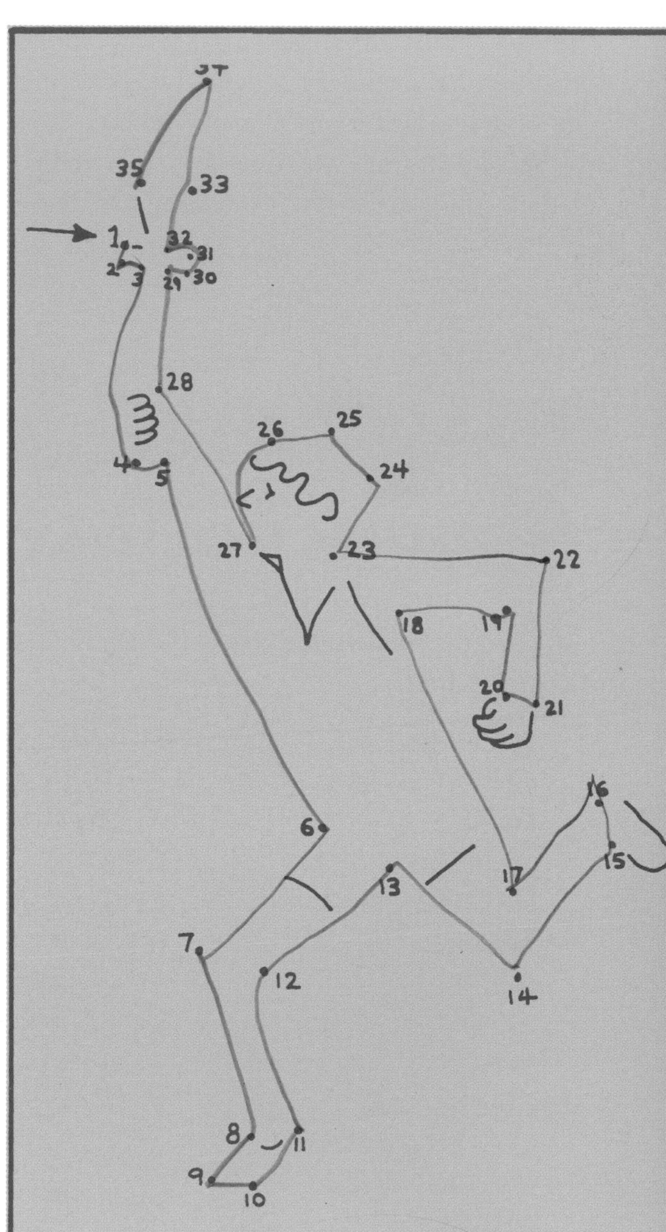

7 ISRAEL CELEBRATES
Holidays Are for Everyone

Here's what Israeli Jewish kids say about holidays:

Rahely: I love Pesach. We have lots of company at the *seder.* And my mother makes a great chocolate cake out of layers of matzah and chocolate.

Uriah: Each holiday is different and special. I love them all.

Sam: Chanukah is the best holiday because we get presents.

Meirav: Pesach! The whole family is together. It feels warm and happy. For each *seder* Grandma cooks a turkey with stuffing.

Ruthy: Purim is fun. We play games at school like Giants and Dwarfs.

Yotam: Israel Independence Day, with its fireworks and balloons, is my favorite holiday.

Abigail: Shabbat is wonderful. I love going back home and relaxing on Shabbat.

Schoolchildren planting trees on Tu Bishevat.

Tu Bishevat

It's still raining, hailing, and snowing. But the almond trees know that the spring is coming. They are covered with white blossoms. Israelis put on boots and raincoats to plant trees on this New Year of the Trees. Once gray rocks and thistles covered many of Israel's hillsides. Rain washed the good brown earth down into the valleys. Then the first Zionists arrived and began to plant trees. Year after year the young forests grew. Today many of the hills are green, although there are still plenty of gray rocks left. But each Tu Bishevat more tiny trees are planted among them.

Purim

Don't ride a bus on Purim in Israel! Godzilla or a grinning skeleton might sit down beside you. Dracula might drool on you.

Purim is the holiday of games, tricks, and costume parties. Even in the synagogue, grown-ups and kids get silly. They read *Megillat Esther* aloud. That's the story of how Queen Esther and Mordecai saved the Jewish people from the evil Haman. Everyone stamps, hisses, and twirls a noisemaker when Haman's name is read. Some towns have Purim parades. Giant floats roll through the streets. Peddlers sell *hamantashen.* Kids bat one another with plastic hammers. And the shopping centers are crowded with kids wearing costumes. It's a wild, funny holiday. If you're in Israel next

On Purim, people dress up in costumes and march in the Purim parade.

Say It in Hebrew

<u>English</u>	<u>Hebrew</u>	<u>How to Say the Hebrew</u>
winter	חֹרֶף	*cho*-ref
spring	אָבִיב	a-*viv*
summer	קַיִץ	*ka*-yitz
year	שָׁנָה	sha-*nah*

Purim, watch for Captain Planet. It might be Yotam.

Pesach

The rains are over by Pesach. The air gets warm. Wildflowers pop up under clotheslines and between garbage cans. Many people pull out their furniture and repaint the walls of their homes. They clean out the closets and unpack the Pesach dishes. Sam's dog, Tic-Toc, hides under the porch, hoping that his family will forget about his Pesach bath. "Not a chance," says Sam. On this holiday everything gets scrubbed. Then people and pets begin again, fresh and bright as wildflowers.

Kids have two full weeks of vacation from school. Adults get holiday gifts from their employers. And then comes the best part—the *seder.* Uncles, aunts, and friends arrive. Some families invite *olim* from Ethiopia or Russia to their *seder*. Together they read the story of Pesach in the *haggadah*. It tells about freedom. Both the

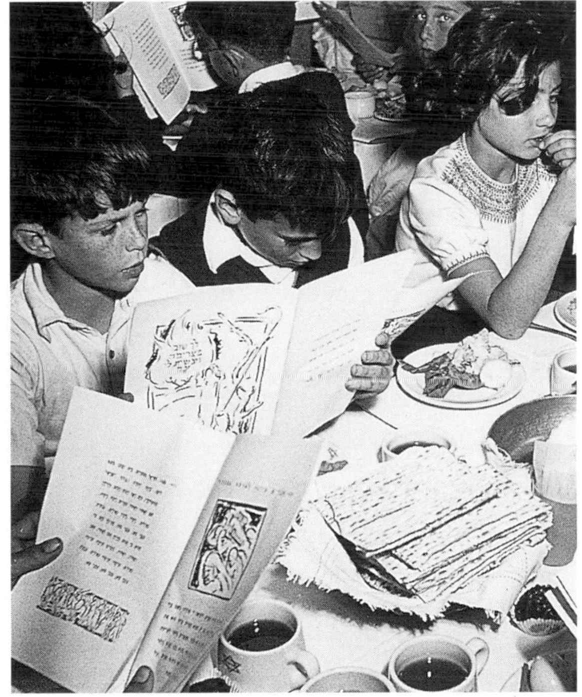

***Children reading from the* haggadah *during a Pesach* seder.**

Israelis and *olim* are happy to be free in their own country. Their kids are very busy. They ask the Four Questions. Then they hunt for the *afikoman.*

Even families that don't read the *haggadah* gather for a holiday meal. The matzah, food, and wine taste special. And welcoming springtime is special, too.

This sculpture stands outside Yad Vashem, the Museum of the Holocaust in Jerusalem.

Yom Hashoah

This is a day of sad memories. Israelis remember the six million Jews who were killed by the Nazis. Many people lost their parents, brothers, and sisters in the Holocaust. Some Israelis lived through the Holocaust. They hid in forests and fought the Nazis or survived the Nazi prison camps.

The two-minute air raid siren makes a crying wail. When Israelis hear it, they stop whatever they are doing. They stand quietly and remember those who died.

Yom Hazikaron and Yom Ha'atzmaut

First comes a sad day and then a happy one.

Yom Hazikaron is a day of remembering. Israelis think about the men and women who died defending their country. Many people have died in Israel's wars. In the middle of the morning, the sirens sound all over the country. On the highways cars pull over to the side and wait. In schools, factories, and stores people stop their work. For two minutes everyone remembers the dead. The whole country says a silent thank you to them. Without them the State of Israel would not have been born and would not have survived.

The happy celebration of Yom Ha'atzmaut, Independence Day, begins at the end of Yom Hazikaron. Bonfires blaze all over the country. People toast marshmallows and bake potatoes in the flames. The next day there are roaring flyovers by air force jets. Many army bases are open. Kids climb all over the huge, grim-looking army tanks and swing from the gun barrels. Guides from the Society for the Protection of Nature in Israel lead hikes all over the country. Meirav might be leading a hike in a few years. Look for her on Yom Ha'atzmaut. Happy birthday, Israel!

Lag Ba'omer

Before Lag Ba'omer, Israelis have to keep a sharp eye on their scrap wood. Kids celebrate Lag Ba'omer by making bonfires in every empty lot, using old wood fences, doors, and boxes.

On Lag Ba'omer, students honor their teachers. Orthodox Jews go up to the village of Meiron in the mountains of Galilee. An

An Independence Day float.

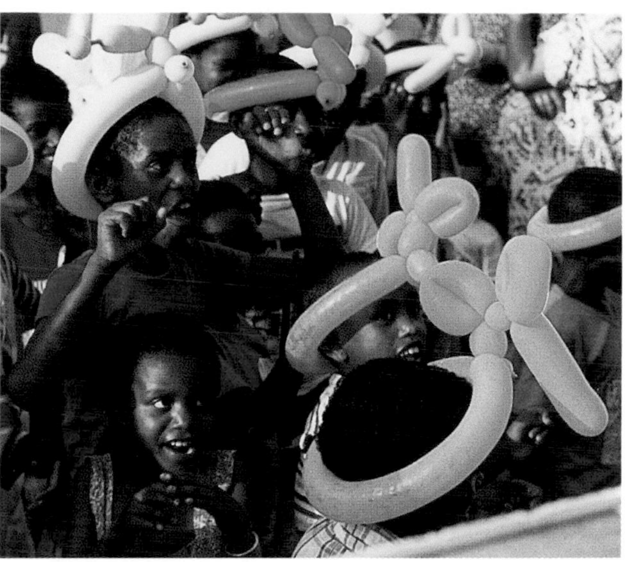

Ethiopian olim *at their first Independence Day party.*

important rabbi named Shimon bar Yochai is buried there. The twisting roads are jammed with cars. And the village is bursting with people. Orthodox three-year-old boys get their first haircut at Meiron. On Lag Ba'omer, tiny Meiron is a noisy hullabaloo. People are dancing and praying, little boys are crying, and picnic barbecues are sizzling.

Shavuot

So much has happened on Shavuot.

Moses brought the Ten Commandments down from Mount Sinai. And the Jewish people promised to obey them.

Much later, Ruth and Naomi returned from Moab to Bethlehem, where Ruth married Boaz. Their great-grandson David became the second king of Israel.

Much, much later the Jews began going to the Temple in Jerusalem on Shavuot. They would bring God the first springtime fruits of their fields.

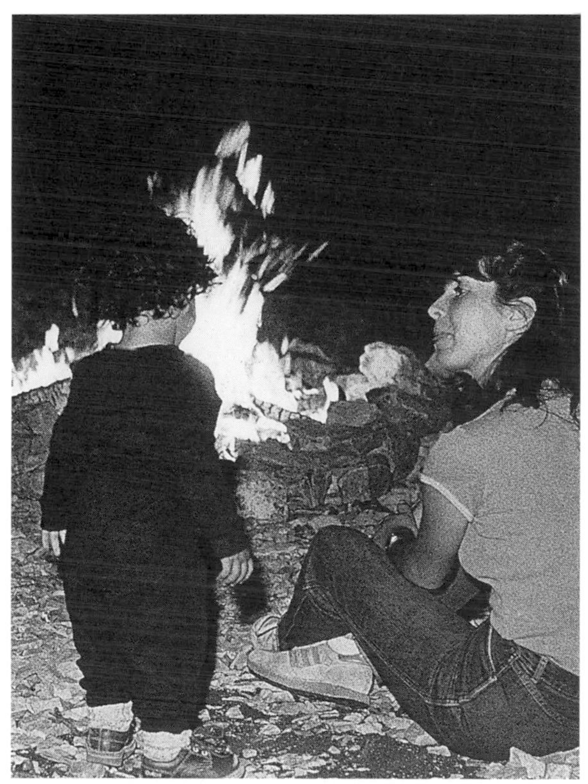

Two Israelis enjoy a Lag Ba'omer campfire.

"Is everybody ready?" calls the tractor driver. The First Fruits parade is almost on its way.

Later still, Reform Jews began to have confirmation ceremonies for boys and girls on Shavuot.

All of those events are important. But in Israel the best Shavuot happening is the First Fruits party on a kibbutz. The kibbutz is like a farm. You'll find out more about it in Chapter 10. In late spring when Shavuot comes, chicks are poking out of their shells. Newborn lambs and goats are prancing around the children's farm. And kibbutz kids are already picking the first radishes and green onions. These are all the first fruits of spring. The kids decorate wagons with bright flowers. They pile leafy branches and baskets of fruit on the back of the wagons. Then they climb aboard, holding wiggling baby animals.

"Is everybody ready?" calls the tractor driver. "Ready!" the kids yell. *"Kadimah!"* ("Forward!") The tractor pulls the wagon forward. Around and around the kibbutz they go. It's a clapping, singing parade of first fruits.

Tishah Be'av

It's mid-summer. The beaches and parks are crowded. But some Israelis sit at home. Quietly they read the sad words of the prophet Jeremiah. The Holy Temple was burned to the ground on Tishah Be'av. Over the years other bad things have happened to our people on this day. In Jerusalem many people go to the *Kotel,* the Western Wall, on Tishah Be'av. They fast and pray all day long.

Closing the Circle of Holidays

Our circle of holidays started on Rosh Hashanah in early autumn. Now it's summer. Yotam, Shai, and other Israeli kids are enjoying their long vacation from school. In only a few weeks it will be Rosh Hashanah again. The circle of Jewish holidays goes round and round.

Get the apples and honey ready!

SUMMING UP

In gray, rainy mid-winter, Israeli kids plant trees on Tu Bishevat. About a month later they celebrate Purim with costumes and noisemakers. Pesach, Lag Ba'omer, and Yom Ha'atzmaut are happy, busy holidays. On Yom Hashoah and Yom Hazikaron, Israelis remember the sad things that have happened to Jews. In the spring Shavuot, with its first fruits and flowers, makes them happy again. Then Tishah Be'av brings another reminder of sad times in Jewish history.

Soon summer will pass. The year will have made a full circle. Rosh Hashanah will be here again.

ACTIVITIES

Use Chapters 6 and 7 to help you answer the questions in this section.

PAIRS OF HOLIDAYS

Column **A** is a list of Jewish holidays. Column **B** is a list of holidays celebrated by many Americans. Draw a line connecting each holiday in Column **A** to a holiday in Column **B** that is similar or that occurs in the same season.

A	B
Purim	Thanksgiving
Yom Ha'atzmaut	Halloween
Chanukah	Memorial Day
Sukot	Independence Day—July 4
Yom Hazikaron	Christmas
Pesach	Arbor Day
Tu Bishevat	Easter

List three of the connected pairs of holidays. Tell how they are alike.

1. ____

____

2. ____

____

3. ____

____

List three other pairs of holidays. Tell how they are different.

1. ____

____

2. ____

____

3. ____

____

The Same and Different

American and Israeli Jews celebrate the same Jewish holidays. Some customs are the same in both countries. Some are different.

Identify five customs that are the same.

1. ____
2. ____
3. ____
4. ____
5. ____

Identify three customs that are different.

1. ____
2. ____
3. ____

❄ HOLIDAY OBJECTS ❄

Below are some objects that are used on certain Jewish holidays. Fill in the missing letters to name each object.

1. S _ _ _ _ R

2. T _ N _ _ _ _ _ _ _ _ _ _ _ _ S

3. L _ _ _ _ and _ _ _ _ G

4. H _ _ _ _ _ _ _ S _ _ _

5. T _ _ _ H

6. T _ _ E

7. F _ _ G

8. _ H _ _ _ _ _ _ _

Identify the Jewish holiday or holidays on which each of the above objects is used.

1.

2.

3.

4.

5.

6.

7.

8.

HOLIDAY CROSSWORD PUZZLE

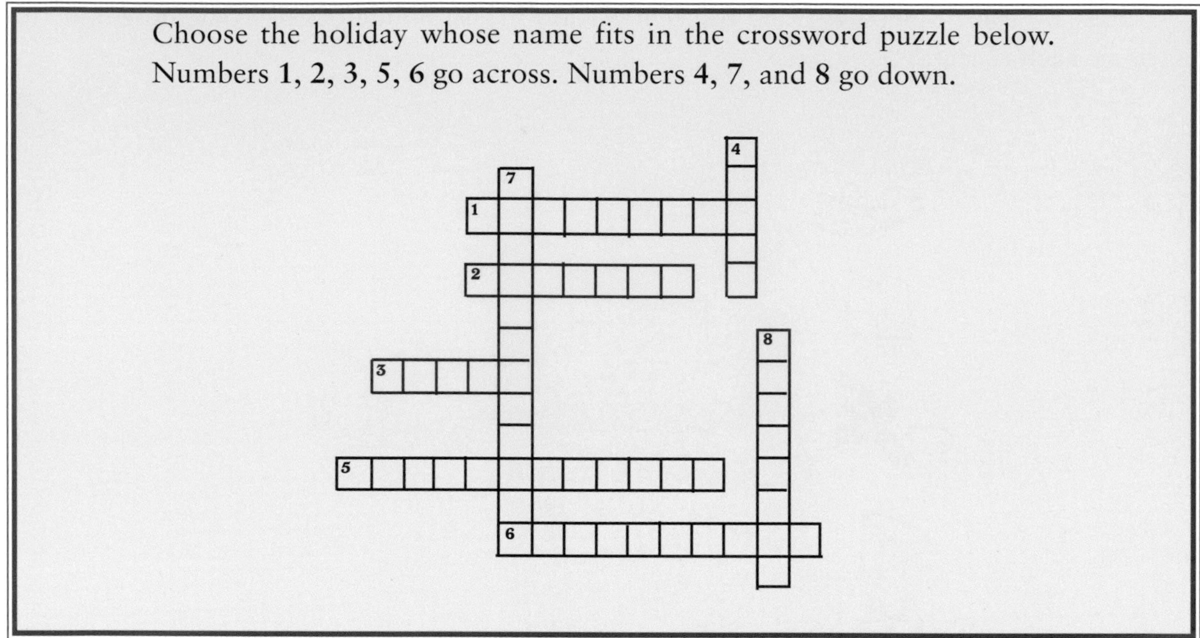

Choose the holiday whose name fits in the crossword puzzle below. Numbers **1, 2, 3, 5, 6** go across. Numbers **4, 7,** and **8** go down.
1
2
3
4
5
6
7
8

WHEN SHOULD WE CELEBRATE?

Write the name of each of the following holidays in the box under the season in which it falls. Make sure to write each holiday in the order in which it occurs in the year.

Shabbat
Rosh Hashanah
Yom Kippur
Simchat Torah
Chanukah
Tu Bishevat
Purim
Pesach
Yom Ha'atzmaut
Lag Ba'omer
Shavuot
Tishah Be'av

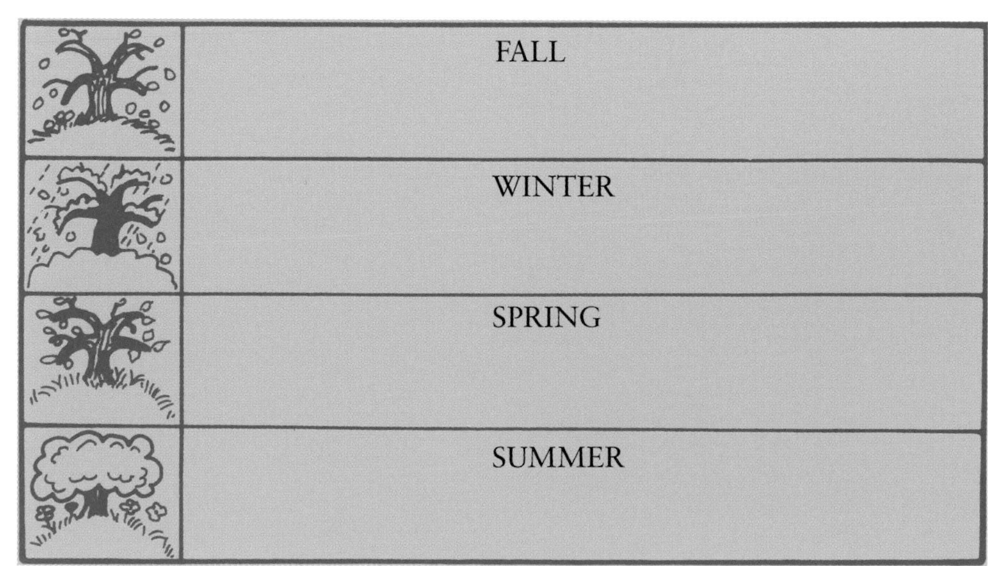

AVIRAM IS A CITY KID

Israel's Cities

Aviram lives in Tel Aviv. He's twelve and a half years old and in the sixth grade. He and his brother Derin are eating falafel sandwiches.

Aviram says: "I belong to *Tzofim*. It's like Boy and Girl Scouts in the United States. Last Pesach my group went hiking in the South. We climbed down into very old caves. Jewish rebels dug them as hiding places from Roman soldiers. Sometimes the Romans blocked the openings and the people who were inside died. It was scary to be down there. We learn about Israel and talk about things at *Tzofim* meetings. For example, we talk about how we feel about Arabs. Arab kids are in *Tzofim* groups, too. We decided that even though some Arabs are terrorists, we can't blame all Arabs.

"Pesach is my favorite holiday because at that time we get the longest school vacation. And I like eating matzah instead of pita for a change. I like school. But mostly I like sports—soccer, basketball, weight lifting. And I compete in shot put. Next year I'll go to a junior high. It's a big school. I think I'll feel a little lost because I won't be with my friends. Friends are the most important thing to me.

"When I grow up, after I serve in the army, I think I'll study to be a coach or gym teacher. I like working with little kids.

"Sometimes I go to the center of Tel Aviv. It's crowded with stores and cars. And it's smoky and smelly. We have a big park near my house. The city built it as a reward to us after the Persian Gulf War. Scud missiles crashed down right on our neighborhood, but nobody ran away. We all stayed in our homes."

Surprising Cities

Tiny Israel is full of surprises. And Israel's cities are also surprising. They're very different from one another. Tel Aviv-Yafo is busy, muggy, and flat. Haifa climbs a breezy hillside. Beersheba pops suddenly out of a huge brown desert. Safed naps on its history-filled mountaintop. And Jerusalem is so special that it needs a whole chapter of its own.

Tel Aviv-Yafo

Tel Aviv-Yafo stretches along the sparkling Mediterranean Sea. Whether it's hot summer or chilly winter, the beach and walkways are always busy. A few tough swimmers ride the waves. Kids build waterways and tunnels in the sand. Peddlers sell balloons, toys, and jewelry. Everyone else strolls and enjoys the fresh salty air.

Behind the beach is a line of tall hotels. Tourists come from many countries for the swimming, the sun, and the "action." "Tel Aviv never sleeps," say the travel agents. There are concerts, plays, discos, museums, movies, and a great safari park. In the summer, rock bands play beside the Yarkon River in northern Tel Aviv. People float past in paddleboats and rowboats and listen. Tel Aviv-Yafo has enough action to keep people awake day and night.

Tel Aviv is also busy buying, selling, and making things. It has a big diamond center. Diamonds are brought to Tel Aviv from Africa and Europe. They are cut and polished and then resold. Israel's stock market is in Tel Aviv. Most of the country's newspapers and books are published here. The city's busy factories make fur coats, aspirins, cornflakes, and other products.

Eighty-five years ago Tel Aviv was just a sandy beach. Yafo was a very old port city to its south. But Tel Aviv grew fast. It outgrew Yafo and joined with it. Today Tel Aviv-Yafo is the world's oldest-youngest great city and the second-largest city in Israel.

Haifa

Some people think that Haifa looks like San Francisco. Both cities are ports on the shore of a great sea. The houses of Haifa climb Mount Carmel the same way that San Francisco climbs the California hills. Mount

The harbor in Yafo, on the shore of the Mediterranean Sea.

The open-air market in Tel Aviv is a good place to buy onions, chocolate bars, toys—anything.

Carmel is so steep that some of its streets are connected by staircases. Haifa is Israel's third-largest city. It's the only Israeli city with a subway. Haifa's tiny subway trains struggle up from the port to the top of the mountain. On the very top is a wild, wooded national park. Deer and wild goats roam through the park. On holidays people from Haifa go there to relax. The deer, the goats, and the people have fun watching one another.

At the foot of Mount Carmel is the port. It's tucked into the curve of the bay. Ships docked at the port are loaded with oranges, tomatoes, and apples for Europe. Tankers unload oil for Haifa's big refinery. And other ships bring lumber, steel, plastic, and more products, which feed the smoking factories along the bay. The products are also carried in trucks to other parts of the country.

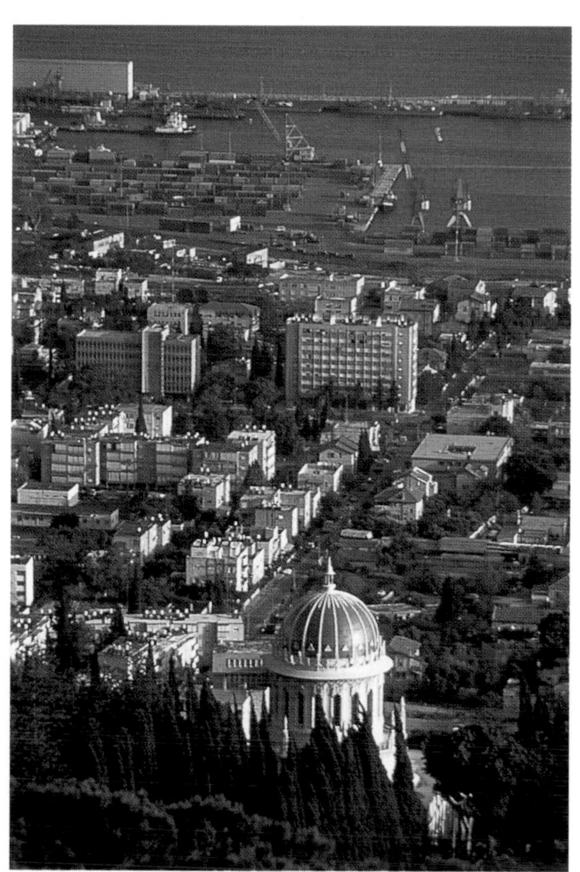

A view of Haifa from Mount Carmel.

Sometimes the big gray ships of the United States Navy dock in Haifa's port. Then the city's streets are filled with happy American sailors on shore leave.

Beersheba

The brown Negev Desert seems to go on for miles as you travel south. Now and then there's a tree. Here and there you see a black Bedouin tent and a herd of goats. Then suddenly, white houses pop up out of nowhere. Beersheba, the capital of the Negev, seems to grow out of the sand. It is a very old city. Abraham and Sarah, our biblical ancestors, wandered through this region. Beersheba was a small, quiet desert town until after Israel's War of Independence. Today it's a center for the farm settlements and smaller towns of the Negev.

Many Bedouin live near Beersheba, where there is a Bedouin market each week. Get there early and buy a camel, a bright rug, or a beautifully embroidered dress.

Scientists at Ben-Gurion University in Beersheba learn about the desert. They study its plants, climate, and soil. The United Nations has asked the university to help other countries that have large deserts. The scientists will teach the people of those countries to grow trees and plants with very little water.

Safed

Tough, little oak trees cover the hills and red poppies sparkle between the rocks of this city. It is located in the Galilee, the

(above) ***Bedouin stop for water in the Negev Desert.***

(left) ***For good cake and the best iced coffee filled with ice cream, come to a café in Nahariya.***

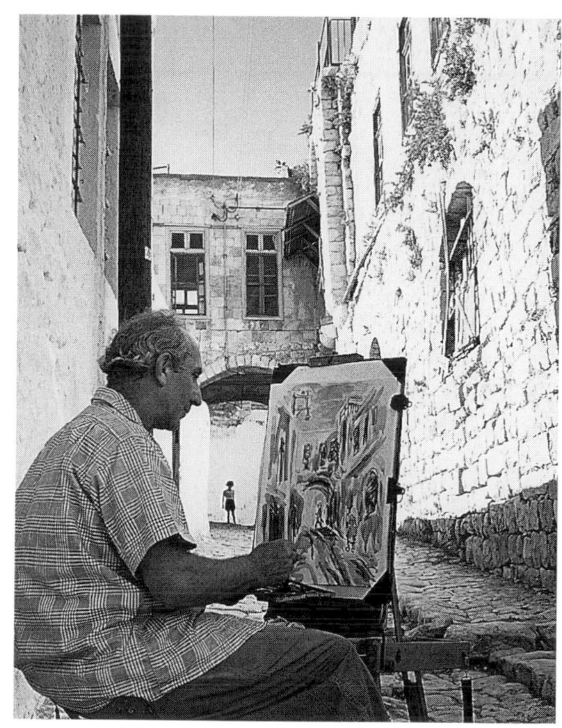

(above) ***The Crusader city of Akko.***

(left) ***Artist Avraham Gilboa painting a street scene in Safed.***

greenest part of Israel. A twisty, turning road leads up to Safed. From the top you can see Lake Kinneret in the East and the Mediterranean Sea in the West. Three hundred years ago Safed was a center of Jewish learning. People went to Safed from Europe to study with its famous rabbis. They built small, beautiful synagogues on winding lanes. Europe's Chasidim borrowed many ideas from the rabbis of Safed.

Today artists go to Safed to paint pictures of the hills and old synagogues. Students study in *yeshivot*. And tourists wander through the city.

More Cities

Eilat in the Far South is the warmest place in Israel. Frostbitten tourists go there to snorkel, skin-dive, and warm up. Eilat is also a port.

Tiberias on Lake Kinneret is another warm vacation city. It has ancient hot baths that the Romans built almost two thousand years ago. Sit on a worn stone. Dip your feet into the steamy water. You may be sitting where a Roman emperor once sat. This is the place where Israel's water carrier starts. From here the water of the Jordan River is carried to the thirsty Negev.

Akko is also a very old city. It was once the home of the Crusaders, Christian soldiers who came from Europe. Underneath modern Akko lies a whole buried Crusader city.

Nahariya sits on the Mediterranean Sea in Israel's Far North. It's the honeymoon capital of the country. A small stream trick-

Say It in Hebrew

English	Hebrew	How to Say the Hebrew
city	עִיר	ir
park or garden	גַּן	gan
port	נָמָל	na-*mal*
desert	מִדְבָּר	mid-*bar*

les down its tree-lined main street. Horse-drawn carriages carry newlyweds along the shore. Many soldiers stationed with the United Nations live in this peaceful town.

Then there's Afula, where the best pita sandwiches in Israel are made. And Hadera with its huge power plant. And Ashdod with its large port. And Ashkelon. And many more cities.

They're all interesting and special. You'll read about the most colorful city in Israel in the next chapter.

SUMMING UP

Israel's cities are very different from one another. Tel Aviv-Yafo, Israel's second-largest city, has a long sandy beach. There are theaters, museums, and many fun things to do in this city. It's also a busy center for business and manufacturing. Haifa, Israel's third-largest city, sits on a hillside. It is an important port. Haifa has many factories and a wooded national forest. Beersheba is the capital of the Negev. At the university located there scientists study the plants and soil of the desert. Safed is a picturesque city perched high in the mountains of the Galilee. It was once an important center of Jewish religious learning. There are many other cities in Israel, all interesting and special.

ACTIVITIES

HELP A TOURIST

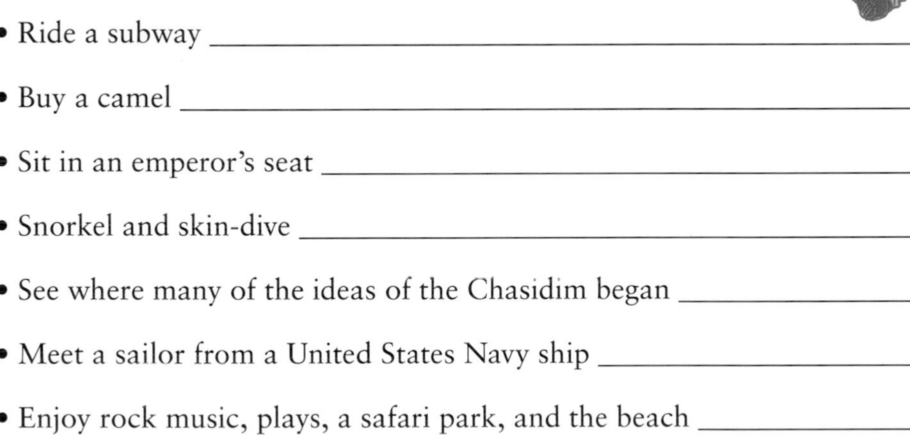

Pretend that you're a tour guide. Tell this confused tourist which city to choose in order to

- Ride a subway ____________________
- Buy a camel ____________________
- Sit in an emperor's seat ____________________
- Snorkel and skin-dive ____________________
- See where many of the ideas of the Chasidim began ____________
- Meet a sailor from a United States Navy ship ____________
- Enjoy rock music, plays, a safari park, and the beach ____________

CHOOSE THE RIGHT WORD

Circle the correct word or words that complete each sentence.

1. Tel Aviv is on the (Dead Sea, Mediterranean Sea, Saint Lawrence River).
2. Crusaders lived in (Akko, Brooklyn, Eilat).
3. The second-largest city in Israel is (Haifa, Nahariya, Tel Aviv).
4. The cities of Akko and Yafo are (new, very old, middle-aged).
5. The capital of the Negev is (New York, Beersheba, Nahariya).
6. The third-largest city in Israel is (Haifa, San Francisco, Safed).
7. Safed is on (Lake Kinneret, the Dead Sea, a mountain).
8. Tel Aviv has a (subway, safari park, underwater observatory).
9. Israel's water carrier starts in (Afula, Tiberias, Ashdod).
10. Beersheba has a (diamond center, university, Bedouin market).

Put Israel Together

On the left are fourteen pieces of Israel to put together. Draw the lines and names you find on each piece onto the correct space in the rectangle on the right.

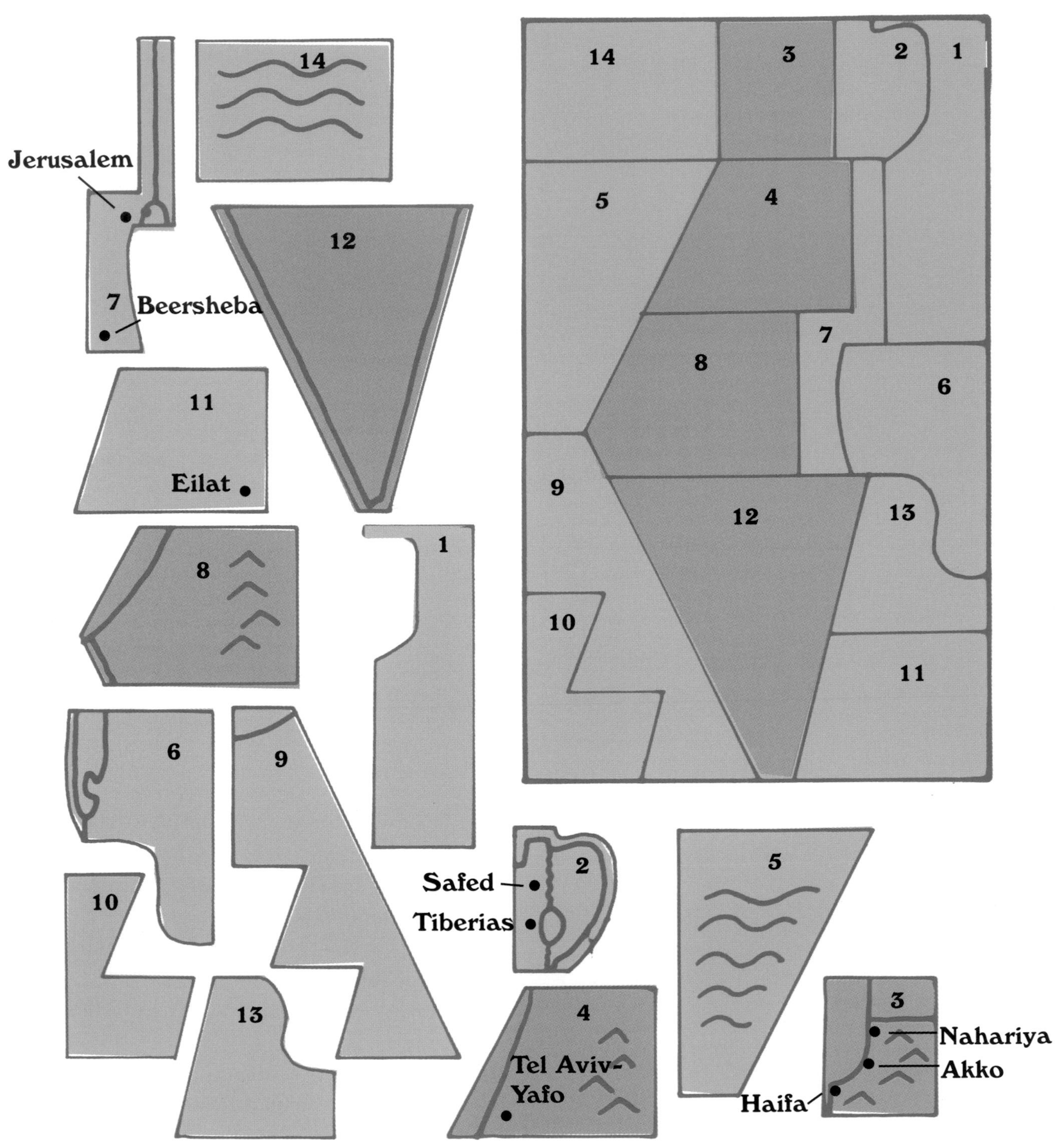

9

RUTHY AND RAHELY IN THE CITY OF GOLD

Jerusalem, Israel's Capital

Ruthy and Rahely live in Jerusalem. They are Sabras. That means they were born in Israel. They are both twelve, but Rahely is eight minutes older than Ruthy.

Ruthy: All the members of our family like to make music. My two older brothers play the flute and the trumpet. I play trombone, and Rahely plays the clarinet. We play in an orchestra and do jazz dancing at our community center. Every morning except on Shabbat we take the city bus to school. And after school we play games like Yahtzee or computer games with our friends.

Rahely: We just started learning Arabic in school. It's an important language for us to know because so many Israelis are Arab. And it's a beautiful language.

Ruthy: There are Arab kids in my class.

Rahely: We're twelve years old now. Almost bat mitzvah. At school we're studying about our family roots and Masada. Our class is going to take a trip to Masada. We'll start at five in the morning and climb to the top.

Ruthy: How do I feel about Jerusalem? I know Jerusalem is important. It's the capital of Israel. And it's where the Temple stood. But to me it's the place where I live. It's my home.

Rahely and Ruthy: To kids in America we say, "Come and visit!"

Jerusalem of Gold

For Ruthy and Rahely, Jerusalem is home.

For the people of Israel, it is their capital city.

For all Jews, Jerusalem is the city they face when they pray. Many Jews believe that Jerusalem is God's city. Long ago God's Temple stood in Jerusalem.

Jerusalem is also a holy city for Muslims and Christians. The ancient Dome of the Rock and the El Aksa Mosque in Jerusalem are important religious centers for Muslims. And Christians revere Jerusalem because Jesus preached and died in that city.

Jerusalem glows in the sunlight. Its round, gold-covered roofs and white stone buildings give it a shining, fairy-tale look. This golden city is important to many people. Take a walk through Jerusalem. Experience the city.

The old city of Jerusalem is holy to Jews, Christians, and Muslims. The golden Dome of the Rock sits on the site on which the Temple stood about 2,000 years ago.

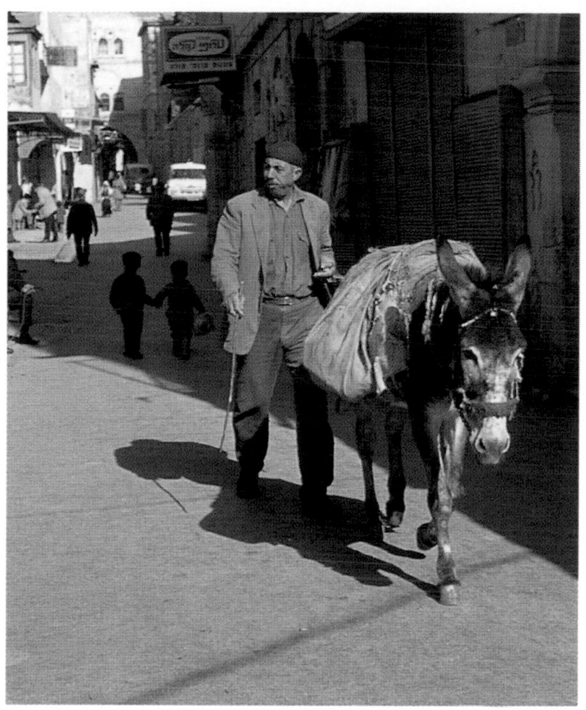

This man walks with his donkey through a market street in the old city.

The Old City

Jerusalem has an old part and a new part. We'll start in the old part, the old city. A thick stone wall was built around the old city many years ago. It protected the people of the city from enemies. Walk through one of the tall gateways of the wall into one of the busy squares. The towers of churches and mosques poke high into the sky above you. Narrow streets extend from the square. They are lined with shops that sell honey cakes, camels carved from olive wood, bright goat-hair rugs, and many other things. The smells of spices and herbs will tickle your nose. You will pass priests wearing tall black hats, Arabs in striped head scarves, and bearded Jews with curly *peot.* They all bump into one another on the crowded streets. And when a loaded donkey comes clip-clopping along, everyone squeezes to the side.

The Temple Mount

The Temple Mount stands in the old city, far from the busy shops. It is a platform of earth and stone, about as big as five football fields. Ancient stone steps lead up to it. In the days of the Bible, the Holy Temple and its courtyards stood on this spot. The Temple was burned to the ground almost two thousand years ago. Only one wall of the Mount was left standing—the Western Wall. In Hebrew it is called the *Kotel.*

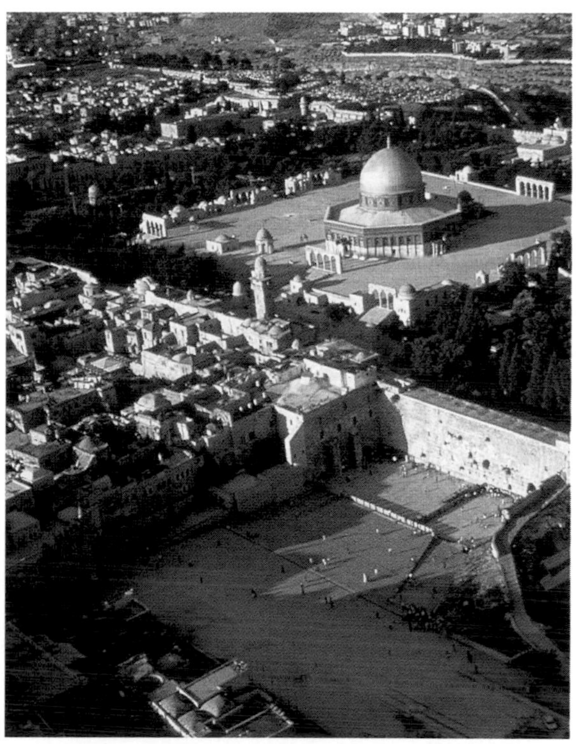

A view of the Western Wall and the Dome of the Rock, located in the old city of Jerusalem.

Through the centuries Jews would come to the *Kotel* from all over the world. They would cry and pray and leave notes to God in the cracks between the stones.

Today Jews still come to the *Kotel*. Some cry, some pray, and some just leave notes to God. At the *Kotel* you might also see a boy reading from the Torah. He is becoming a bar mitzvah. Men are gathered around him. Women and girls are watching from the women's section. As soon as the boy finishes reading, everyone throws candy at him. The kids race around picking up the candy, the women cheer, and the men might dance in a joyous circle. The *Kotel* is a happy place today.

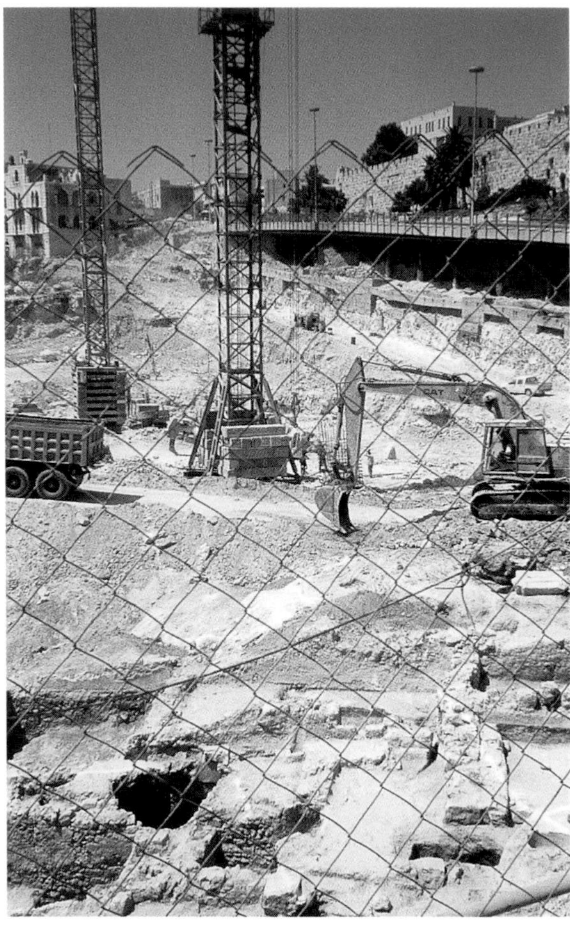

Here's a builder's nightmare and an archaeologist's dream. While digging for a shopping center near old Jerusalem, the builders uncovered a 3,000-year-old suburb. The bulldozers had to wait while the archaeologists studied the ancient walls.

Two religions consider the top of the Mount a holy place. Jews believe that Abraham brought his son Isaac there, intending to sacrifice him to God. Later King Solomon built the Holy Temple on this hill. And much later the Muslim prophet Mohammed dreamed that he flew up to heaven from the Mount. The Muslims built two beautiful mosques on the Mount, the Dome of the Rock and the El Aksa Mosque. Tourists and art lovers come to admire their bright tile walls and shiny roofs.

Digging into History

As you leave the old city, you might see people digging near the city walls. They are archaeologists. They are trying to find out about the people who lived in this area many years ago. But why are they digging? Because Jerusalem is made of layers, like a giant cake. And each layer tells a story. Long before the Bible was written, people had built a town there. They had cooked and made toys for their children, squeezed oil out of olives, and prayed to their gods. One day the town was destroyed by enemies. The people were taken away or killed. Slowly the walls of the houses fell and were covered by dust and weeds. The town became a hidden layer.

Years later new people came and built another town over the hidden layer. Eventually they also left. When their town

Say It in Hebrew		
English	Hebrew	How to Say the Hebrew
mosque	מִסְגָּד	mis-*gad*
church	כְּנֵסִיָּה	ke-ne-si-*yah*
[the Western] Wall	כֹּתֶל	*Ko*-tel
Israeli parliament (Knesset)	כְּנֶסֶת	*Kne*-set

crumbled, a new layer was added to the giant cake. A hill made of layers like these is called a tell.

As they dig, archaeologists find very old walls, broken toys, mosaic floors, and coffins. "Finds" like these are being discovered all over the country. Ben found an ancient paved cistern (water storage pit) near his house. The "finds" tell archaeologists what kind of people lived in a place. If the diggers were to uncover a *mikveh*, a *menorah*, or a *shofar* carved on a rock, they would probably decide that Jews lived there. The discovery of a cross or a fish design would probably mean that the town had been Christian. The small carved figure of a goddess or a square stone altar might mean that the town had been Canaanite.

Ben-Yehuda Street in new Jerusalem is a popular spot for shopping or sitting at a café.

The New City

Jerusalem's new city is just outside the old city wall. Cars honk, buses growl, and people hurry along the streets. New Jerusalem has

FOCUS

Talking Stones

The Crusader castle of Nimrod.

An archaeologist in Israel is like a kid who has been let loose in a giant toy store. From the Crusader castle of Nimrod in the North to the ancient city of Avedat in the South, Israel is full of exciting "toys" for archaeologists to discover. For thousands of years, people have wandered across this land. Some, like the Jewish people, settled down and lived there. Others went blazing through with chariots, spears, and elephants, looting and burning. All of them have left a mark on the land.

Ben likes to walk along gray stone walls that circle a hill near his village. The walls were built one thousand five hundred years ago by Byzantine farmers. Dafna, whom you will meet in Chapter 10, squeezes through narrow underground passages at Bet Guvrin. These passages were dug out of the rock by Jewish fighters and were used as hiding places from the Roman enemy by Jews.

Next to the Temple Mount, archaeologists have dug deep and found a thick stone wall. It was built by the Hasmoneans (Judah Maccabee's family) after they had driven out the Greeks and celebrated the first Chanukah. And in the Far North, students of Hebrew Union College-Jewish Institute of Religion are digging. They have already uncovered Tel Dan, a busy market town from

ARCHAEOLOGICAL TIME LINE

Pre-Temple	Iron Age	Persian Period	Hellenistic (Greek) Period	Roman Period
4000-c. 950 B.C.E.	1200-586 B.C.E.	586-330 B.C.E.	c. 330-63 B.C.E.	63 B.C.E.-330 C.E.
	First Temple c. 950 B.C.E.	Second Temple c. 516 B.C.E.		

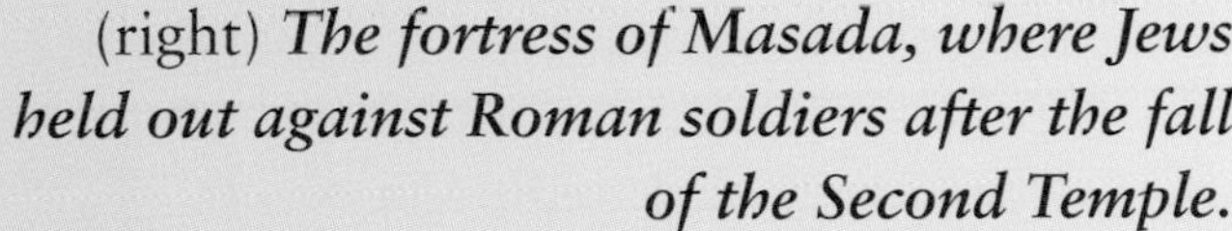

(above) *At Tel Dan, students uncovered this ancient sanctuary.*

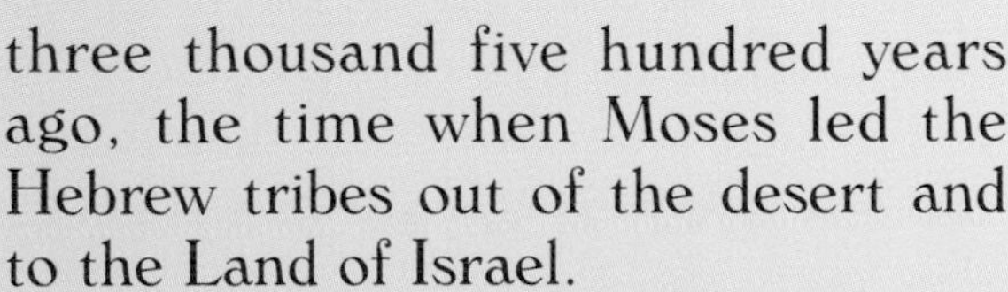

(right) *The fortress of Masada, where Jews held out against Roman soldiers after the fall of the Second Temple.*

three thousand five hundred years ago, the time when Moses led the Hebrew tribes out of the desert and to the Land of Israel.

The stones of Masada, Gamala, Tzippori, and many more sites tell us thrilling stories. People fought bloody battles at these places with burning oil, rocks, and sometimes their bare hands. There were also quiet years in these places when people tended their olive trees and vineyards, built homes and synagogues, and studied their holy books.

As the archaeologists uncover and examine each site, they begin to understand the lives of the people who had lived there. It's as if the stones speak to the archaeologists and through them to us.

Byzantine Period 330-640 C.E.	Muslim Period 640-1099 C.E.	Crusader Period 1099-1291 C.E.	Mameluke Period 1291-1516 C.E.	Ottoman (Turkish) Period 1516-1918 C.E.

Ice cream trucks line up across the road from the Knesset (Israel's Congress). Perhaps the ice cream will cool the hot tempers of the lawmakers.

department stores, tall hotels, office buildings, and houses. It also has the Knesset building. Israel's elected lawmakers meet in the Knesset. You can sit in on one of their meetings. But you'd better bring ear plugs. Israel is a noisy democratic country whose lawmakers yell at one another a lot. The chairperson usually has to bang on the table again and again to get them to quiet down.

After visiting the busy Knesset, you'll want to relax with a pita sandwich and a drink. Sit at a sidewalk table on Ben-Yehuda Street, a tree-lined walkway. If you're lucky, you'll see jugglers, musicians, or even a puppet show as you eat. Rested enough? Then it's time to check out some Jerusalem museums.

At the Israel Museum you can see special scrolls, which are rolls of thin leather. Parts of the Bible were written on these scrolls two thousand years ago. The owners put the

The Hadassah Hospital in Jerusalem exhibits Marc Chagall's famous stained-glass windows, depicting the twelve tribes of Israel.

scrolls into clay jars. They hid the jars deep in a cave near the Dead Sea. That's why the scrolls are called the Dead Sea Scrolls. The scrolls were not found until 1947, the year before Israel became a state.

On a nearby hill is a low stone building. It is the Museum of the Holocaust, called Yad Vashem. It houses many photographs and records, all of which tell a sad story. They remind us of the six million Jews who were killed by the Nazis. In another building tiny lights twinkle like stars. Each light represents a Jewish child who died in the Holocaust. The names of the children are read aloud so that we never forget them.

There are many other interesting places to visit. There's Hebrew University, Hadassah Hospital (your mom may belong to Hadassah), Hebrew Union College-Jewish Institute of Religion (your rabbi may have studied there), the Jerusalem Great Synagogue, and much more. You could also visit the Jerusalem Zoo, where you will find some strange birds and animals that you read about in the Bible. There's an onager, a water buffalo, and a hoopoe bird. Another good place to visit is King Hezekiah's tunnel. It's an ancient, dark water channel under Jerusalem. Hezekiah, a king of Judea, built it many years ago. If you visit it, you'll get wet up to your belly button and have to pray that your flashlight battery is strong. You'd rather not go there? Then it's time to move on to the next chapter.

SUMMING UP

Jerusalem is the capital of the State of Israel. It is a holy city for Jews, Christians, and Muslims, with many synagogues, churches, and mosques. The city has an old and a new section. Narrow, twisting streets and small shops fill the old section. The ancient Western Wall of the Holy Temple is in the old section. Above it, on the Temple Mount, stand two mosques.

Archaeologists are digging around the walls of the city. They are discovering objects that help them to understand the people who once lived there.

The Knesset is in the new section of the city. In this building Israel's laws are made. The city also has many tall office buildings, hotels, homes, and museums. Two important museums are the Israel Museum and Yad Vashem. And for fun, visit the Jerusalem Zoo or King Hezekiah's tunnel.

ACTIVITIES

POST OFFICE TO HEAVEN

At the Western Wall, people often feel very close to God. They leave messages for God between the stones. Write a message or a prayer that you would like God to receive.

____

____

____

____

FILL IN THE BLANKS

Choose one of the following words or set of words to fill in the blank in each sentence below.

Knesset, *Kotel*, mosque, archaeologists, Hebrew Union College-Jewish Institute of Religion, Hadassah Hospital, King Hezekiah's tunnel, Temple Mount

1. ______________________ is a wet walk under Jerusalem.
2. Muslims pray in a _______________.
3. Students learn to become Reform rabbis at ______________________.
4. ______________________ study history by digging up buried towns.
5. The ____________ is the only wall left of the Holy Temple.
6. Israel's lawmakers argue and vote in the _______________.
7. American women raised money to build ______________________.
8. Many years ago the Holy Temple stood on top of the ______________________.

❄ GARBAGE CAN ARCHAEOLOGY ❄

Archaeologists learn about ancient people from their garbage. Broken clay pots, animal bones, and bits of jewelry tell stories. They tell about the food that the people ate, the tools that they used, and the kind of clothing that they wore.

Empty the wastepaper basket in your room or classroom. Make a list of the things that you find. What does the list tell about your life? What would a stranger learn about the food you eat, your tools (pencil, pen, computer paper), your toys or books, and your religion?

Your List	**What Does the Item Tell?**
______________	______________________
______________	______________________
______________	______________________
______________	______________________
______________	______________________

IMPORTANT PLACES

1. The city of Jerusalem is important to many people. Why is it important to Jews? ______________________

   ____

   To Muslims? ______________________

   ____

   To Christians? ______________________

   ____

2. The Knesset is important to all citizens of Israel. Why? ______________________

   ____

3. Yad Vashem tells a sad story. About what events does it remind us? ______________________

   ____

   ____

4. Archaeologists like to dig in Jerusalem. Why? What have they found? ______________________

   ____

You're the Archaeologist

Archaeologists have just dug down to the layer shown below. Help them decide who once lived on this layer. Darken each space that has a dot. Then answer the questions below.

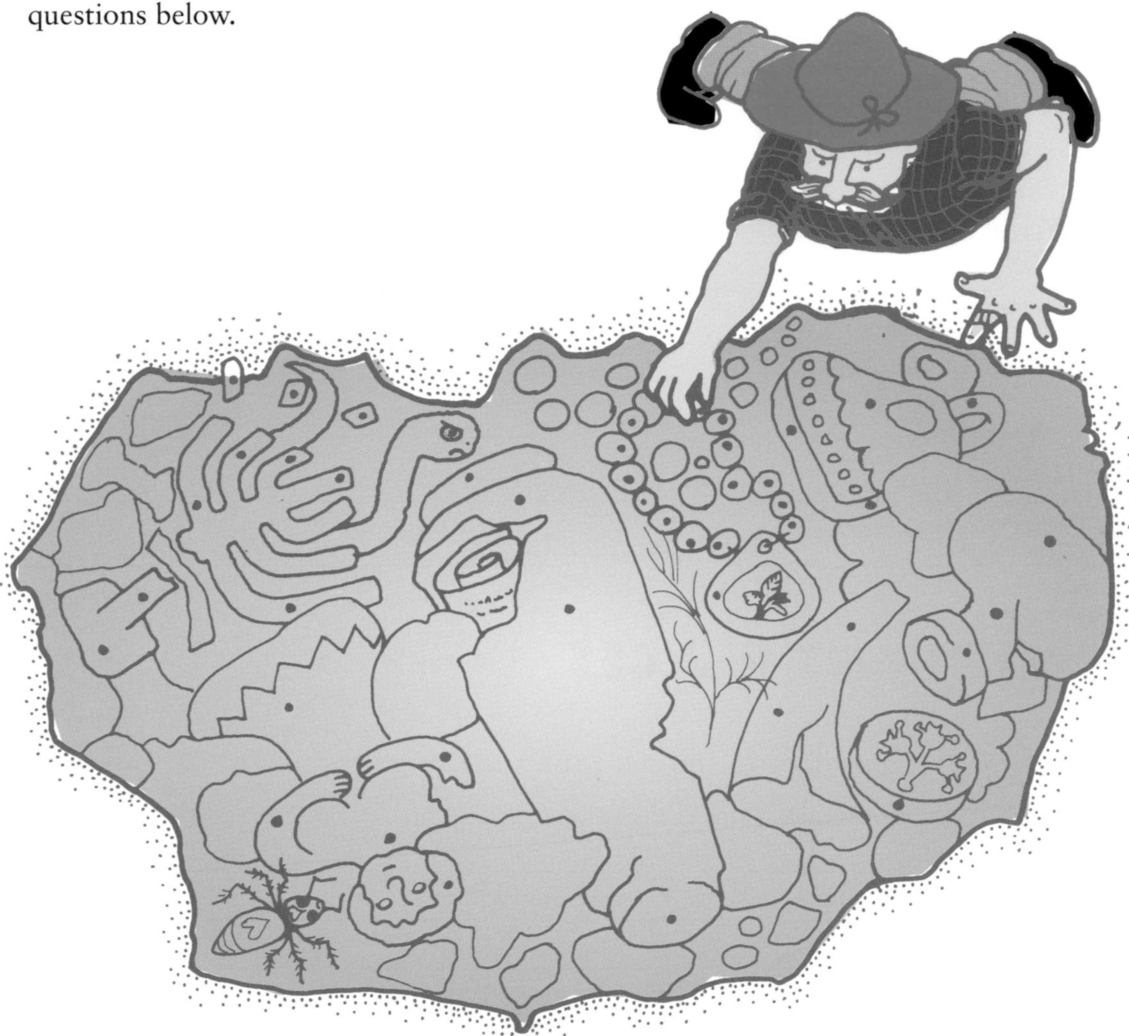

1. What was the religion of the people who lived on this layer?

____

2. How do you know? ____

____

10

DAFNA RAISED HAMSTERS
Country Life

Dafna lives on a kibbutz, a farming village, in southern Israel.

Dafna says: "I'm thirteen and a half, right in the middle of my bat mitzvah year. I think that becoming a bar or bat mitzvah is different on our kibbutz than it is in the United States. Here all the thirteen-year-old kids spend a year doing bar and bat mitzvah work. We study Jewish history and take trips to learn more about being Jewish. My class went to Jerusalem and to a history museum in Tel Aviv called the Museum of the Jewish Diaspora. And we try to help other people. Once we took blankets and dishes to a center in which new immigrants live. These people needed things they couldn't bring with them from their old country. On Purim we baked lots of cookies and *hamantashen*. We took them to soldiers at an army camp.

"We study about our roots, too. We asked our parents and grandparents questions about their childhood. Then we wrote down their stories. We collected old photos, letters, and all the stories and made a "Roots" book.

"In the spring we'll have a big bar and bat mitzvah party for our families and friends.

"I like the way in which we share work and property on the kibbutz. Each Sunday afternoon after school, we help out on the kibbutz. My big sister works in the cow barn. I work in the nursery school. And Yoni, my younger brother, works on the children's farm. He takes care of the hamsters. That used to be my job.

"My friends and I feel very free on the kibbutz. It's not like a city. We can be out after dark. We visit each other and take walks. Our parents don't worry about us."

Country Life

Did you ever live in the country? If you did, you may think that you know about everything in this chapter. But country life is different in Israel than it is in the United States. Israel has individual farms, with cows and chickens and fields of vegetables, just like the farms in California or Pennsylvania. But Israel also has large farming villages in which everyone shares the work, as well as other farming villages in which people share machinery. In addition, Israel has ordinary villages whose people just share baby-sitters or lawn mowers.

The Kibbutz

Dafna's kibbutz, Kfar Menahem, looks like a sleepy village. It has broad green lawns and small houses tucked under tall trees. Children and grown-ups ride bicycles along the shady paths. It's so peaceful that even the dogs just nap in the sun instead of chasing the bicycles.

Some kibbutzim are farming villages. The farmers raise cows, sheep, goats, and chickens and grow fruits and vegetables. Other kibbutzim do some farming but also have factories. All kinds of products, from

A quiet lane in Kibbutz Hatzor.

Just fill your tray. Eating with friends in the kibbutz dining room is easier than cooking at home.

This man works in the kibbutz dairy. Can you read his T-shirt?

vegetarian hamburgers to kitchen faucets, are made in the factories.

So far the kibbutz sounds like a village that has farms and a factory. But remember that Dafna said, "I like the way in which we share work and property on the kibbutz"? The kibbutz isn't like an ordinary village. Dafna was referring to the fact that on a kibbutz, all the members own all the property and share all the work. The big barn filled with mooing cows belongs to every kibbutz member. So does the factory with its humming machines. The groves of orange trees and fields of cotton also belong to everyone.

Kibbutz people do all kinds of jobs and are all paid the same wages. Dafna's father works in the kibbutz office. Her mother teaches kindergarten. And her older sister milks cows. Many of the "housework" jobs are done by members of the kibbutz instead of by each family. Assigned people do everyone's laundry and mending. And cooks prepare meals in a big restaurant-style kitchen. Most members eat in the large kibbutz dining room. But sometimes Dafna and her family take their dinner home. Or they make pizza and sandwiches in the tiny kitchen of their own house.

Dafna and the other children used to sleep in the children's house, where teachers would care for them and teach them. At the end of the workday and on Shabbat, they'd go home to play with their parents, but they would return to the children's house to sleep. However, many of the parents missed their children and wanted them to live at home. They went to the monthly meeting of kibbutz members and said, "We want our kids at home!"

A kibbutz is a democracy. When most of the members want things to change, the kibbutz tries to make the changes. In many kibbutzim today kids go to school in the morning and return home to their parents' house to sleep, just as you do.

The kibbutz kids study math, social studies, language, science, and computers at school.

Say It in Hebrew

English	Hebrew	How to Say the Hebrew
kibbutz (collective farm village)	קִבּוּץ	ki-*butz*
moshav (cooperative farm village)	מוֹשָׁב	mo-*shav*
pioneers	חֲלוּצִים	cha-lu-*tzim*
Zionist	צִיוֹנִי	Tzi-yo-*ni*

After school, they have hobbies and jobs. Yoni, Dafna's brother, helps out on the children's farm. The pigeons, hamsters, goats, and ponies need to be fed. Some classes tend fruit and vegetable gardens. Working on the kibbutz teaches the kids to love nature and the land.

Yahel and Lotan—Kibbutzim in the Aravah

Why did young Americans from Columbus, Ohio, San Francisco, California, and many other American cities make the long schlepp to Israel's Aravah? And why did young Israelis leave Tel Aviv, Jerusalem, and Haifa for the Aravah? During the day the Aravah is hot and dry. At night it's freezing. The loudest night noises are made by howling jackals and by wild pigs digging for roots and bulbs. Shopping malls, movies, concert halls, and museums are far, far away.

These three young children go to nursery school at Kibbutz Yahel.

Picking grapes at Kibbutz Yahel.

"We could've stayed in the United States if we wanted shopping malls and bright lights," one settler laughed. She and many of the other Americans were members of the National Federation of Temple Youth. They felt a strong connection to Israel and Jewish culture. As a result, they decided to join a group of Israeli Reform Jews and build a new community in Israel.

Yahel was formed in 1976. Lotan began in 1983. The members built Reform synagogues in which they conduct Shabbat services and celebrate holidays together. They have weekly study groups. At Lotan the members are learning about Maimonides, the great Jewish philosopher. Both settlements grow date palms and vegetables and have herds of milk cows. Yahel and Lotan are patches of green in the stony beauty of the desert.

Why did these settlers end up deep in the desert on the border with Jordan? They are there because it's a tough place, and kibbutzim have always been built in tough places. Individual families might have trouble coping with the harsh climate, the loneliness, and the dangers of the Aravah. But people find strength working together in a group on a kibbutz. That was true of Degania, the first kibbutz, many years ago, and it's true of Yahel and Lotan today.

Rabbi Alexander Schindler carries a Torah scroll at the dedication ceremony of Kibbutz Yahel.

Different Kinds of Kibbutzim

Most kibbutz members do not observe religious rituals. Many kibbutzim don't even have a synagogue. But members enjoy celebrating Jewish holidays together. Remember the Shavuot party described in Chapter 7?

Some kibbutzim, like Kibbutz Lavi, are associated with the Orthodox movement. Some, like Kibbutz Hannaton in the Galilee, belong to the Conservative movement.

FOCUS

Degania, the Grandma of Kibbutzim

The young olim from Russia in this picture built a farming village nearly seventy years ago. They chose a steamy, hot place near Lake Kinneret. Although it was full of swamps and whining, disease-carrying mosquitoes, the settlers were determined to make it fruitful and beautiful. They called the village Degania. The word degania means "cornflower" in English.

In Russia these young people had lived in cities and towns. They had been students and shopkeepers. But they refused to be city people in Palestine. They said, "Palestine won't be a Jewish homeland unless Jews plant and harvest with their own hands. We'll be chalutzim, pioneers. We'll learn to be farmers!"

They began working the muddy earth. At first they were very poor. Many of them got sick. Often they went hungry. But they shared everything that they had and tried to take care of one another. They wanted to create a community in which everyone would be equal. Nobody would be the boss. They called their community a kevutzah, which means "community settlement."

Slowly wheat and vegetables began to grow. The swamps were

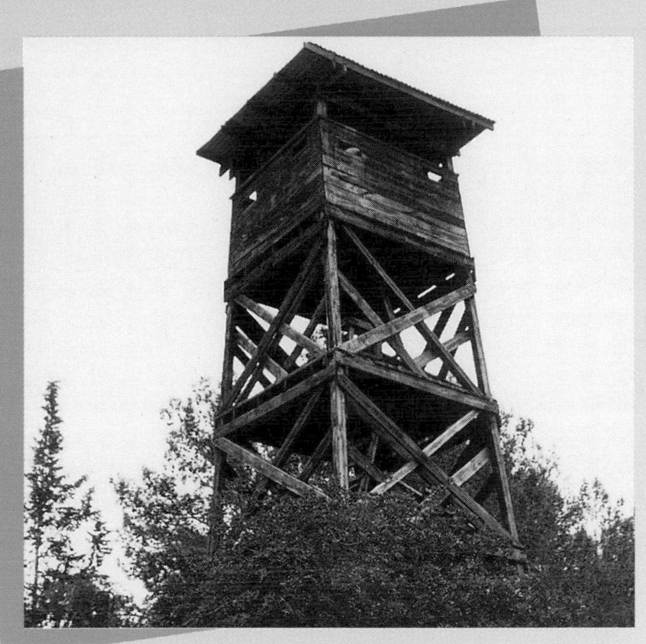

Before the State of Israel was founded, many kibbutzim were built in places far from the main cities. The first structure built on a kibbutz was a watchtower, like this one at Kibbutz Hanita.

dried up. And more people arrived to join the first small group.

Other young people learned from Degania's settlers. They built their own villages and shared their money, clothing, and food. This kind of village was called a kibbutz, which is a large kevutzah. The young kibbutz members chose to settle on dangerous borders or on rocky, dry soil. They said, "Jews must settle in all parts of Palestine. And we can go to the tough places because we're strong. Working and sharing on a kibbutz makes us strong."

This mud hut was the first home of Degania's settlers.

Two members of Kibbutz Yahel celebrate Shabbat.

The Jezreel Plain, the largest plain in Israel. It stretches from the Samarian foothills in the South to the slopes of the Galilee in the North.

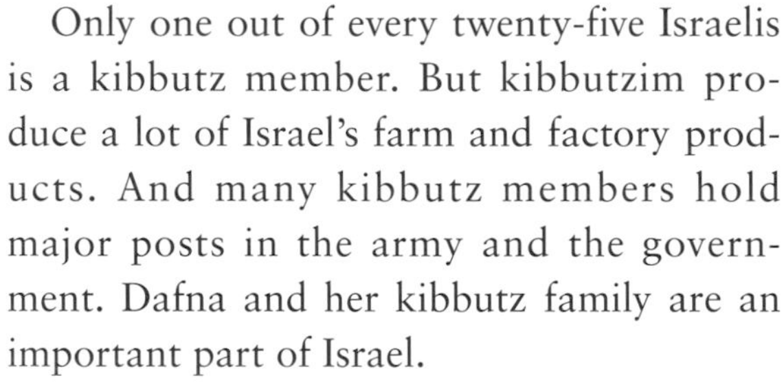

Only one out of every twenty-five Israelis is a kibbutz member. But kibbutzim produce a lot of Israel's farm and factory products. And many kibbutz members hold major posts in the army and the government. Dafna and her kibbutz family are an important part of Israel.

The Moshav

A moshav is another kind of farming village in Israel. The members of a moshav often share big farm machines like tractors and harvesting machines. They may send their crops to market together. But the members of each family take care of their own cow barn and chicken house. They live in their own house, cook their own meals, and raise their own children. Remember that in Chapter 2 you read about Tamar's work as a nurse? She worked with new immigrants on a moshav called Ein Yaakov.

Private Villages

Arab and Jewish villages are scattered all over Israel's countryside. Families live in their own home, just as you do in the United States. Har Halutz in the Galilee, where Sam lives, is a tiny village. It is part of the Israeli Reform movement. Many of its settlers came from the United States. The adults work at jobs in nearby towns. The kids take a school bus to and from school.

Learning to Love the Land

Today most Israelis live in cities. But the early Zionist farmers left a mark on all Israelis. They valued each tree and wildflower. Modern Israelis love exploring their beautiful country. Every holiday the roads leading to the hills and forests are crowded with cars and buses.

SUMMING UP

Israel has several kinds of villages. They include the kibbutz, the moshav, and the private village. All the property on the kibbutz is shared by its members. The money that is earned is also shared. Each member on a moshav has his or her own farm. But the members may share farm machinery. Or they may take their crops to market together. The people in a private village live apart from one another. They live just as you do.

Degania is an old farming village. The young people who built the first kibbutzim learned from the settlers of Degania. They learned to share and work together. They built farms in difficult, dangerous places. Their goal was to establish Jewish villages throughout Palestine.

Today country life is easier than it used to be. Dafna says, "It's good on the kibbutz. I have lots of freedom. I love being there."

ACTIVITIES

TRUE OR FALSE

Put a **T** in front of each true statement. Put an **F** in front of each false statement.

1. ____ A kibbutz is exactly like a village in the United States.
2. ____ Only husbands are allowed to do housework on a kibbutz.
3. ____ A kibbutz is a democracy.
4. ____ Degania is the newest moshav in Israel.
5. ____ Most Israelis live in small towns.
6. ____ Moshav members often share big farm machines.
7. ____ A kibbutz is a small *kevutzah*.
8. ____ Kibbutz members own all the property and share the work.
9. ____ The *olim* who came to Palestine from Russia nearly seventy years ago wanted to be farmers.
10. ____ Degania is near the Dead Sea.

❄ WHAT DO YOU THINK ❄ ABOUT THE KIBBUTZ?

1. You may share your sweater with your sister or brother. You may even lend your bicycle to a friend for a day or two. But how would you feel about sharing most of your things with your friends?

____

____

____

2. Give two reasons why the early kibbutz members decided to share everything.

____

____

____

____

3. What do you think about the bar and bat mitzvah year on Dafna's kibbutz?

What do you like about it?____

____

What don't you like about it?____

____

Would you like to have a kibbutz-type bar or bat mitzvah? Why or why not?

____

____

____

COUNTRY LIFE CROSSWORD PUZZLE • • • •

Fill in the spaces across and down.

Across

5. When the *chalutzim* first made *aliyah*, the Land of Israel was called ___________.
8. A ________________ works to build a Jewish homeland.
9. A farming village whose members share machines is called a________________.
10. The early *olim* didn't want to live in the city. They wanted to be________________.
11. The name of a kibbutz that belongs to the Reform movement is________________.

Down

1. The name of a kibbutz that belongs to the Conservative movement is ______________.
2. The name of the grandma of kibbutzim is ______________.
3. Most Israelis don't live in the country. They live in _______________.
4. The *olim* to Degania came from a country called ____________.
6. Everyone is equal on the kibbutz. No one is the ___________.
7. Dafna's brother takes care of the __________________.

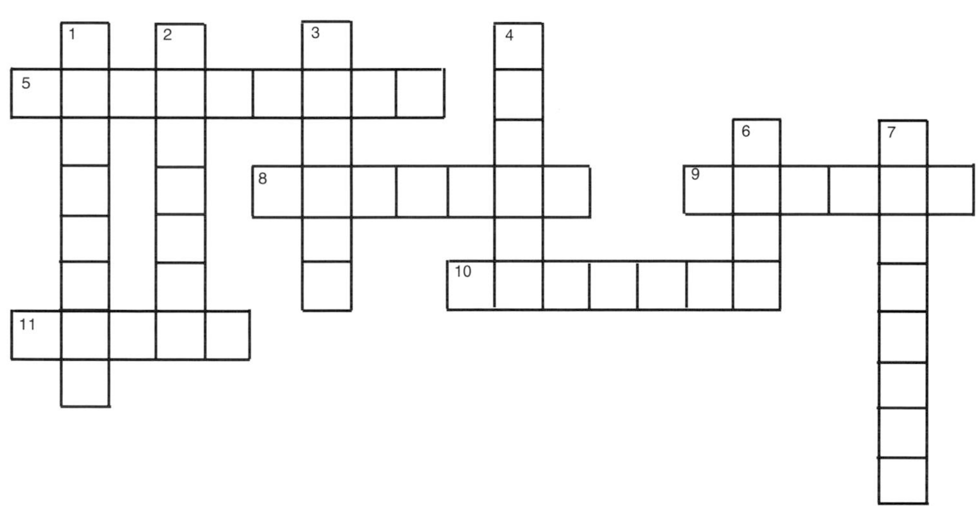

Who Is the Enemy?

Connect the dots to discover what the most dangerous enemy of the first settlers of Degania was.

Why was this enemy dangerous? ____

____

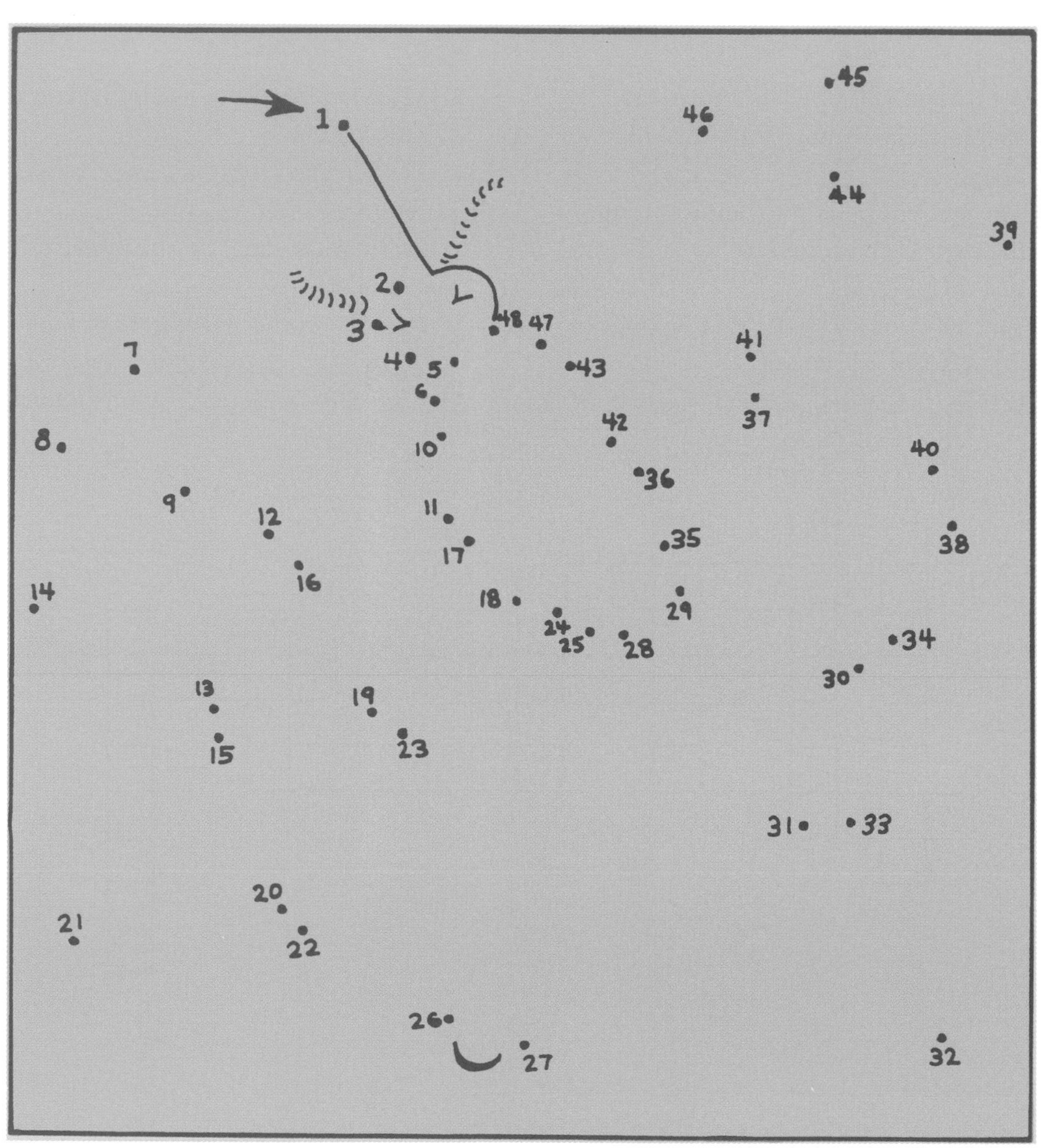

11

MOHAMMED, SIMA, AND ISRA
Arabs in Israel

Mohammed is fourteen, Sima is thirteen, and Isra is ten. They are Arabs who live in Jerusalem. They are Muslims.Their religion is called Islam.

Mohammed: My sisters and I go to different schools. In my school I study math, English, history, and other subjects. And I study the Koran–the Muslim Bible.

Sima: Of all the subjects I take, I like English the best. I want to be able to speak to Americans.

Isra: In my school we start learning Hebrew in the fifth grade. Until then all our lessons are in Arabic. Maybe I'll be a Hebrew teacher when I grow up.

Mohammed: I want to be a garage mechanic or a carpenter. My uncle is a carpenter.

Sima: I want to go to the university, like my big sister. Maybe I'll be a doctor. Or maybe I'll work in an office.

Mohammed: Our most important holiday is Ramadan. It lasts a month. We pray each morning, and we don't eat all day. We're not allowed to eat until after it gets dark. But we go to work and to school. At the end of Ramadan, there's a big feast called Id el Fitr. Then we eat all day long. We eat roast mutton and little cakes made with dates and nuts.

Isra: You know why we're not allowed to eat during Ramadan? It's so that rich people should know how it feels to be poor and hungry.

Sima: I like to learn about Arab history. I watch films about Arab religion and history on TV.

Isra: I like cartoons. And I like to go walking with my friends. We draw on the sidewalk with chalk and play hopscotch.

Mohammed: After school I go to the playground and play soccer. I like to watch TV. But when I watch the news, I get angry. Why do Arabs and Jews throw rocks and shoot at each other? My favorite TV programs are about cops and robbers because they have a lot of action.

The People of Israel

Over five million people live in Israel. Four and a half million of them are Jewish. Almost all the rest, about one million people, are Arab. Most of them are Muslim. There are also Christians, Druse, and people who belong to smaller religious groups.

Mohammed's Family Is Muslim

The sky over Jerusalem is gray. The air is fresh and cool. Most people are still asleep. Suddenly a singsong cry sounds through Mohammed's neighborhood. *Allahu akbar*! ("God is great!") wails a voice. It is coming from a tall tower beside the mosque, the Muslim house of prayer. The priest is waking people up to pray. He calls them five times a day. As soon as they hear the call, some Muslim men stop whatever they are doing. They spread a small rug, get down on their knees, and pray to Allah.

Mohammed's family follows religious customs carefully. On Friday, the Muslim Sabbath, Mohammed's father prays at the mosque. Sometimes he walks to the large mosque on the Temple Mount. The family fasts all day during the Arab month of Ramadan and gives money to help poor people. Mohammed's mother and older sisters cover their heads with a white scarf and wear a long skirt.

Feast Days

Even those Muslims who don't follow religious laws carefully enjoy the feast days. Many families roast a whole sheep over an open fire. Then they serve big platters of mutton and greens. For dessert they have small cakes made with honey and nuts. And they drink sweet mint tea or thick black coffee.

Id el Adha is a feast day that tells a story you might know. On that day Allah ordered Abraham, our forefather, to do a difficult thing. Allah told Abraham to sacrifice his son Ishmael. At the last second, just as Abraham was raising his knife to kill Ishmael, an angel flew down. "Stop!" cried the angel. And he gave Abraham a sheep to sacrifice in place of Ishmael.

Sound familiar? It's like our own Torah story but different. The prophet Mohammed who started the religion of Islam told many stories based on events in the Torah. Those stories became part of the Muslim Bible, the Koran.

In the Village

Mohammed is a city boy. In Israel most people live in cities. Mohammed's cousins Ahmed and Hadiya live in a village in the hills. They have a house with a flat roof. Grapevines grow up the sides of the house and over the roof. The leaves give shade in the summer. When the grapes hang in bunches, the roof looks like a *sukah*.

Sometimes on hot summer nights, Mohammed's cousins sleep on the roof. In the valley below the house are many olive trees. Once the villagers planted vegetables and tobacco. But they earned very little money from farming. Now some of the people build houses. Others work in nearby offices and factories.

At harvest time they become farmers again. The kids stay home from school. The grown-ups take time off from work. Everyone goes down to the valley. The kids climb the trees and shake off the ripe olives. The villagers fill sacks with olives and take them to the olive press. Ahmed and Hadiya

The Dome of the Rock was built over 1,300 years ago. Muslims from many countries come here to pray.

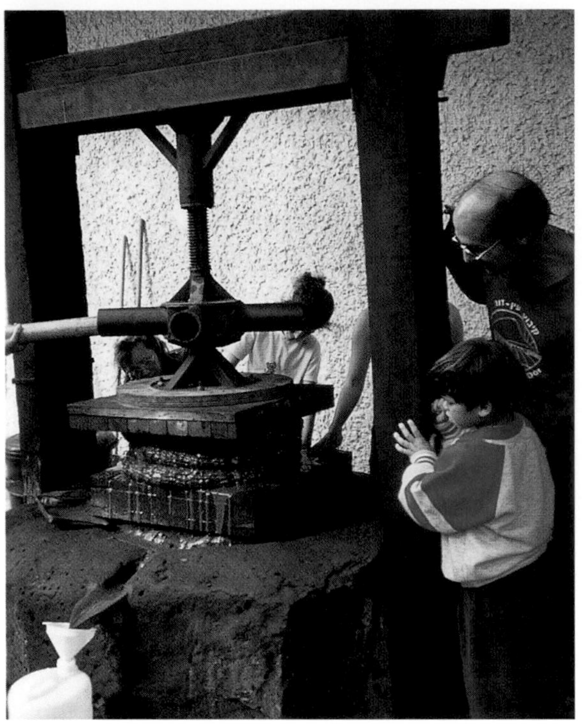

Olives are squeezed in this heavy press. The fresh, warm olive oil runs into the container below the press.

bring Mohammed a big jar of fresh olive oil when they go to Jerusalem.

Bedouin

Bedouin are also Muslim Arabs. But they don't live in the city. They usually have large herds of goats and sheep. And they like to move around. The Bedouin shepherds lead their herds from pasture to pasture. When all the grass in one area has been eaten, the Bedouin roll up their houses. They load them onto their camels and donkeys and move on. How do they roll up their houses? It's simple. Bedouin houses are large tents made from the woven hair of sheep, camels, and goats. These houses are rolled up like a carpet.

A Bedouin woman and girl are working in their tent. The girl is grinding kernels of wheat between two round stones.

It's not easy to be a Bedouin. The women are always busy sewing up holes in the tents. The kids miss a lot of school because they are often needed to watch the goats or because their family may decide to move away in the middle of the school term. Some Bedouin have settled down in permanent houses and have taken jobs. But to many of them, a permanent house doesn't feel like home. So they put up their old tent in front of their house. That's really home!

Two Bedouin sisters.

Bedouin are good scouts and trackers. Some of them serve in Israel's army and police force. They follow the trails of people who break the law.

Christian Arabs

Christianity began in the Land of Israel. Christianity is based on the teachings of Jesus. Jesus was a Jewish teacher who lived in the Land of Israel about two thousand years ago. Jesus traveled to many places in Israel. These places are now Christian holy sites. Visitors come to explore the holy places and celebrate the Christian holidays. During Easter they walk in Jerusalem along with the Christian Arabs. Hundreds of bells ring from church towers to honor the holiday. At Christmas, people gather in Bethlehem, the birthplace of Jesus. The Christian Arabs and the visitors light candles, sing, and pray.

Christmas and Easter are important holidays for Israel's Christians. Although the country doesn't usually have a snowy, white Christmas, it does have Christmas trees. The Jewish National Fund cuts and sells small pine trees from its forests, which some people put up and decorate, just as your Christian neighbors do.

Druse

According to their religion the Druse are close relatives of the Jews. They're relatives by marriage because Jethro, the most important Druse prophet, was the father-in-law of Moses. The Druse religion, which is kept very secret, has much in common with Islam.

Christmas Mass at the Church of the Nativity in Bethlehem.

Most Druse live in villages in northern Israel. The men serve in Israel's army, police force, and border patrol. The security guard in Sam's village is Amin, a Druse from a nearby town. He wears a uniform because he is in the border patrol. And like most Druse men, he has a wide black mustache. All night he patrols the village, carrying his rifle.

Sam, whom you met in Chapter 4, and the other people in the village were invited to the wedding of Amin's son. Sam's mother sat with Amin's wife, the bride, and the other women. Sam, his brother, and his

These Druse soldiers are marching in an Israel Independence Day parade.

father sat with the men. The street in front of Amin's house was crowded with guests. A drummer and two flute players made wailing, thumping music. The air was blue with the smoke of roasting meat. The wedding 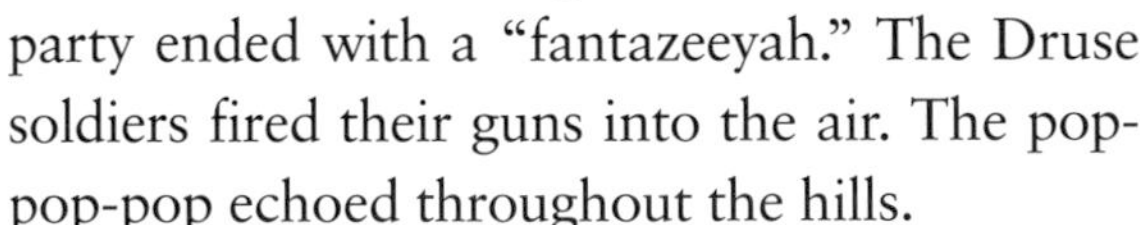party ended with a "fantazeeyah." The Druse soldiers fired their guns into the air. The pop-pop-pop echoed throughout the hills.

Cousins

Jews and Arabs share a great-great-grandfather, Abraham. The Bible says that Abraham's son Isaac was the father of the Jewish people. Arabs believe that Abraham's other son, Ishmael, was the father of the Arab people. So Jews and Arabs are cousins. But cousins are not always friends. The Arab countries of the Middle East have gone to war with Israel many times. You'll read about those wars in Chapter 12.

Living Together and Hoping

About one million Arabs live in Israel. How do you think that they feel about the many wars that have taken place in the region? They have different opinions. Some feel sad and mixed-up. Although they are citizens of Israel, they also have friends and relatives in the nearby Arab lands. They may disagree with many of the government's ideas about war and peace. Other Israeli Arabs don't have mixed feelings. They complain about taxes and health care, just as

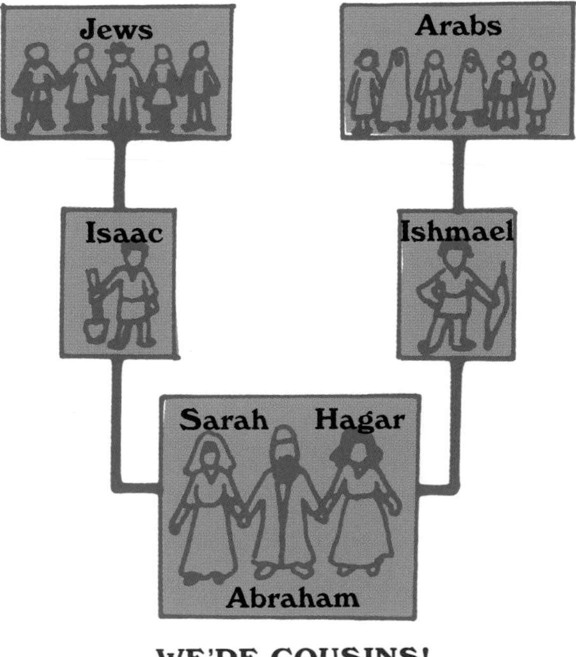

WE'RE COUSINS!

Say It in Hebrew

English	Hebrew	How to Say the Hebrew
Arab	עֲרָבִי	A-ra-*vi*
brother	אָח	ach
sister	אָחוֹת	a-*chot*
Muslim Bible (Koran)	קֻרְאָן	Kur-*an*

Israeli Jews do. But in general, they support the government.

Both Arab and Jewish citizens vote in the elections for the Knesset. Several Arab Israelis are members of the Knesset. Others are soccer stars, TV actors, and diplomats. Arab kids like Sima plan to study at a university. Some will serve in Israel's armed forces. And Arab doctors and dentists work in Israeli hospitals and clinics.

The arrangement sounds okay. Israeli Jews and Israeli Arabs live together and share their small country. But life would be better if there were no more wars. Israeli and Arab diplomats continue to meet and talk. They argue about borderlines, refugees, and terrorism. And Israelis wait with hope. They wonder whether Abraham's great-great-grandchildren can ever be friends.

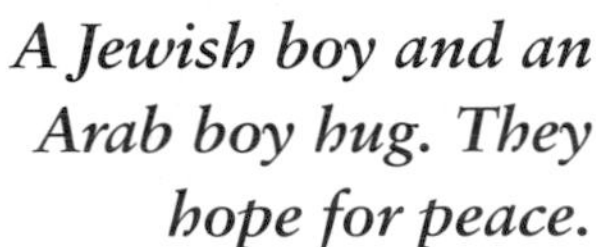

A Jewish boy and an Arab boy hug. They hope for peace.

SUMMING UP

Israel has about one million Arab citizens. Most of them are Muslim. Some are Christian, Druse, and of other religions.

Many Muslims pray five times each day. During the month of Ramadan, they don't eat during the day, only at night. They also have many feast days.

Today most Arabs live in cities. Those Arabs who live in villages often have groves of trees and do some farming. Bedouin are Muslim Arabs. Some of them have large herds of goats and sheep. They live in tents and move around with their herds. Some Bedouin serve in the Israeli army.

Christian Arabs welcome many visitors from faraway lands who come to Israel to celebrate Christmas and Easter. Israel has many Christian holy places because the Christian religion began in this country.

Most Druse Arabs live in northern Israel. The men serve in the Israeli army.

Abraham is the great-great-grandfather of both Jews and Arabs. Although Arabs and Jews are cousins, the people of Israel have had to fight many wars against neighboring Arab countries. The wars make the Arab citizens of Israel sad because they feel close to both sides.

ACTIVITIES

FILL IN THE BLANKS

Circle the correct word or words that complete each sentence.

1. Most Arabs in Israel are (vegetarian, Muslim, Christian).
2. The Koran includes many ideas from the (Bible, Constitution, encyclopedia).
3. (Judah Maccabee, Jethro, Jeremiah) is a Druse prophet.
4. Ramadan is a (famous Arab general, Muslim month, TV hero).
5. Abraham was the father of (Ishmael and Isaac, Jacob and Esau, Falafel and Hummus).
6. (Apache, Bedouin, Egyptians) are scouts and trackers in the Israeli army.
7. The Christian religion began in (Rome, Chicago, the Land of Israel).
8. Id el Fitr and Id el Adha are (Arab brothers, famous mosques, Muslim feast days).
9. A "fantazeeyah" is a (Walt Disney movie, shooting celebration, soft drink).
10. Christian Arabs celebrate (Ramadan, Christmas, Yom Kippur) in Bethlehem.

A BIBLE STORY

Change the story below from the Koran to make it like the story in the Torah. Cross out the words that you change. Write the new words above each line.

Allah ordered Abraham, our forefather, to do a difficult thing. Allah told Abraham to sacrifice his son Ishmael. At the last second, just as Abraham was raising his knife to kill Ishmael, an angel stopped him. The angel gave Abraham a sheep to sacrifice. Ishmael was saved.

Two Rebuses

1. Solve this rebus and unscramble the answer to find the name of a Muslim prophet.

2. Now find the name of a popular Bedouin vehicle.

❄ MISSING WORDS ❄

Learn about Israel's Arab citizens by filling in the blanks below. There are letter clues in each missing word.

Israel's Arab citizens may be _ U _ _ _ _, Christian, or D _ _ _ _. _ U _ _ _ _ S pray in a M _ _ _ _ E. The most important Muslim holiday is R _ _ _ _ _ N. The people don't eat all D _ Y. They eat only after it gets D _ _ K. At the end of R _ _ A _ _ _, there's a big holiday and feast called _ D _ _ F _ _ R.

C _ _ _ _ T _ _ N Arabs enjoy Christmas and Easter. They ring C _ U _ _ H bells, light C _ _ D _ _ _, sing, and P _ _ _.

Many D _ _ S _ Arabs serve in Israel's A _ _ Y. They like to fire their G U _ _ at weddings.

J _ _ S and A _ _ B S are cousins. We hope that they will be F _ _ _ _ D S.

ABIGAIL FIXES JETS
Israel's Army of Citizens

Abigail is twenty years old. She is a soldier stationed at an air base in the center of Israel.

Abigail says: "My job is to make sure that all the electric and electronic connections in a plane are working properly. My crew checks each plane before it takes off. Sometimes we're at work at six in the morning. Other times we work all night. I'm the only woman in my unit. I feel as though I always have to prove that I can do everything. People say, 'Let me help you.' But I'd rather do everything by myself, even lifting heavy boxes or machine parts.

"My first days in the army were hard. We arrived in camp and right away got shots in both our arms and our bottom. Then they gave us uniforms that didn't fit and looked awful. Our drill sergeant looked us over and yelled, 'Take off those earrings! Wipe off your lipstick! You'll have to cut off that ponytail!' We hiked to our barracks with our pant legs dragging. It was a big, cold, uncomfortable room. I remember thinking that I wanted to go home, I wanted my mommy.

"There was no time to be lonely. We were up at five. We ate, cleaned, hiked, jogged, and listened to lectures. We learned to shoot guns. We carried each other on stretchers. And we put up a tent in record time—four minutes! Going home on leave was so great. I dragged home my load of dirty laundry. The Shabbat table was set and looked beautiful. I could take a hot shower and eat and sleep as long as I wanted.

"After a few months we were tested and given special jobs. That's how I got to work on planes. I've learned a lot. I work with all kinds of Israelis. There are new Israelis like Russians and Ethiopians and also Sabras. We all mix together. I've made good friends. You really care about the people you work with.

"Before I went to the army, someone told me, 'Being in the army can make you hate Israel and want to leave. Or it can tie you to the country so that you'll never leave.' I've fallen in love with the country. When I walk down the street in my uniform, I feel that I am a daughter of Israel."

Tzahal, the Israel Defense Force

Even little kids in Israel know about the army.

Early one morning Yoav's little sister Noa came into the kitchen. She saw that her father was wearing a light brown uniform. He was carrying a gun and a backpack. He put down the gun, picked up Noa, and hugged her. "Bye-bye, Noalleh," he said. Then he took the gun and left.

Noa ran to the window to wave. "Where did Aba [Daddy] go?" she asked her mother.

A father returns home from army reserve duty.

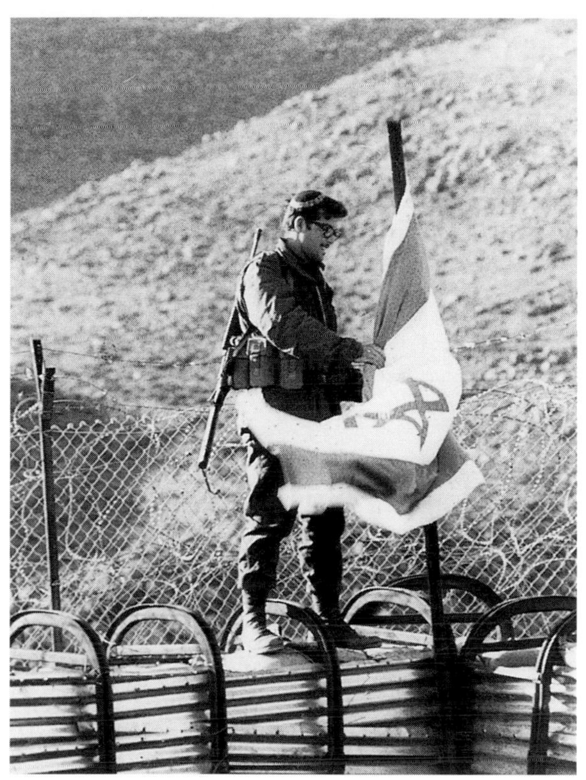

A soldier raising an Israeli flag at a border outpost overlooking southern Lebanon.

"To *miluim* [army reserve duty]," her mother replied. "He goes to *miluim* every year."

"And so does Ari's father and Anat's father and almost everyone's father," Yoav told her.

Noa was happy when her father came home the next Shabbat. But it was just a visit. He told Noa and Yoav, "I'll be finished with *miluim* in four weeks." After Shabbat he went back to his army camp.

To understand why Noa's father goes to *miluim*, we have to know about Israel's army.

Before Israelis do *miluim*, they must serve in the army. The army's Hebrew name is *Tzeva Haganah Leyisrael,* which means "Israel Defense Force." Everybody calls it *Tzahal* for short. Most Israeli Jewish boys and girls don't start college or jobs when they finish high school. Instead, they go right into *Tzahal.* Druse and Bedouin boys also serve in *Tzahal.* Sam, Meirav, and most of the other kids who appear in this book expect to join *Tzahal* when they finish high school. Boys serve in the army for three years, girls for two.

New soldiers are sent to an army camp. Abigail told you a little of what happens there. After basic training, soldiers are assigned to all kinds of army jobs. They may strap parachutes on their back and jump from planes. They may drive tanks or shoot big guns. Or they may repair planes, tanks, and guns.

A soldier on duty, 1968.

Some women soldiers work with complicated machinery, as Abigail does. Many become teachers. They teach new soldiers how to use guns. Or they teach new immigrants about Israel. Those who lead hikes carry guns, so they are guides and guards at the same time.

After army service some people stay in the army. But most leave the army, and the men become part of the reserves. Most women don't do *miluim* unless they have special jobs.

Miluim—the Reserves

Israelis don't finish reserve duty until they are forty-five years old. Each year an Israeli man is called to do *miluim*. He leaves his job and goes to his army base. He may be gone for four to six weeks. And he may be sent anyplace in Israel. He could guard a village on the border. Or he may drive a big tank in the dusty Negev. He may even patrol the coast in a boat or fly a plane.

Israel needs to have a reserve army because it's a small country. Its army has had to fight many wars. Israelis know that they must always be ready to protect their country. In the event of a sudden attack, the people in the reserves will rush to their bases. In a few hours they'll be ready to fight alongside the country's regular army soldiers.

Long before Tzahal There Was Hashomer

Even before there was a State of Israel, Jews had to learn to protect themselves. The Zionist settlers who went to Palestine one hundred years ago had a hard time. Palestine was like the Wild West. In those days a country called Turkey ruled Palestine. Cattle rustlers stole the cows, horses, and donkeys of the settlers. Wandering shepherds took the vegetables from their fields and the chickens from their front yards. The settlers paid the local police for protection. But sometimes the police were as bad as the crooked sheriffs in Westerns are.

A few young Zionists became guards for the settlers. In 1908 they formed a group called Hashomer, which means "The Guard." The watchmen learned to shoot rifles and ride horses. They grew bushy mustaches and carried knives and guns. They patrolled the forests and fields, protecting the Jewish settlements.

An early shomer *(guard) in Palestine.*

Say It in Hebrew

English	Hebrew	How to Say the Hebrew
Israeli army	צַהַ"ל	*Tza*-hal
Jewish army in Palestine ("The Defense")	הַגָּנָה	Ha-ga-*nah*
peace	שָׁלוֹם	sha-*lom*
war	מִלְחָמָה	mil-cha-*mah*

Next Came the Haganah

A Jewish army was formed in 1920. It was called Haganah, "The Defense." It was a secret army. It had to be secret. The British, who were the new rulers of Palestine, did not like the idea of a Jewish army. When they caught Haganah members, they put them in prison.

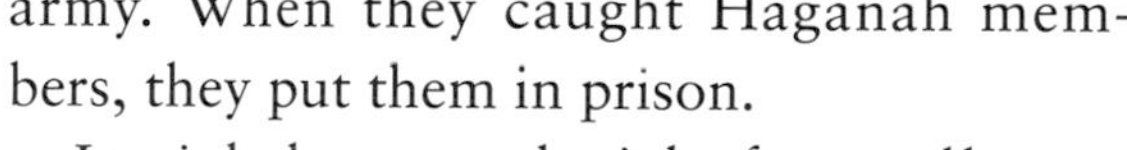

Jewish boys and girls from all over Palestine joined the Haganah. You read about Tamar's sister in Chapter 2. She was an officer in the Haganah. Its members learned to make weapons and use them. When Arabs attacked road traffic or settlements, Haganah members drove the attackers away. Two smaller secret armies were also formed. They were called the Irgun and Lehi.

Haganah and Irgun people went to Europe before World War II. They tried to rescue Europe's Jews from the Nazis. During the war Haganah members entered Europe

Jewish refugees on the biggest ship yet to come illegally to Palestine, July 1947.

secretly. They were in constant danger of being captured and killed by the Nazis. But they managed to save some Jews and take them back to Palestine. After the war Haganah ships kept taking Europe's Jews to Palestine, although British warships tried to stop them.

And Finally There Was Tzahal

In May 1948, the State of Israel was born. The secret Haganah fighters became the proud army of Israel called *Tzahal*. Some of the youngsters who had fought with the Haganah became the leaders of *Tzahal*, including Moshe Dayan, Yigal Allon, and Yitzhak Rabin. Do you recognize any of these names?

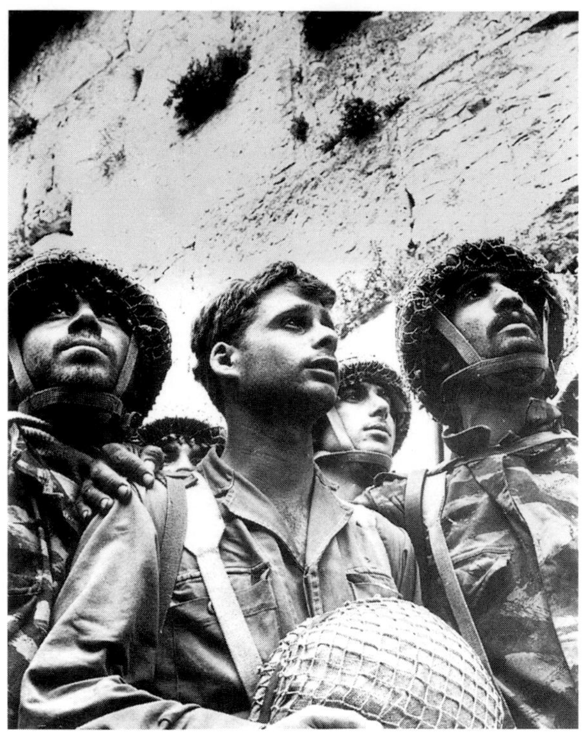

Israeli paratroopers reached the Western Wall during the Six Day War.

The First Two Wars

From the minute that it was formed, *Tzahal* had to fight. The first war it fought was Israel's War of Independence. You read about that war in Chapter 2. In the years following Israel's independence, Egypt sent raiders across the border to attack farms and towns in the Negev. In defense, *Tzahal* fought a second war in 1956 called the Sinai Campaign. During that war Israel sent *Tzahal* into Egypt's Sinai Desert. *Tzahal* succeeded in driving back the enemy armies.

The Six Day War and Its Results

In the spring of 1967, Egypt and Syria joined forces. They threatened to go to war against Israel, and they stopped Israel-bound ships from reaching the Israeli port of Eilat. War broke out in June 1967. For six days Israel fought against Jordan, Syria, and Egypt. Israel successfully defended itself against the enemy armies and captured land from each of them.

Israel conquered the Golan Heights in the Northeast from Syria. It captured the West Bank of the Jordan River from Jordan. The old city of Jerusalem and the Western Wall of the Temple, the *Kotel*, are in this region. Israel also captured the Sinai Desert and the Gaza Strip in the South from Egypt.

But the lands that Israel captured already had people. One million Arabs lived in the Golan, Gaza, Sinai, and West Bank. Some of them had fled from Israel in 1948. Others had lived in these lands for a long time.

Arguments about the Captured Lands

Israeli Jews began to argue with one another.

"We should make Palestine and the Golan part of Israel," some said. "Arab Palestine is part of the land that God promised to Israel. Its real name is Judea and Samaria. And the holy city of Jerusalem is in this area, as is the Western Wall of the Temple. We can't give these lands up!"

Others said, "Israel is too small. Our enemies can easily drive tanks right across our country. We need these added lands to be safe." They began to move into these areas and build towns.

There were also Israelis who argued against keeping the captured lands. "We can't make all these lands part of Israel," they said. "One million Arabs live there. If they become citizens of Israel, we won't have a Jewish country anymore. There will soon be more Arabs than Jews. Besides, the Palestinians should have a land of their own. We must give back most of these lands."

The Arabs of Palestine and the nearby countries also argued with one another.

Some said, "We can make peace. But first the Jews must give back all the Arab lands that they took."

Other Arabs said, "We will never make peace with Israel. We must drive the Zionists out of Israel and Palestine." These Arabs formed groups like the Palestine Liberation Organization (P.L.O.) and Hamas, which fought against Israel. They staged many terrorist attacks, killing and wounding hundreds of civilians.

The Yom Kippur War and a First Peace Agreement

On Yom Kippur in 1973, Syria, Jordan, and Egypt attacked Israel. Israeli soldiers and reservists rushed to their bases from their homes and synagogues. Again they fought tough, bloody battles and drove their enemies off.

Finally in 1979, a first step toward peace was taken. Israel signed a peace treaty with its southern neighbor, Egypt. In return for peace, Israel gave back the Sinai Desert. Look at the map on page 37. Sinai was the largest of the captured lands.

Egyptian President Anwar Sadat, American President Jimmy Carter, and Israeli Prime Minister Menachem Begin sign the Camp David Accords, a peace treaty between Egypt and Israel, March 26, 1979. It is the first treaty between Israel and an Arab nation.

The War in Lebanon

Although there was peace on Israel's southern border, the fighting did not stop on the country's other borders. For years, Israel's settlements had been shot at from Lebanon. In 1982, *Tzahal* was sent into Lebanon to stop those attacks. But after *Tzahal* left Lebanon, the attacks started again. In order to protect its border, Israel continues to patrol this area.

The Intifada and the Gulf War

In December 1987, Arabs living in the West Bank and in Gaza rebelled against Israeli rule. This rebellion became known as the *intifada*, Arabic for "uprising." For the next several years Arabs threw stones at Israeli soldiers, held violent demonstrations, and went on strike. The P.L.O. and other Palestinian groups hoped that the *intifida* would help them establish their own state.

The Gulf War marked a turning point in the Middle East. In August 1990, Iraq invaded its neighbor Kuwait, an ally of the United States. In response, the United States and many other countries—including Egypt and Saudi Arabia—sent troops to free Kuwait. Although Israel was not involved in the war, Iraq launched forty missiles at Israel. Jordan and the P.L.O. supported Iraq. But when Iraq lost the Gulf War, both Jordan and the P.L.O. realized that violence would not help them regain any of the lands captured by Israel in 1967.

A Second Peace Agreement

In September 1993, Israel and the P.L.O. signed a peace agreement in Washington. Israel agreed to give autonomy (partial independence) to Jericho and the Gaza Strip. In return, the P.L.O. agreed to recognize Israel as a state. On that historic day Israel's Prime Minister Yitzhak Rabin stated, "Let me say to you, the Palestinians, we are destined to live together on the same soil in the same land. We, the soldiers who have returned from battles stained with blood; we, who have seen our relatives and friends killed before our eyes...we say to you today in a loud and clear voice: enough of blood and tears. Enough!"

People on both sides hope that now the fighting and terrorism will end and the P.L.O. and the Israelis will become good neighbors.

On the lawn of the White House, President Clinton congratulates Israeli Prime Minister Yitzhak Rabin and P.L.O. Chairman Yassir Arafat as they shake hands after signing a peace accord, September 13, 1993.

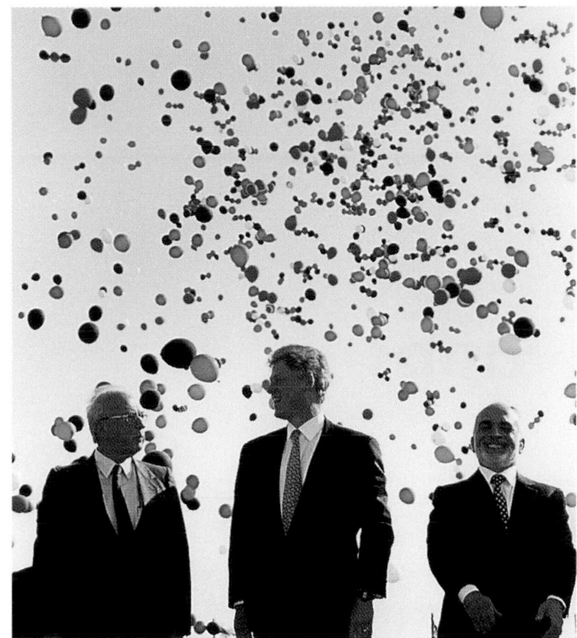

Israel and Jordan sign a peace treaty on October 26, 1994. From left to right: Yitzhak Rabin, Bill Clinton, and Jordan's King Hussein.

Peace with Jordan

In October 1994, Jordan also signed a peace treaty with Israel, ending forty-six years of war. The two countries agreed on final borders and on how to share the water of the Jordan and Yarmuk rivers. After the two countries signed the peace treaty, colorful "peace balloons" were released into the sky.

What's Next?

Many tough problems still have to be solved. Terrorism continues. Some Israelis and some Arabs believe that there will never be real peace. They say that the peace agreements can't work. But in spite of the pessimism and terrorism, the talks are continuing. Israeli and Syrian diplomats keep meeting. The P.L.O. and the Israeli government are discussing elections, borders, and the hardest problem of all–terrorism.

By the time you read this chapter, the diplomats may have given up. Or they may still be talking. Or, best of all, they may have signed a fourth peace agreement and a fifth! Then *Tzahal* will be able to relax a little and Noa's father and the other reservists will be able to put down their weapons and stay at home.

SUMMING UP

After high school most Israeli Jewish boys and girls serve in *Tzahal*, the army of Israel. Druse and Bedouin boys are also in the army. The citizens of Israel are always ready to defend their country.

Hashomer was the first defense group formed to guard the Jews of Palestine. It was created about ninety years ago. The Haganah was the country's first army. It was a secret army, formed in 1920. When the State of Israel was born in 1948, *Tzahal* was formed.

Tzahal has fought many wars against Israel's neighboring Arab countries. In the Six Day War in 1967, *Tzahal* captured a lot of land. Israel gave the Sinai Desert back to Egypt after that country made peace with Israel. Now Israel has signed peace agreements with the P.L.O. and Jordan. Peace talks are also going on with Syria. But terrorist attacks on Israelis are continuing. Peace or no peace–we still don't know.

ACTIVITIES

CHOOSE THE RIGHT WORDS

Draw a circle around all the answers that are true.

1. Most Israeli men go to
   - *miluim*
   - army service
   - hairdressers

2. Right after high school most Israeli kids go to
   - *Tzahal*
   - Disney World
   - college

3. Hashomer means
   - The Guard
   - The Pioneer
   - The Secret Jewish Army

4. The following Israeli leaders fought in the *Haganah*:
   - Moshe Dayan
   - Theodor Herzl
   - Yitzhak Rabin

5. Irgun and Lehi are the names of
   - an Israeli singing group
   - spices used in a vegetable soup
   - two secret Jewish armies

6. Israel needs the reserves because
   - it has a small army
   - Israeli men like to have a vacation away from home
   - all Israelis must be ready to protect their country

7. Among Israel's wars were
   - the Sinai Campaign
   - Star Wars
   - the War of Independence

8. In the Six Day War, Israel captured
   - Tel Aviv
   - the East Bank
   - the Sinai Desert

9. The 1967 War is known as the
   - Six Day War
   - Sixty Days War
   - Six Months War

10. Israel has signed peace agreements with
    - Egypt
    - the P.L.O. and Jordan
    - Syria

❄ ARGUMENTS ❄

1. Write two different opinions that Israeli Jews have about the captured lands.

   a. ______________________________

   b. ______________________________

2. Write two different opinions that Arabs have about the captured lands.

   a. ______________________________

   b. ______________________________

SYMBOLS

Symbols are pictures or designs that make us think of an idea.

On the right is the symbol of *Tzahal*. It includes an olive branch, which is a symbol of peace.

What else is on *Tzahal*'s symbol? ______________________________

____

What does the design make you think of? ______________________________

____

צבא הגנה לישראל

On the right is the symbol of the State of Israel.

What is on it? ______________________________

____

What does it make you think of? ______________________________

____

ישראל

Think about the name of your temple. What does it mean? Think about what you do at the temple. Use the space below to draw a symbol of your temple.

WHAT DO YOU THINK?

Moshe Dayan was a commander of *Tzahal*. He said, "Our army does not depend on size but rather on excellence. We want courage and boldness.... We want officers who say, 'Follow me!' not 'Forward!'"

What kind of soldier did Moshe Dayan want *Tzahal* to have? ______________________

____

What kind of officer did he want *Tzahal* to have? ______________________________

____

Did he think that it was important for Israel to have a very big army? ________________

____

Peace Headlines

At the time that this book was written, Israel had already signed peace agreements with Egypt, the P.L.O. and Jordan. Perhaps by the time you read this book, Israel will have made peace with all its neighbors.

Imagine that peace has come. Write a headline and a short story for your local newspaper about the peace agreements. Include the following: Where did they take place? Which countries signed them? What did these countries agree to do and not to do?

JACOB AND JESSIE LOOK AT ISRAEL
Connections

Jessie and her sister Sydney.

Jacob and Jessie are cousins who live in Seattle, Washington. Jacob is thirteen and Jessie is twelve. They have both visited Israel.

Jacob says: "Two years ago I stayed at a village in the Galilee. The kids were nice. They spoke English to me even though it was hard for them. I was studying Hebrew for my bar mitzvah, but I couldn't speak the language. We visited many places. We went swimming in the Kinneret and ate good pizza at a café. That was fun. And we went to the Wall in Jerusalem. It was strange to see people standing at the Wall and praying and sticking notes between the stones. I'm not into history very much, but the Wall made me feel a connection to long ago.

"I know we Jews need our own country. But I wish the Palestinians could have a homeland, too. Sometimes I worry about Israel and what will happen there. My friend Shmulik lives in the Galilee village. He's just about to go into the Israeli army. I hope that he'll be careful and that things will be peaceful so that he'll be safe."

Jessie says: "I got off the plane and—bang—the bright sunlight hit me in the face. Then I saw the palm trees and rocks and wildflowers. Israel is so different from Seattle, where everything is green and wet. It feels more special than other places I've been. I love Seattle. It's my home. But Israel is my ancient home. It's where my people started out.

"I was overwhelmed when we climbed Masada. It's so old. The thought of our people fighting from up there and the sight of the attack ramp and the Roman army camp made me shiver.

"I'm studying Hebrew now. It's not as hard as French. I guess I put more effort into it because I want to know it, because it's part of being Jewish. I think I'd like to live in Israel some day, if my family would also decide to go."

A Thousand Connections

What's the connection between American Jews and Israel? That question was raised at the beginning of this book. Jacob and Jessie gave you their answers. Here are some of the other connections between Americans and Israelis. There must be a thousand.

- American basketball players play on Israeli teams.
- Israeli musicians perform in American concert halls.
- Loud American rock music blasts from Israeli radios.
- Spicy Israeli-style pita sandwiches are sold from Maine to Florida.
- American-style ice cream, pizza, and hamburgers are popular from Eilat to Haifa.
- American college kids attend Israeli colleges and *yeshivot*. And Israeli kids go to American colleges and universities.
- Americans bathe in the Dead Sea, the lowest spot on earth. And Israelis gape

Jacob and his sister Rivka with a friend at Disneyland.

at the Grand Canyon and Manhattan's skyscrapers.

- Israelis and Americans share their connection to the land of the Bible. Many Israeli towns still have their five thousand-year-old Bible names. Jerusalem, Beersheba, Yafo, and Hatzor were all cities in biblical times. The ground that people walk on today is filled with stories and history.
- Most important is the religious tie. For Jews, Israel is the Promised Land, where Jewish history and religion began. Today Israel is once again an important center of Jewish life.

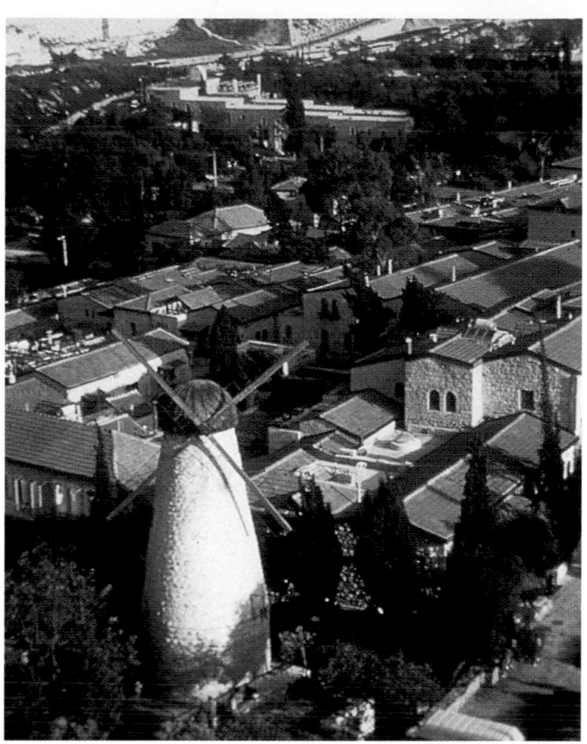

The development of Yemin Moshe, which was supported by American Jews, marked the beginning of new Jerusalem.

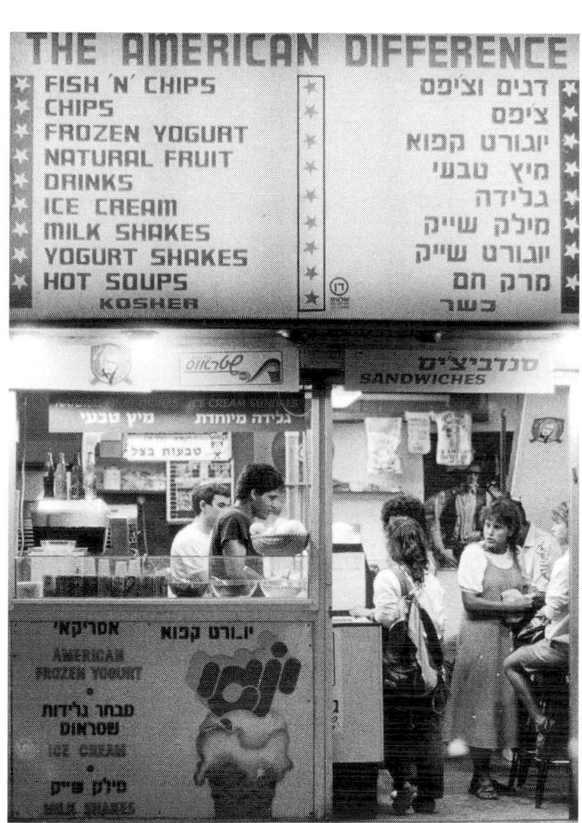

America's tastiest contribution to Israel–frozen yogurt.

The Connections Started Long Ago

The first connections were made when the United States was a very young country. At that time Israel was still Palestine and was ruled by Turkey. In the 1820s some of the Jews of Jerusalem wanted to move out of the city because it was crowded and unhealthy inside the old walls. Judah Touro, a rich Jew from New Orleans, sent them money to build a new suburb.

Much later, about eighty years ago, an American woman named Henrietta Szold visited Palestine. She was shocked to find many sick people and no health care. Henrietta and other Jewish women raised money to send nurses to Palestine. Their group was called Hadassah. Ever since,

Say It in Hebrew

English	Hebrew	How to Say the Hebrew
Jewish National Fund	קֶרֶן קַיֶּמֶת לְיִשְׂרָאֵל	*Ke*-ren Ka-*ye*-met Le-yis-ra-*el*
connection	קֶשֶׁר	*ke*-sher
American	אֲמֵרִיקָנִי	A-me-re-*ka*-ni
Israeli	יִשְׂרְאֵלִי	Yis-re-*e*-li

Hadassah has built many hospitals, schools, and clinics in Palestine and Israel. Other American Jewish organizations have also done good work, and non-Jewish groups have raised money to help them.

Non-Jewish Americans worked with American and Palestinian Jews in the 1940s. They sailed small ships crowded with Jewish refugees out of Europe. They saved thousands of people from Nazi death camps and took them to Palestine. Later they helped other Jewish refugees slip past British warships and reach Palestine.

Many Americans went to fight beside the Israelis in Israel's War of Independence. Mickey Marcus, an American army officer, was killed while commanding Israeli soldiers near Jerusalem. And the first pilots in Israel's new air force were American fliers who had fought in World War II.

Ever since the State of Israel was created, the connections have grown stronger. Organizations like the United Jewish Appeal continue to raise money for Israel. They build schools and homes for immigrants. Other groups build parks, playgrounds, and tennis courts. Did you ever buy a tree certificate from the Jewish National Fund? If you did, then you have also helped Israel.

Youth Aliyah children aboard a ship sing and dance upon reaching Israel.

Middle East. For a long time it was impossible to get Israel and its neighbors to talk to one another. But in 1978 the leaders of Egypt and Israel met in the United States. American President Jimmy Carter kept them talking until they finally signed a peace agreement.

Israel and the United States Also Have Connections

The United States has been a good friend to Israel. In 1947 the United States supported the plan for a Jewish state and an Arab state in Palestine. When Israel was founded in 1948, the United States quickly recognized Israel. Other countries did the same.

Israel and the United States are both democracies that prize freedom. That's one reason that the United States worked to bring freedom to Jews in Russia and Ethiopia. For many years Ethiopia and the former Soviet Union kept their borders closed. Jewish citizens and others were not free to leave. The United States persuaded and argued with the two governments, both of which finally opened their doors. Now many Russian and Ethiopian Jews have settled in Israel.

The United States has helped Israel with loans and gifts of money and arms. It has also worked hard to bring peace to the

Your Connection

People express the ties that they feel to Israel and the Bible in different ways. Jessie says, "I love Seattle. It's my home. But Israel is my ancient home. It's where my people started out." And Naama, whom you met in Chapter 1, says, "Israeli Jews are like a mosaic. We have people from all over the world, from China and Paris and California. But the center of the mosaic is Jerusalem."

To figure out your own connection to Israel, make a list of the things that you care about: your friendships, your family, baseball, your dog, your home, your town or country. Many of you will put your synagogue, your religion, and Israel on that list. It may seem strange to put baseball, your family, your country, and your synagogue on the same list. But all of those things are a part of you. They help make you the person that you are. And since you are a Jew, Israel is also a part of you.

Come and visit. Sam, Meirav, Rahely, and all the others are waiting to say "Shalom! Welcome home!"

SUMMING UP

Americans and Israelis like to sample each other's foods, music, and sports. And they like to visit each other's countries. Many Americans feel a close tie to biblical sites in Israel. There are many connections between Israel and the United States.

The connections started a long time ago. In the 1820s Judah Touro, a rich American Jew, helped some of the Jews in Palestine. More than one hundred years later American women formed Hadassah. Hadassah has worked to provide better health care for the people of Palestine/Israel. In the 1940s American sailors helped take European Jews to Palestine. And many Americans helped Israel fight its War of Independence.

The United States government is a good friend to Israel. In 1948 it quickly recognized Israel as an independent country. It has also lent and given money to Israel. Americans have pressed Russia and Ethiopia to let their Jews leave. And Americans have worked hard to bring peace to the Middle East.

You also have a connection with Israel. Your family, friends, religion, and country are all a part of who you are. Because you are a Jew, Israel is a part of you, too.

ACTIVITIES

CONNECTIONS

List three ways in which you, your family, and your temple help Israel.

1 ____________________

2. ____________________

3. ____________________

List three ways in which Israel helps you, your family, and your temple.

1. ____________________

2. ____________________

3. ____________________

❄ WORD SEARCH ❄

Search for the following words in this mishmash of letters. Look across and down. Circle each word that you find.

ISRAEL
DEMOCRACIES
PITA
UNITED JEWISH APPEAL
TELL
JUDAH TOURO
RUSSIA
PEACE TALKS
ETHIOPIA
JEWISH NATIONAL FUND
MICKEY MARCUS
HADASSAH
EGYPT

```
J E W I S H N A T I O N A L F U N D
U N I T E D J E W I S H A P P E A L
D E M O C R A C I E S A R E E G H F
A W O L Y U S H L T E L L A A Y O A
H A D A S S A H P H S I L L C P B R
T L I L N S O R P I T A Y C E T I N
O L V T A I Y I Z O T Z U E T C H E
U S S A L A T Y U P M E I N A G E I
R I S R A E L Y O I R E N I L F I N
O Y I S T Z U M I A R A L B K E R U
V A Y M I C K E Y M A R C U S S T N
```

Now use the words from the Word Search to complete these sentences.

1. ________________ ________________ helped build a new suburb of old Jerusalem.
2. ________________ is a women's organization that supports hospitals in Israel.
3. An Israeli sandwich bread is called ________________________.
4. ________________ ________________ was an American officer who fought in Israel's War of Independence.
5. The ____________ ______________ ______________raises money for Jewish causes.
6. The ________________ ______________ ____________ plants trees in Israel.
7. Israel and the United States are both ____________________________.
8. The United States persuaded the countries of ________________________ and ____________________ to allow their people to leave.
9. A ____________ is a hill made of layers of towns, one on top of the other.
10. In 1978 leaders of ________________ and ________________ met in the United States to make peace.
11. The United States has worked hard to keep ________________ ________________ going.

TAKE A TRIP

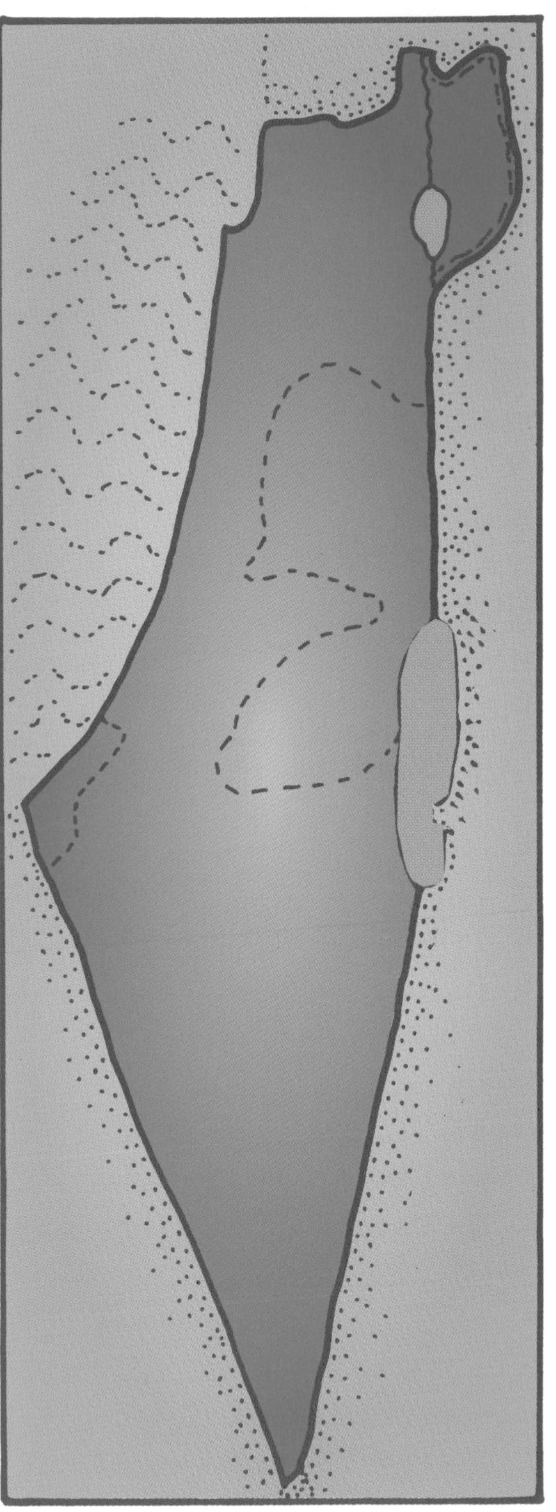

Now that you've read this book, you know a lot about Israel. Choose four places in Israel that you'd like to visit. Locate the places on the map. Draw a star at each location. In the numbered spaces below list each place and write what you expect to see there.

1. ______________________________

____

____

2. ______________________________

____

____

3. ______________________________

____

____

4. ______________________________

____

____

OUR LAND OF ISRAEL Database

A Few Important Events in the History of Israel and Zionism

1882 Members of BILU, an early Zionist group, came from Russia and started to build farms and settlements in Palestine.

1897 In Switzerland, Theodor Herzl called together the First Zionist Congress to work to establish a Jewish state.

Theodor Herzl

1917 Great Britain issued the Balfour Declaration, which called for a Jewish homeland in Palestine. In 1922 the League of Nations (an early United Nations) gave Great Britain the mandate to help establish a Jewish homeland.

1939–1945 Six million Jews were killed by the Nazis in the Holocaust in Europe. Many of the Jews who had survived demanded to go to Palestine.

1947 The United Nations voted to partition Palestine into a Jewish state and an Arab state.

1948 The State of Israel was established. Israel won a war for independence and became a member of the United Nations.

1967 The Six Day War brought new land under Israel's control. Jerusalem was unified as Israel's capital city.

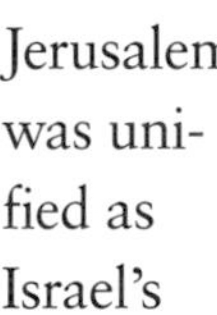

First Independence Day parade (July 1949)

1979 Egypt and Israel signed a peace agreement at Camp David in the United States.

1993 Israel and the Palestine Liberation Organization signed a peace accord.

1994 Israel and Jordan signed a peace treaty.

Israel's Form of Government

Israel is a democracy. Every four years country-wide elections are held. Israeli citizens vote for the political party they want. Like the American Congress, the Knesset is made up of representatives of the various political parties. It makes the laws. A president, prime minister, and cabinet set policy and carry out the laws. Courts review the laws. Elections may take place before the government's four-year term ends if it loses its support in the Knesset.

Political Parties

The many political parties in Israel range from the Communist Rakah to the Orthodox Shas. The two largest political parties are Likud and Labor. To get enough votes in the Knesset to run the government, a large party usually forms partnerships with several smaller parties.

Israel's Population

A total of 5,195,900 people live in Israel.

4,239,855	Jews
727,426	Muslims
140,289	Christians
88,330	Others

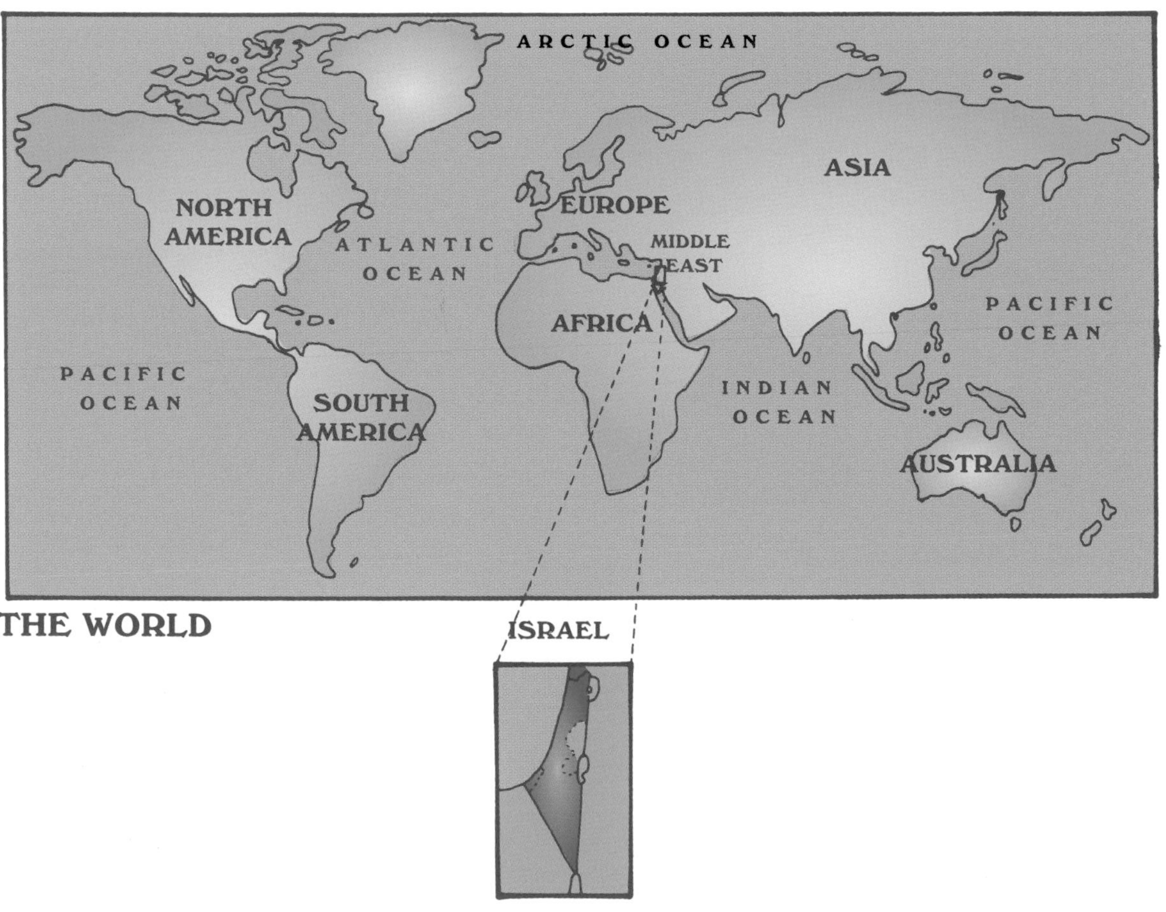

THE WORLD

Israel's Size and Climate

The country covers 8,000 square miles, which is about the size of New Jersey. It has rainy, windy winters and warm, dry summers. Sometimes there's a *chamsin*, a hot, dry wind that sends everyone to the beach or the shower. In general Israel's climate is like that of central and southern California.

The Economy

Most Israelis live in cities. Farm products produced by the kibbutzim and moshavim are important exports but also feed the people at home. Citrus fruits, flowers, and cotton are all major crops. Factories produce textiles, electronic products, plastic products, and pharmaceuticals (medicines). Israelis also mine chemicals from the Dead Sea and chop limestone for cement out of the country's mountainsides.

Presidents of the State of Israel

FIRST—**Chaim Weizmann,** 1874 –1952
A very early Zionist leader and scientist who helped bring about the Balfour Declaration and convinced Harry Truman, the president of the United States, to vote for the establishment of the State of Israel

SECOND—**Itzhak Ben-Zvi,** 1884 –1963
Scholar and leader of the Histadrut before the State of Israel was formed

THIRD—**Zalman Shazar,** 1889–1974
Scholar and writer

FOURTH—**Ephraim Katzir,** born 1916
Scientist

FIFTH—**Itzhak Navon,** born 1921
Scholar and political leader

SIXTH—**Chaim Herzog,** born 1918
Former ambassador to the United States and army general

SEVENTH—**Ezer Weizman,** born 1924
Former air force chief of staff

Prime Ministers of the State of Israel

FIRST—**David Ben-Gurion,** 1886–1973
Leader of Palestine Jewry before the State of Israel was formed and one of the founders of the Haganah

SECOND—**Moshe Sharett,** 1894 –1965
Foreign minister in Israel's first cabinet and political leader

THIRD—**Levi Eshkol,** 1895–1969
Leader of the Histadrut and statesman

FOURTH—**Golda Meir,** 1898–1978
Israel's first ambassador to the Soviet Union

Golda Meir

FIFTH—**Yitzhak Rabin,** born 1922

Army commander in chief and former ambassador to the United States

Menachem Begin

SIXTH—**Menachem Begin,** 1913–1991

Leader of the underground Irgun before the State of Israel was formed and political leader

SEVENTH—**Shimon Peres,** born 1923

Former minister of defense and political leader

EIGHTH—**Yitzhak Shamir,** born 1916

Leader of the secret army Lehi before the State of Israel was formed and political leader

NINTH—**Yitzhak Rabin,** born 1922

A Few of the Heroes of Zionism and Israel

We could fill a hundred books with the names of Israel's heroes. Here are just a few important, wonderful people to know about.

Theodor Herzl, 1860–1904

Herzl founded modern political Zionism. He called together the First Zionist Congress in 1897 in Switzerland. At that time, he said there would be a Jewish state within fifty years. People cheered and clapped, but not many believed him. Israel was born fifty-one years later!

Eliezer Ben-Yehuda

Eliezer Ben-Yehuda, 1858–1922

Ben-Yehuda was an educator and linguist who made biblical Hebrew a modern language. He published a Hebrew newspaper and wrote a fifteen-volume Hebrew dictionary that contained words for daily use.

Henrietta Szold, 1860–1945

With Reha Freier, Szold led the work of Youth Aliyah, which rescued thousands of children from death in Nazi Europe. She also founded Hadassah, a large women's Zionist organization.

Hannah Senesh

Hannah Senesh, 1921–1944

During World War II, young Hannah was in Israel training to be a fighter. She hoped to enter Europe secretly and lead Jews and others in battle against the Nazis. Hannah was dropped by parachute into Nazi-occupied Europe. But she was unable to carry out her mission. She was captured and executed. Her poems remind us of her bravery. One of them begins with the words "Blessed is the match that is burned up in its own flame."

Yonatan Netanyahu, 1946 – 1976

Yonatan, an Israeli paratroop commander, led a daring rescue of Israeli airline passengers who had been hijacked by Arab terrorists and were being held in Entebbe, Uganda. Israeli planes managed to evade detection by radar and flew 2,200 miles into Africa. They surprised the terrorists and rescued the passengers. Yonatan was killed in the action.

Israeli Symbols

Magen David

These words mean "Shield of David" in English. A six-pointed star, the Magen David is often used in synagogue decorations. It also appears on the blue and white flag of Israel.

The Flag

Israel's white flag with blue stripes was designed to look like the traditional white *talit* with its blue stripes.

Menorah

A *menorah* is a candle holder or oil lamp that has several branches. It is one of the oldest Jewish symbols. A golden six-branched *menorah* stood in the Temple in Jerusalem. The *menorah* is pictured on the seal of the State of Israel.

Hatikvah

This is the Hebrew word for "The Hope." "Hatikvah" is the anthem of the Zionist movement. You'll find some of the words to "Hatikvah" on page 12.

Index

"there's nowt so queer as folk."

—Old English proverb

POCKET BOOKS
New York London Toronto Sydney Singapore

queer as folk

the book

paul ruditis

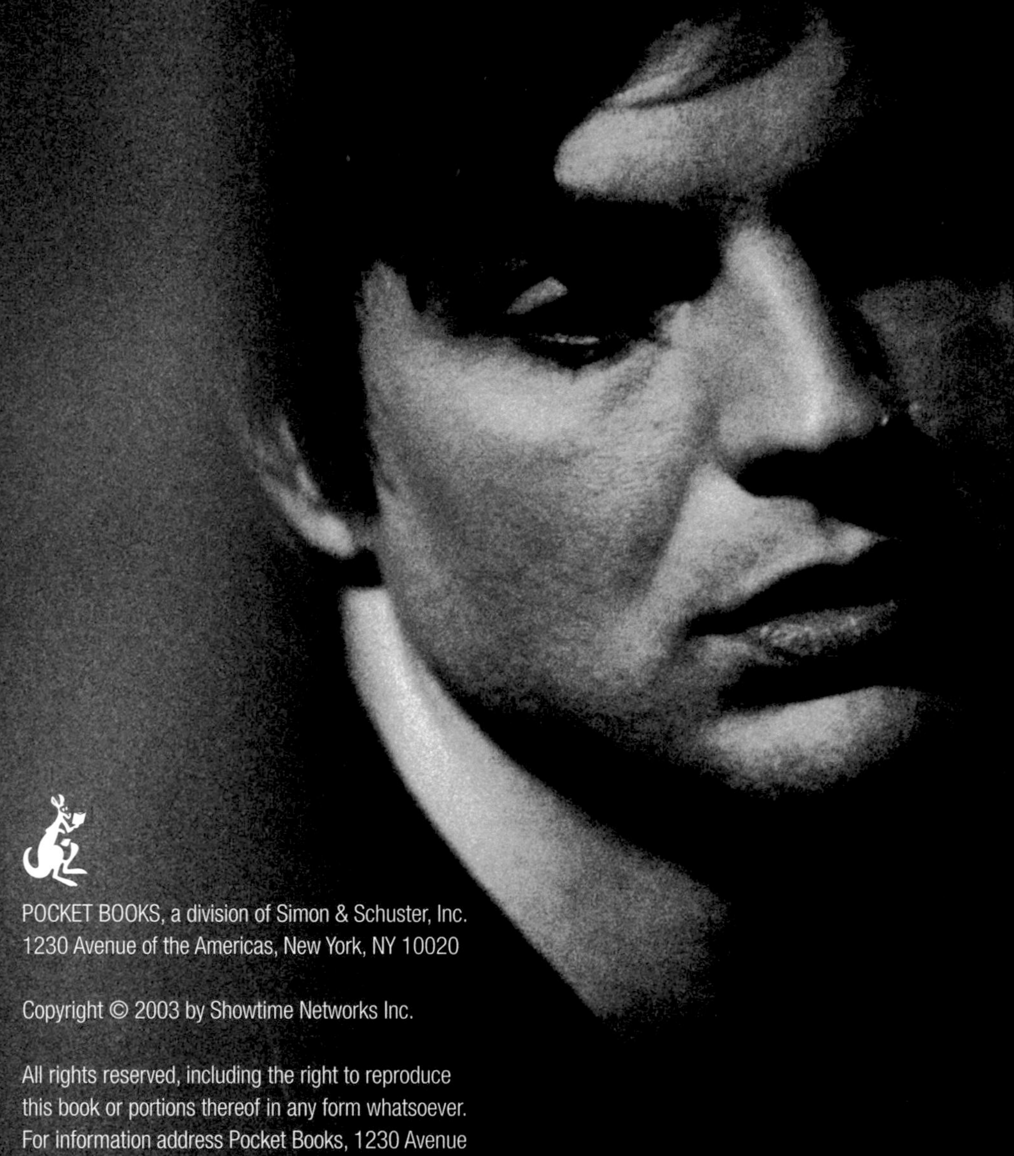

POCKET BOOKS, a division of Simon & Schuster, Inc.
1230 Avenue of the Americas, New York, NY 10020

ISBN: 0-7434-7636-0

First Pocket Books trade paperback edition November 2003

10 9 8 7 6 5 4 3 2

Manufactured in the United States of America

Design by Joel Avirom and Jason Snyder
Design assistant: Meghan Day Healey

This book is dedicated to all those creative and courageous people who have helped to make *QAF* a landmark in gay and television history.

contents

Theater—And then the dinner party conversation turned to Neil Simon. Page 3
Movies—Almodóvar & Co. Page 4 • Music—Pianist Mari Kodama rolls out Beethoven. Page 6

SUNDAY

Calendar

Some Like It Not Too Hot

You'll probably never see the British miniseries sensation "Queer as Folk" on American TV, despite its cult following. But a cable adaptation is in the works—minus the more explicit parts, of course.

BY KRISTIN HOHENADEL AND PAUL BROWNFIELD PAGES 8-9

introduction

The first time we became aware of that most curiously incomprehensible phrase "queer as folk" was in the cover article in the Sunday Calendar section of the *Los Angeles Times* (November 21, 1999). There was this TV series about gay life in Britain, you see, that was so unflinching, so graphic, so shocking, that you could bet that we would never see it on these provincial shores. The article went on to say that any attempt to do an American version would be so lame, so ball-less, so sanitized, that it would be laughable.

Well, that certainly got our attention.

That, followed by the news that it was Showtime that was negotiating for the rights to this certain-to-be-doomed venture. Coincidentally, Showtime was the very network we were producing a series for. Or trying to. The financing had just fallen through. Preproduction had halted. The phones stopped ringing.

Fortunately, the phone did ring a short time later. It was the Powers That Be at the No Limits Network. Would we be interested in writing and producing the American version of this British import with the confounding title *Queer as Folk*?

Let's see—would we be interested? Well, first we needed to see it. And see it we did. To say it was unflinching, graphic, and shocking was an understatement. We were stunned. Speechless. Thankfully, we did manage to get out one word—"Yes!" But with a very explicit proviso of our own. We felt compelled to accept the challenge of that article in the *Times*. Our version had to be as bold and as daring as the original. We had to do what they said could never and would never be done on American television—or there was no reason to attempt it at all.

And, by God—Showtime agreed. And it was written. And it was shot. And the audiences came. And it became a big fucking hit!

Well-l-l—it wasn't quite that simple. There were the usual—and not so usual—stumbling blocks along the way. You'll read about some of them in this book. (After all, what's a good triumphant tale without a few setbacks, right?) But the important thing is, the guys at Showtime lived up to their No Limits mantra and left us alone to do what we felt had to be done. The sex would be hot. The characters would be flawed. The show would live up to its mandate (an appropriate word if there ever was one) to be outrageous, in-your-face, uncensored, and unapologetic. And, as anyone who's seen the show knows, we fulfilled that mandate—and are still doing so as we begin our fourth season.

So, why did we jump at the chance to take on this queer project? Well, for one thing, we'd simply never seen anything like it. No one had. We knew—no matter how the show was received—it would be a true one-of-a-kind, never-been-done-before original. And not just for TV. Anywhere.

For another thing, we were immediately attracted to the unique voice of Russell T Davies (creator of the British *QAF*). It was graphic and shocking, all right—but it was also oddly sweet, charming, witty, and naughty (as, indeed, Russell—a gentle giant and our long-lost brother—is himself). The boys and girls of Liberty Avenue started speaking to us almost immediately. That's the test. You know you can surmount any obstacle as long as your characters speak to you. It's spooky and mystical. But they do. Really.

Queer as Folk (there's that bizarre title again. Should we change it for an American audience we thought?) gave us an arena in which to portray gay people as they've never been portrayed before. As the very first line in the very first episode states, "The thing you need to know is, it's all about sex." For gay people that's especially true. And not just about having it. But being free to have it. Happy to have it. Celebrating it, instead of being ashamed, fearful, condemned, punished. The world of Liberty Avenue presented a chance to show a gay world in which gay men and women would be complete. That means being sexualized human beings. Sex, we need not tell you, is a vital human behavior. A behavior that can illuminate character. Unfortunately, in our culture, that behavior is limited in its depiction—for both gay and straight characters. We must be polite. Close the bedroom doors. It's nobody's business. But not on *QAF*.

Also, for the first time in the history of the whole damn world, gay people would be the stars of a TV series. Not just the funny sidekick at the office or the sexless best friend. And they'd be fucking their brains out to make up for all that lost time.

Through our characters, we are able to tell stories that must be told, that have not been told, could not be told anywhere else or in quite the same way as on *QAF*. Stories about discrimination, harassment, gay-bashing, AIDS, gay parenting, being accepted—or rejected—by one's family, being HIV-positive, being HIV-negative, steroids, drug use and abuse—all the issues that gay people struggle with and that to a large degree define their lives.

QAF is intended as a celebration of gay life. We made an early decision never to moralize or judge our characters or their world. To let it stand as it is and show all of its colors. But that doesn't mean it's always pretty. Sometimes it can be downright ugly. *QAF* is not (surprise! surprise!) "politically correct." That said, it doesn't mean we're out to offend. Our job is to tell the truth. Whatever that truth may be and wherever that truth takes us. And let's face it, sometimes the truth hurts.

Now, in contradiction of ourselves, the show is obviously not "all about sex." If it were, our faithful viewers would have turned off long ago. Those shirtless guys dancing nightly in Babylon might be hot, and Brian and Justin's love scenes might make not only our gay audience but also our straight female fans swoon (there's a psychology book waiting to be written about that!), but we like to hope it's something else that keeps the audience coming back: compelling characters and story lines. TV series do not survive on gimmicks. We've learned that there is a fantasy element to any series. No, not necessarily angels coming to earth or a housewife who turns out to be a witch. A simple fantasy: I wish those characters were my sisters or my brothers or my friends or my family. And that's what *QAF* is really about. Aside from our much repeated "boys becoming men" theme. It's about being a family. A family of one's own choosing. Gay people seem to have an abundantly loving knack for that.

And we chose our family, too. Our creative one, that is.

We have truly been blessed to be able to work with amazingly talented men and women. All of them—our writers, directors, artisans, technicians, and staff—are so gifted, so courageous, so dedicated and passionate.

And then there's our cast. As remarkable as human beings as they are as actors. You'll discover more about them as you read on—as well as others who help us make Liberty Avenue come alive every episode. They're our heroes—every one of them. They have made our jobs a joy—and one of the highlights of our lives and careers.

So, here it is: *Queer as Folk: The Book.*

With no apologies and no regrets—but with great appreciation.

—RON COWEN AND DANIEL LIPMAN

P.S. As you may have noticed, we never did change that title. And there's good reason. Because—well—because *Queer as Folk* is—queer as folk! That says it all. "There's nothing stranger than people"—be they British, American, Canadian, men, women, gay, or straight. Politically correct or incorrect—that's something we can all agree on.

setting the tone

The ads warned, "It's Here. It's Queer," and it was coming. Something unlike anything ever seen on North American television. British audiences had both embraced and been outraged by the series created by Russell T Davies that depicted an in-your-face view of gay lifestyles. Was America ready?

But the better question was, were the producers ready?

Bringing a new version of *Queer as Folk* to American shores was a tremendous undertaking for executive producers Ron Cowen, Daniel Lipman, and Tony Jonas. Even with the full support of Showtime behind their audacious pilot script, the producers had a colossal task before them. Few British series had been successfully translated for American audiences, often because American production companies did not follow the formula of the original. The producers decided early on that, while they were going to strive to set a standard of unique programming, they would never forget the original vision on which their version was to be based.

Bringing a series to television often involves a difficult preproduction process in setting the tone for the series. But the producers had a little help in that endeavor as director Joel Schumacher, known for the hit films *St. Elmo's Fire* and *Batman Forever,* was already on board through an existing arrangement with Channel 4 in England. Together, they started laying out their plan for the show, and that's when they hit their first snag. The pre-production ran a bit longer than usual and Joel stepped out to take on a film. The glitch was a blessing in disguise.

Tony, Ron, and Dan

Seemingly rudderless, the search began for the right director to blend with the existing team. As Daniel Lipman explains, "We had a lot of directors interested in doing the show who did nice pieces. But we said 'No, this project needs a driving energy.' And that's why we got Russell Mulcahy. He really invested the pilot with a sexual, kinetic energy. We wanted the tone of the show to reflect gay sexuality, but a powerful masculine gay sexuality as embodied by the character of Brian."

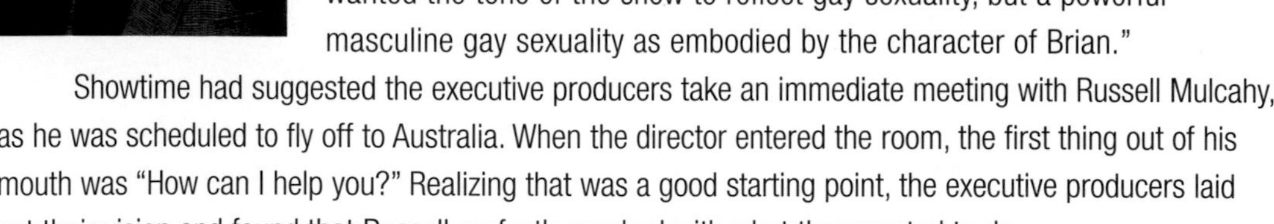

Showtime had suggested the executive producers take an immediate meeting with Russell Mulcahy, as he was scheduled to fly off to Australia. When the director entered the room, the first thing out of his mouth was "How can I help you?" Realizing that was a good starting point, the executive producers laid out their vision and found that Russell perfectly meshed with what they wanted to do.

Traditional drama series have a slicked-up "television look" of perfect people in perfect shots, with a perfect underscore. But *Queer as Folk* would be different. Since the characters were far from perfect, the look of the show would be just as far from perfect as well. They weren't going for some big-budget look; instead they decided the series would have more of an independent-film feel.

"When we first saw the British version, we saw it had grittiness to it that we liked," Dan explains. "We didn't want it to look like a television show. We had done *Sisters* and that had a little bit of a slick look to it, which seemed to work for that particular show. We felt this show required more of a realistic feel. When we hired Russell Mulcahy to do the pilot, he set a lot of that tone. There was a lot of handheld camerawork and that sort of intimacy."

Russell helped establish the look of the series, and the episodes that followed stayed true to the original. Subsequent directors on the series worked to match that style while bringing their own ideas to the table and expanding that independent-film tone. This is where filming the show in Toronto has definite advantages.

Sheila Hockin

The Canadian city has an independent-film scene—one that producer Sheila Hockin is closely keyed into. Among her many responsibilities in keeping the show up and running is to continue bringing in directors that have a résumé of independent-film work where they are accustomed to doing things quickly and creatively. She looks for directors who are able to take risks and, more importantly, *want* to take risks so the show is not necessarily bloated with television work that's all by the numbers.

Ron, Dan, Tony, and Sheila also looked to the local film community to fill out their creative staff—starting with Thom Best as their director of photography. Thom came in with a sample reel that had the exact look they were going for and although he had a considerable amount of film work, he had never done a television series before.

"On an indie feature film, you have a period of prep and then you have a finite amount of shooting," Sheila explains. "It's usually twenty-five or thirty days, if you're lucky. Then it's all over. So anybody can make their way through that. On a series, when it goes on week after week, and you're lighting standing sets and you're running a very large crew, it's a very different experience."

Production designer Ingrid Jurek was in the same boat. "Her experience was in independent feature film," Sheila explains. "She had never done a TV series. For a production designer it's a massive job. People don't build a lot of sets in indie features because they can't afford it, so they tend to shoot on location a great deal. This was a huge shift for Ingrid to have to conceptualize all these peoples' homes and for our set dressers to be able to start from scratch and conceive of what these people owned."

What these people brought to the table in terms of their creative vision far outweighed their lack of experience in this particular medium, and the practice of hiring from the indie scene carried over to the rest of the creative crew. "Pretty much everybody in the key creative positions was new to series television," Sheila admits. "We think that it really worked out. And the culture of the show has that indie feel to it as well. It's a very committed group of people. They care so much about it. They're people who are used to doing a project that they're intimately involved with."

The tone was set. Thanks to Russell Mulcahy's work with the producers, *Queer as Folk* had found its look. The production team would approach the series as if they were putting together a mini-independent film each week, and they continued to gather talent that could work within those parameters. In the end, they would fulfill their own edict to present something that had never before been seen on television.

That was the easy part.

finding folk

Before *Queer as Folk* even began filming, words like *groundbreaking* and *revolutionary* were being used to describe the show in and around the entertainment industry. The original series had created a lot of buzz in Britain. The pilot script for the American version was being touted as even more powerful and in-your-face. Everything looked to be falling into place with the show, and the executive producers began casting riding on a wave of positive vibes. Who wouldn't want to be associated with their show?

"As it turned out, everybody was very scared," Tony Jonas admits of the shocking discovery when they started the search for actors. "It went down a lot of different roads because there were issues about playing a gay character. Largely it was the issue of actors wondering if that would change the audience's perception forever so that the actor could only play gay roles afterwards. Then it became the general sense of homophobia about everything, which included not wanting to be associated with the project even if they were going to play straight characters. That was probably the first real wake-up call that it was going to be really tough to get actors."

When any show is being cast, the casting agents, in this case, Linda Lowy and John Brace, produce a list of N/As or "not availables." Generally this list of N/As is a couple of pages long and contains names of actors who generally cite prior commitments. But Daniel Lipman found their list to be a different case entirely. "Linda Lowy brought a thirty-five-page, single-spaced list of N/As," he recalls. "It wasn't just because they were getting married or going on a trip. It was because of the show. So we would then go in to have a casting session and Linda would say, 'There are only five people coming today.' And we'd ask, 'Five?' Then she'd say, 'Well, there were supposed to be twenty-five, but they're all no-shows.'"

When actors did show up, the producers found that they were still not going to have an easy time. A lot of actors who were not gay felt that they needed to state that up front. Then, some went out of their way to make sure that Ron, Dan, and Tony knew that they *were* gay so the producers would be more open to their performance. Some of the actors even felt they needed to start taking off their clothes at the audition to appeal to what the producers were looking for, which was, needless to say, not the right approach.

The casting process wasn't entirely a disaster. In fact, it started out rather well according to Ron Cowen. "The easy part was knowing who is right for the role. Within ten seconds you know, unless they have some terrible problem like they can't act for shit. The hard part was having them come through the door. In some cases it was less difficult than others. **Peter Paige** (opposite top) walked in the first day. **Scott Lowell** (opposite bottom) walked in the first day, followed by Hal. In fact, I think Scott was the very first actor we saw for the show. We said, 'Oh my God, this is going to be easy. They're just coming right in. We'll be done by four o'clock.'"

Although casting wasn't close to being done by four on the first day, certain actors needed less convincing than others to come in to audition. Scott Lowell received the pilot script for the series the

same day he received the script for a TV movie about firefighters. The two scripts could not have been more different, but for Scott the choice of going up for Ted was easy. "I read *Queer as Folk* and it scared me," he recalls. "I kept checking to make sure it was a TV show. I didn't quite know what it was going to be, but this character really drew me in. Ted's not in the pilot a lot until the end, but there was something about him I really, really hooked into and related to on a very personal level, having been that guy and felt like him at various stages in my life."

Physically the character was described differently in the original script. The producers later told Scott that they hadn't had Ted entirely defined in their minds when he came in, but in the pilot script he was supposed to be a lot heavier and balding. Although Scott didn't fit exactly what it *said* they were looking for, he felt he understood the character and went in with the attitude "Here's my take on the guy, and if you like it, you like it." It worked because he ended up being the first one cast in the series.

At the same time, Peter Paige also came in to audition for Ted. "When I read the script, I certainly related emotionally to Ted," says Peter, echoing Scott's reaction. "We all feel like a schlub sometimes. So I went in and I gave a kick-ass audition for Ted, but as soon as I finished, I said to the casting director, 'Let me read for Emmett.'" Linda Lowy immediately told the actor that she was giving him a callback for Ted. But something about the other character stuck with Peter and he asked again to read for Emmett. Linda indulged his request, and when the audition was over, she made an almost unheard-of offer, asking him to choose which role he would like to come back to audition for in front of the producers.

Since they had originally brought Peter in to read for Ted, he decided to come back for that role and claims it's the smartest thing he has ever done. During his callback for the producers, Dan and Ron watched him read for the role of Ted, but made the connection to try him out as Emmett on their own. When they asked Peter to shift from Ted to Emmett, they asked how he felt doing that. His answer was simple: "I was like, I feel fine with that because I've already prepared the lines."

In the next step in the casting, Scott and Peter came in to audition for the Showtime executives. That's where they met some of the other hopefuls and future castmates. "Everyone had to report at eight o'clock in the

morning," Dan recalls. "I mean, this is Hollywood. Eight o'clock in the morning? To audition?" Scott picks up the story: "And being the anal guy that I am, I got there early and Peter was also there early. So the two of us sat down in the hallway outside Showtime's offices because they were still locked up. The newspapers were being dumped off in the hallway with us. We both sat there sizing each other up trying to figure out if we were there for the same audition. When we found out we were up for different roles, we relaxed and were comfortable with each other."

Scott and Peter weren't the only actors giving each other the once-over that morning. **Michelle Clunie** (top) had also been brought in to meet the executives for the role of Melanie. "I auditioned three times," she recalls. "And then we had to audition a fourth time because they wanted to see Thea and I read together. So they flew her down to Los Angeles, and it was some asinine hour like eight-fifteen in the morning that they wanted us to come in and read. I remember thinking, 'It's hard enough being Michelle at eight-fifteen in the morning, much less Melanie.'"

When Michelle arrived, lots of people were already there besides Peter and Scott. "I looked over and I saw this girl with sandy blond hair in overalls with her foot up on a bench," Michelle says, regarding the first sighting of someone she was about to get to know well. "I remember thinking, 'Oh, that's Lindsay. That's definitely Lindsay. There's no doubt about it.' I went over and introduced myself and said something like 'Are you nervous?' I can't remember what she said, but I said, 'We're gonna do great. We're gonna do great.' I remember looking her up and down and thinking to myself, 'This is the girl . . . this is Lindsay.'"

Thea Gill (above) also recalls the first meeting of Lindsay and Melanie. "I remember Michelle taking control, going in with a real confidence and a sense of accomplishment," she explains. "Like we were meant to be these roles and we were meant to be these characters. She kind of grabbed me and said, 'I love her and we have the best chemistry and you'd be fools not to cast us.' She went in

there as Melanie and I was Lindsay. It really helped the whole audition process, because it was very nerve-racking."

Thea was not the only actor to travel for the audition. **Randy Harrison** (left) had also flown in for the early-morning meeting with the executives. His original audition for Justin was included in a collection of tapes sent to the producers from a New York casting director who was looking for actors in that city. A list accompanied the tapes that had certain names checked off suggesting actors the producers should look at. "These tapes came on a daily basis," Ron explains. "It was getting to be the eleventh hour and we didn't have a Justin. Someone had the brilliant idea of going back and looking through these tapes and this time looking for names that were not checked off just to see if we may have overlooked someone. And there was Randy, whose name had not been checked off."

They knew that they had found a wonderful actor, but were concerned that he looked a little too much like a teenager. It was important that the actor be at least eighteen years old. When the producers checked his résumé and saw that he had graduated college, it eased some of their concerns. "We were terrified because he was awfully young," Ron admits. "Brian was going to become sexually involved with a guy who was several years younger than himself and a teenager in high school. We were scared because Randy was really young, but he was not as young in real life as he looks. He was the same age that I was when I had my first play done in New York."

Although Randy was the youngest and newest to the business, it seemed that most of the other parts as well were filled by relatively undiscovered actors. When **Hal Sparks** (right) was added to the mix, he brought a familiar name to the project, although this kind of drama was not something he was known for. "I had just finished *Talk Soup*," Hal recalls of the time he first heard of the show. "I was working on *Dude, Where's My Car?* when my manager got the script and thought it was great. He called me up and said, 'It's based on a British show that's terrific. It was a big hit, but it's very controversial. There's a lot of sexual content,

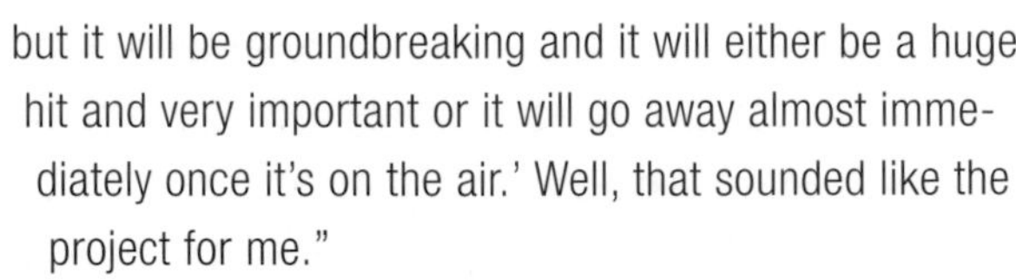

but it will be groundbreaking and it will either be a huge hit and very important or it will go away almost immediately once it's on the air.' Well, that sounded like the project for me."

Hal got the script from his manager and thought it was fantastic, but when he brought it to the attention of his agent, he was definitely reluctant. "He was a bit worried," Hal admits. "Saying that a lot of actors and a lot of agents wouldn't read the script or pass them on or even agree to go in. Everybody was chickening out. And that was reason enough for me to go in, because everybody's afraid to do it. That's why I had to go audition." Hal did audition, although at the time he suspected that the producers had only brought him in to have a laugh in the middle of a difficult day of auditioning by bringing in a comic. But he impressed them with his dramatic interpretation and got the role.

If the producers thought casting the show was difficult in general, it was nothing compared to the experience of finding someone to play Brian. The producers knew that without the right Brian there would be no show. Unfortunately, the right person to play Brian was also a no-show and time was running out. That eight-o'clock, Monday-morning audition with the Showtime executives was fast approaching. "So it was Wednesday and it was Thursday and there was no one for the role of Brian," Dan recalls of the tension-filled week. "And Linda, to her credit, kept saying, 'Don't worry, he'll come. I'm telling you he'll come.'" But as the week progressed, Dan grew more and more skeptical.

"Friday morning I kept checking in with her," Dan continues. "And she'd say, 'Don't worry, Dan, he'll come.' And I was thinking, 'Oh, God, what are we going to do?' Noon . . . One . . . Two . . . At quarter to six on Friday the phone rings and all I hear is 'He's here.'" At first Dan didn't believe it, but he and Ron were in their car a moment later heading down the street to Linda Lowy's office. "**Gale Harold** (above) walked in," Dan recalls, "and he read the scene. I thought to myself, 'Am I desperate or is he fabulous? I'm thinking, he's pretty fabulous.'"

Afterward the executive producers asked Gale if he could go to the pilot test Monday at eight o'clock. But the actor had a commitment on Sunday night that he suspected would interfere with the call time and told the producers that he couldn't make it. "So we gave him the script so he could see the first episode," Ron says, admitting that they weren't about to give up. "At noon on Saturday, we were writing, and the phone rings. Dan gets the phone and all he hears is 'Hello, this is Brian Kinney.' The rest is history."

Though the auditioning was difficult, one bright spot in the casting came about through a fortunate coincidence. **Sharon Gless** (opposite) was performing in a play in Chicago while preparing to work on the play *A Lion in Winter*. To help her with the new role she had hired a drama coach who had been an agent as well. He called her and mentioned the pilot script for *Queer as Folk* and the role he knew she would be perfect for. "So he messengered it over," Sharon says. "And I went nuts. I read that thing and instantly I picked up the phone. I'm usually shy and not very aggressive about my career, but something just came over me when I read this script and I read the part of Debbie. I said, 'Oh, man, could I do something with that.' And I wanted it."

This is the point where the stars aligned for everyone involved. As fate would have it, the former assistant to Sharon's husband, producer Barney Rosenzweig, was currently the assistant to Jerry Offsay, President, Original Programming, Showtime Networks Inc. Carole had been with Sharon's husband for years and was considered family, so it was not out of the ordinary for the actress to give her a call. Sharon remembers that Carole reacted to the news a bit skeptically at first. "She said, 'Sharon, there's no money. There's no money in this show. You don't want to work on this show.' I said, 'Yeah, I really do. I don't care about the money.'" So Carole ran the idea by Jerry Offsay and got back to Sharon and told her, "Jerry loves the idea and says he thinks you'll add a little class to the project." Naturally, Sharon's response was "Tell Jerry class is not what I had in mind."

Sharon met the producers on one of those days when nobody would return their phone calls. "I told the guys that I hadn't gone after a role since the seventies," she admits. "It's the first thing I said when I walked in the door."

Ron says, "She came in and said, 'I haven't been on an audition in twenty-five years, but I read this and I had to at least meet you guys, because I have to ask you a question. How the fuck are you going to do this?'"

The truth was the producers still didn't know how they were going to do it. But they did know that they weren't going to ask Sharon Gless to audition for them. Once they learned that she shared their vision for the series, Sharon was offered the part of Debbie. No other actress was even considered for the role.

queer writes advocates

Executive producers Ron *Cow*en and Daniel *Lip*man are the men behind the *cow* and the *lip* at Cowlip Productions and have been partners in writing and in life for over thirty years. They met at the Eugene O'Neill playwrights conference in Connecticut, where Ron had prepared a three-act play for the summer program and Dan had a one-act. Knowing there was little that could be done with a one-act play, Ron approached Dan to suggest writing a companion piece to add to Dan's. "Then we realized that it was two-thirds of an evening and we needed a third act," Ron recalls. "So we decided to write it together. The concept was that our characters would meet each other in the third act, and then we thought, 'Why don't we make it a musical, too, just to be ridiculous?'"

Together, Ron and Dan wrote the songs for their third act and turned the play into a musical. The play was done the following summer at the Berkshire Theater Festival in Massachusetts and optioned for production off-Broadway. Ron remembers it as an exciting time, except for one thing.

"The play was terrible," he admits with a laugh. "It was the most godawful thing I had ever seen. So Dan and I had the rare distinction of going to the Palace Theater building on Times Square and begging these producers not to produce our play."

Although the initial effort of the writing team may not have been a success, it was the start of a great collaboration. Over the next few years they continued writing both separately and as a team. "We discovered we really enjoyed working together," Ron says. "At that time we each brought things to the collaboration that the other didn't. Dan is a very funny guy and I was a much more serious writer at that time. I think over the years, working with Dan, I've allowed myself to express more of my humor in my writing."

Dan agrees that the experience was mutually beneficial. "When you work with someone for a very long time as a team, you develop a voice," he explains. "It's something that just happens. You can't just meet a writing partner and have it gel like it did for us. Once you have a voice with another person, you meld both voices and lose your sense of ego. You never really know who writes which line, and you're just as thrilled for the other person who writes the great line as for yourself."

When Ron and Dan moved to Los Angeles and started working in television, they found it became almost a necessity to write together because of the pressure of delivering scripts in a tight time frame. "Writing is a very lonely business anyway," Ron adds. "I think, perhaps, that's why a lot of writers are crazy. Not that we aren't crazy, but at least we have the benefit of being crazy together."

The collaboration really began to pay off, and the duo became writer/producers. Their first big breakthrough project was *An Early Frost* in 1985, the Emmy Award–winning television movie about a man living with AIDS. "It was very controversial," Ron says. "We actually started writing it in 1983. It took about a year and a half and fourteen drafts to get *An Early Frost* on NBC. If you think about how they approach gay projects now on network television and what you're allowed to see and not see, well, if you go back eighteen years, it was the dark ages. So doing that project was extremely controversial." Despite strict network censors and a lack of advertisers, *An Early Frost* was a huge hit, scoring higher ratings than its competition, including *Monday Night Football.*

Ron and Dan continued writing for television together and their next major collaboration was the hit NBC series *Sisters.* Although Ron and Dan didn't have any sisters of their own, they did understand the complexities of that kind of sibling relationship and hooked into a concept they related to. Ron explains, "*Sisters* and *Queer as Folk* both deal with minority groups who I don't think are given full-class citizenship in the world and have to struggle harder to be accepted. I think in many cases, women and gay men are both devaluated in our culture and treated almost like second-class citizens. There is a similarity between those two shows."

Dan adds that there's another important similarity that also affects the way they write *Queer as Folk.* "*Sisters* began with us and it ended with us," he says. "We were there the day we started the pilot and we were there the day the series wrapped. I think it's going to be the same thing for *Queer as Folk.* A lot of writers don't do that, but I get very invested. I think the show is very important to a lot of people and it's very important to us."

straight from the cow's lips

RON COWEN: Going into *Queer as Folk* we knew that we had to be outrageous and brave. And it scared us because we never wrote that way before. In television, we were never given the opportunity to write that way, and back when we were writing for the theater, if you said "fuck" onstage or showed nudity, everybody gasped. So, this was really the first chance we had to be as explicit as we are on this show. That scared us, but it was also a challenge. As it turns out, it was the best therapy I never paid for.

Working on this show is great therapy for everyone, because you're put in this situation—possibly for the first time in your life—with straight people, gay people, men, women . . . all different ages. All of a sudden you're having very explicit conversations about sex. At first it's a little embarrassing, but then everybody starts to laugh and it turns silly. At that point it's the most liberating feeling.

DANIEL LIPMAN: On television, characters have to be good. They have to be balanced and likable. That was the whole thing on network television: "balance and likability." I understand that, but luckily Showtime has given us the opportunity to have more adult drama. I think people really respond to that kind of ambiguous character that does good things, but then makes a mistake. Flawed characters are more interesting to write than the likeable character who can't do anything. Being politically incorrect is not something we intentionally try to work in. It just means that we tell the truth. And sometimes the truth is not what people want to hear. But that's our job, to tell the truth of these characters.

I think every good television series is basically a fantasy, because you want to be part of that world. You wish those people were your family, or your friends. I heard it all the time on *Sisters.* "I wish that I had sisters that were friends like that." I hear it all the time on this show. "I love those characters. I wish I had a mother like Debbie. I wish that Brian, Michael, and Ted were my friends." I think that's a compliment to any show that you'd get so invested.

hal sparks as **michael novotny**

Michael Novotny: Everyman.

He is attractive, but not unattainable; smart, but not intellectual; witty, but not a clown; and surprisingly self-aware for as lost as he may be at times. He is the epitome of the average gay male.

"In many ways, Michael is the emotional center of the show," says Daniel Lipman. "Michael is the Everyman. And he is flawed, like the Everyman. Michael has lied and he has been a coward. But he's sweet and adorable, so sometimes you overlook that. But he basically has a very good heart and I think that he is somebody who will succeed in becoming a man."

In this group of boys growing into men, Michael is the one who has the most growing to do and numerous obstacles to overcome. "There are several events in Michael's life that have made him somewhat immature and insecure," Ron Cowen notes. "Growing up without a father was a problem for him, and having a very domineering mother probably stunted his emotional growth."

Much of Michael's "stunted growth" comes out through his interest in comics and in that the decor of his apartment looks eerily similar to that of his childhood bedroom. His ambiguously gay fictional superhero, Captain Astro, does not provide the real hero he's looking for in life. Ron says, "In a lot of ways, Brian

michael

". . . in ways that maybe no one intended, those superheroes were a lot like me. At work they're meek, underappreciated . . . they're the guys that never get laid. And when they're around other people, they can never let anyone get too close for fear that their true identities will be discovered."

was that superhero figure. Michael has fantasized about having a superhero as an imaginary father. He wanted to have someone who would come to his rescue because he's a fatherless boy with a very overpowering mother. And now that's why the two men he's been involved with in his life—David and Ben—are somewhat older, bigger guys who are sublimated superhero figures who will look after him and take care of him."

At the same time, Michael plays the role of the superhero, too, as the caretaker of the group. This was clear from the start in how he tried to look after Brian when he was out partying hard, and in his having taken Emmett in temporarily—two years earlier. It shows in the way that he thinks, such as when Ted was in a coma, it was Michael who realized the condo could use a thorough porn cleaning before Ted's mom was scared straight. But nowhere is his caring personality more evident than when he tries to look after his own mother.

Michael's growth from boy to man continues into the third season, and Dan acknowledges that he's come a long way. "He's got his own business now and you can see the arc. You see where a character like Michael began. He started with junior college and working at Big Q, and now he has developed this comic book, owns a comic-book store, and he's in this relationship with Ben, which is a very interesting and important relationship. He's parenting this kid with Melanie and Lindsay, and he's also parenting Hunter. So you see the range of what's happened to him."

It is those experiences and that growth that have made him a much stronger character. The Michael seen fleeing with Hunter at the end of the third season is very different from the one seen running down the hospital hall with Brian and Justin in the pilot. He finally comes around to Brian's line of thinking and realizes that the police are not there to help and he has the confidence to take Hunter and bolt. But the biggest change is that Michael's strong enough to go out on his own, only stopping to get Brian's car keys, but not asking his superhero to lead the way.

michael and hal: face-to-face

"If God had wanted me to be on ice, he would have made me a vodka martini."

Michael's not a comedic character at all. The humor comes from how things happen to him rather than his reaction to how things happen to him—it's the environmental factors. He's the guy who's hit in the face with the pie, not the guy who wipes it off and mugs for the camera. It's a very different space to perform, which is something that attracted me to the role.

On *Talk Soup* I'd been creating sketch-level characters in prosthetic makeup and stuff like that. I was really looking to find a character that was totally different from myself, and in many ways this was the natural progression in creating a guy who was sweet and naive and gay and nerdy. In reality I couldn't be more straight or have a bigger ego—truthfully, I'm a professional wiseass. That's what I do for a living. Michael is nowhere near that. Sarcasm doesn't work in his method of communication.

"Like I said, it's all about sex . . . except when you're having it. Then it's all about 'Will he stay? Will he go? How am I doing? What am I doing?'"

Sometimes I feel like I'm not playing a gay man, I'm playing a woman. In the Brian/Michael relationship, he's the feminine role. Brian is very masculine, very male, very penetrative, while Michael is more submissive, adaptive, and passive. He has more classically feminine desires such as long-term love, and he's not focused entirely on physical contact. It's great to play because very few men get to play those emotional arcs because they don't exist in straight story lines.

A lot of people's preconceptions about the show are that it's just about sex and drugs and clubbing.

If you peel that away and have the heart of it, you have Michael, who is looking for a partnership to last his whole life to the point where he dates someone with HIV because he loves that person and he ultimately doesn't mind that it could shorten Ben's life. It's about lifelong connection, not about the length of that life and how many connections he makes.

"You're always there for me. Taking care of things. Fighting off the bullies at school and giving me the answers to tests and taking me to the hospital the first time I got gonorrhea. But this is my mom. And this is something I have to do for her, for myself."

Michael has been kind of refathering himself. Up until now Brian has been his de facto father figure. Brian is his hero, his idol, and his source of adoration. That's usually the role that a father plays. Since Michael never knew his father, somebody had to fit the bill and it was always Brian—which isn't necessarily the best choice. But Michael knows what's lovable about Brian more than anybody else does. Other people think Brian's completely a robot with no emotions. Michael knows he isn't. There's a history that they've been through. There are things that Michael has been through in his life that Brian saved him from and vice versa. There are moments like when Brian's going to strangle himself and Michael's the one that shows up and shocks him back to life. Michael sees the hurt that nobody else sees. If Brian truly was a robot, Michael would be completely stupid. But if you have the sense that Michael's supporting someone that he knows is just hiding, then you go, "Okay, maybe he's smarter than we think and he's trying to protect someone he loves."

"But there is no 'always.' There's only now. That's all we have. Isn't that what you're always telling me?"

Michael has never backed away from a fight with regard to the people he loves. Loving Brian is such a pain in the ass, so he's cut his teeth caring for someone based on something other people would find totally unacceptable. Dealing with David—someone who initially thought he was straight and was still coping with the issues of his ex-wife and having a kid—was small potatoes next to unrequited love for his best friend for fifteen years.

The great thing about the Ben story line is that when Michael fell in love with Ben, he didn't know about the HIV. When he found out, it made it difficult. He had to make a choice and ultimately he made a great choice. We caught a lot of hell from a lot of people for the scene where Michael can't have sex with Ben. No matter how real that is, people were mad. But that's the arc of a story. I've got to start at a low point so I can get someplace high. You don't have a victory unless you play the game. In those scenes I really tried to back off and emotionally play it completely real.

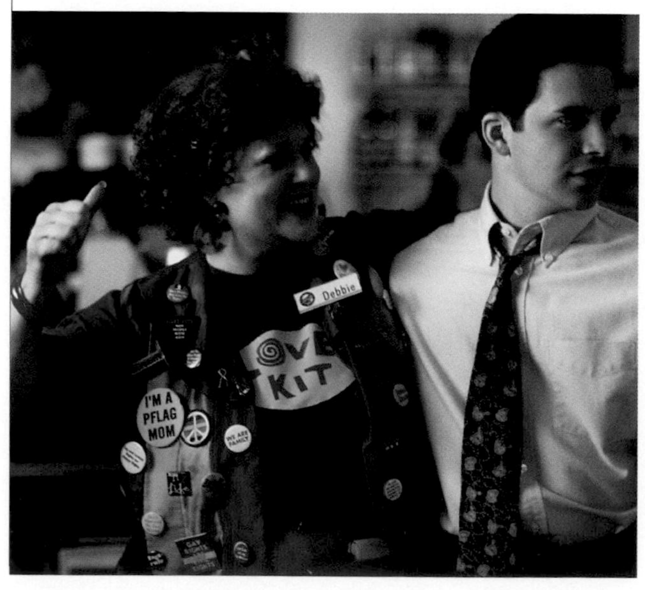

"What was *that* for?"

Sharon and I were shooting the scene where Michael and Debbie return Justin to his mother, and when we're walking away, she pops me in the back of the head. In the script it says that she smacks me really hard. Well, Sharon hates to hit. In fact, when she was doing *Misery* in the West End of London, they had to remove the fight scene because she can't stand the fighting. I think it's great that after years of *Cagney and Lacey,* who knew? The idea of hitting another person is really hard for her and she would pull the hit. I'm a martial artist. I've been beat to snot a couple times. One of the reasons they use so much body makeup on my legs is because I have permanent scars and bruises that don't go away from years of taking bags and bamboo stalks and crap like that. So I can take a pop from Sharon.

I had to take her hand and show her how hard she could hit me in the back of my head. I said, "This is the base of my skullcap. It is all bone for nearly an inch. It's okay. You can just pop me and it won't be a big deal, but the audience reaction will be immediate in that this is a real relationship. If she pulls it, we're faking it. But if she smacks me somethin' hard to where it's jarring even to me, we're all there."

"When you spend your entire life keeping it a secret . . . who you really are. You learn to stop trusting people and it becomes second nature."

With Debbie in such an extreme situation of being so outlandishly supportive, we get a really good look at Michael's psychology. If you really ask yourself why is he still in the closet at thirty years old with a mother that's that supportive, then obviously there's a lot more psychologically going on in Michael than just his homosexuality. It's been a great thing to play out. In a lot of ways, Michael's homosexuality is less of a factor in his life than for anybody else on the show. In this world that we say is all about sex, his longest and most important relationship has been nonsexual. His relationship with Brian has been for the better part completely nonsexual and yet based on a long-term love.

"Everybody knows you don't have sex with your friends."

Most of the negative parts of friendships that are portrayed on television are relegated to minor in-fucking like "You're trying to sleep with my boyfriend" and lame crap like that as opposed to the genuine difficulties of life. For instance, someone thinking that his friend is a loser, but still hanging out together, like the Brian/Ted relationship. Or the fact that Emmett is sometimes embarrassing to Michael and the guys in his flamboyance, and yet they still love him and they still keep that friendship.

A lot of times you don't see annoying traits, like Michael's naiveté and his puppy-doggishness, played consistently on some shows. If he were a friend of mine, I probably wouldn't still be friends with him after all these years if he hadn't found some way to break through that before, because it's frustrating. But then, since they hang on to the little things, you get to see them play out so much deeper story lines about friendships.

HAL SPARKS: We're up there on this eight-story roof in downtown Toronto and we've got it set up so there's a crane shot that curls around us and sees our faces and then pans down and you see an ambulance pull away. It's all timed very specifically. Gale and I had to stand up there and run our lines until our legs stopped shaking, because your body is going, "This is stupid. Please step away from the ledge." No matter how psychologically prepared you are for it, your body is going into survival mode. So you just had to dull it down and do 'em and do 'em and do 'em.

Gale's up there with his wire attached to his back that's holding him still so he can't go any further. But I'm supposed to stand up next to him, step in front of him, and then turn around and hug him. So I've got rope instead of wire and there's a guy pulling a series of eight knots. Now if I fall, I'm going to fall maybe twelve feet and bang against the side of the building. Knowing that doesn't make you feel any better, but I had to do it because that crane shot is just magical because you can see it's us.

The best part—this drove everyone crazy—was I wanted to give it this sense that we were really up on this ledge. Gale was right up against me in the back and there's like a foot and a half of space for both of us to stand. I was standing with just my heels on the ledge. My toes were actually over the side. So, I would let one foot slip down so that occasionally it would look like I might fall off the edge and heighten that sense of fear.

I kept running through worst-case scenarios, and then once I was past that point, it was like, "Now I've got to focus on the scene and care about loving him and really have that look in my eyes when I go, 'Congratulations, Dad,' when I kiss him." That was after dealing with the fact that there was a guy sixteen feet behind me with a series of black knots loosening and tightening them so that I can move.

the ledge

BRIAN: I could end it all! Right now!

MICHAEL: That would be dramatic. Just like *ER* . . . birth and death in the same episode. Now, get down!

BRIAN: You'll have to come get me . . .

MICHAEL: I'm serious. Stop clowning . . .

BRIAN: Or I'll jump!

(Michael climbs up onto the ledge. Brian grabs him in a tight, sexy embrace.)

BRIAN: Come on, Mikey . . . let's fly! Like in all those comic books. I'm Superman! I'll show you the world!

MICHAEL: Why am I always Lois Lane?

(Michael turns to face Brian. They're so close now, their bodies pressing against each other.)

MICHAEL: Congratulations . . . Dad.

The audience is told from the start, "It's all about sex." Certainly, the early scenes in the back room at Babylon and in Brian's loft would not dispute that. But *Queer as Folk* is more than just about sex. The show uses sex as a means of looking deeply into the different lives of the characters. The way Brian fucks is very different from the way Melanie and Lindsay make love. Ted's solo jerk-off scenes serve in stark contrast to Michael's search for a soul mate in life and in the bedroom.

Michael's introductory monologue introduces a world of friendship and love that doesn't always adhere to the norm. Likewise, the Pittsburgh presented on *Queer as Folk* is a somewhat fictional place where Brian, Michael, Justin, Ted, Emmett, Melanie, Lindsay, and Debbie live a free life, "out" in the face of the often homophobic world around them. But it is also a reflection of mainstream America, where gay men and women exist outside of the flashier sections of big cities like New York, Los Angeles, and San Francisco.

The show is a blend of drama and comedy with a little fantasy thrown into the mix in such a way that one episode can both examine the rights of same-sex parents and follow a character as he struggles to be more like his chat room alter ego. It's a place to see serious issues preached by a woman wearing crazy T-shirts, a rainbow vest, and a flaming red wig. It is a show that knows no boundaries.

By the end of the first season the audience will have witnessed love between two men and two women, assorted flings and affairs, recreational drug use, an overdose, a coma, a broken family, hustlers, dildos, gay-bashers, conversion therapy . . . and lots and lots of sex.

season one

". . . they say men think about sex every twenty-eight seconds. Of course, that's straight men. With gay men, it's every nine."

episode 101

Written by: Ron Cowen & Daniel Lipman
Directed by: Russell Mulcahy

A simple night of cruising gets complicated for Michael, Brian, Ted, and Emmett when two new arrivals hit the Pittsburgh gay scene. Seventeen-year-old Justin makes his Liberty Avenue debut—developing an instant attraction to Brian—and Lindsay gives birth to Brian's son with her partner, Melanie.

DANIEL LIPMAN: The moment Justin decided to cross that street to go to Babylon was not in the script—it was Russell Mulcahy's invention. I saw the dailies and I thought, "Now, why is Russell focusing on Justin stepping into a puddle?" And I realized that it was because he is becoming baptized. It's a brilliant image. Justin is standing there smoking and he's very nervous, because the first time you would go into a bar, you're very, very nervous about it. He puts out the cigarette and then you see him step into that water and he's baptized into the world.

"The thing you need to know is, it's all about sex."

episode 102

Written by: Ron Cowen & Daniel Lipman
Directed by: Russell Mulcahy

Brian avoids Justin while continuing his sexual antics with a client from his ad agency. Michael attempts to avoid a female coworker with a crush on him, but is ambushed into a date with her. Lindsay tries to keep Brian from avoiding his financial responsibility by asking him to take out a life insurance policy for their son. And Debbie meets Sunshine.

SHARON GLESS: I was always calling Ron on the phone saying things like "I've got this great idea. She has a different wig every day. Wouldn't that be great?" And when I got here, they wouldn't let me use the wigs. I'd brought seventeen of them. They said that Showtime didn't want to hide the fact that it was Sharon Gless. I said, "Once I open my mouth, everyone will know it's me."

"His eyes were closed and his mouth was open in a sort of smile. Like he was in another place. A beautiful place. And that place was me!"

episode 103

Written by: Ron Cowen & Daniel Lipman
Directed by: Russell Mulcahy

Melanie and Lindsay host a nice bris for their son, which Brian initially ignores and eventually crashes, announcing he has no intention of letting his son be "mutilated" instead of being accepted the way he was born. Emmett falls in love with an Asian hustler and mistakenly believes his feelings are being returned. Ted brings a cute guy home from Babylon, OD's on GHB, and is left for dead.

"Why do I always give my heart away to trash?"

PETER PAIGE: Some guy was trying to pick me up at a club one night. He was offering me drugs, saying, "Come back to my place, I've got some really good coke." And I'm like, "No, I'm good, thanks." And then he figured out who I was. And he was like, "Oh, you're from that show, *Queer as Folk.* I don't watch that show. I don't know anybody like that." Seriously, I didn't know what to do with that statement. He was just trying to get me to go home with him to do some blow, and he doesn't know anybody like that? Interesting.

episode 104

Written by: Richard Kramer
Directed by: Kevin Inch

While Ted lies in a drug-induced coma, Brian is annoyed to find that he has been named executor of Ted's living will. Michael and Emmett give Ted's place a thorough porn cleaning before his mom gets there and they stumble across a photo shrine to Michael. Jennifer asks Justin the question that she has been afraid to ask. And Ted awakens to find Brian fucking an orderly in the hospital room.

"You only do drugs with your friends because they're the only ones who give a fuck about you."

RON COWEN: We had the most outrageous dildos—light-up, glow-in-the-dark, all sizes, all colors—it was insane. The PA dumps them in the middle of Sheila Hockin's office, and the director Kevin Inch is there. He's a really nice straight guy with four kids, who's very funny and very open-minded, and he's just had over thirty dildos dumped at his feet. Well, we were staging a sword fight with two of them in this particular scene, so Kevin's showing us how he's going to stage it. And he's jumping on the sofa and the chairs and running around the room with this dildo. It was hilarious. Then Dan took one of them, which was huge. It must have weighed like twenty pounds. I don't know what you would possibly . . . well, I do know what you could do with it, but I wouldn't want it done to me. Dan takes this thing, that has this tiny suction cup for this girder, and he sticks it on the wall. Of course it immediately falls off onto the fax machine and breaks it. The next day there's a sign on the wall over the new fax machine that says, "No dildos allowed within twenty-five feet—Dan, this means you."

episode 105

Written by: Jason Schafer
Directed by: Kari Skogland

Michael goes on his first date ever with the cute chiropractor Dr. David, while continuing to avoid the pursuit of Tracy at work. In light of his near-death experience, Ted takes stock of his near-life. A potential client dangles a high-priced contract in front of Brian so long as Brian will dangle a bit of himself in front of the client in return. Justin deals with issues over his mom, forcing Brian to deal with issues concerning his own dad.

HAL SPARKS: All of Michael's sex scenes are potential love scenes, with rare exception. There are a couple of times when he tried to live the life of Brian and the rest of the guys and failed miserably. For instance, at the end of their date David doesn't want to have sex with him and Michael doesn't understand what's wrong. So he goes into the back room and gets a blow job. And he's miserable. You can see it in his eyes. We finish the episode looking at how vacant he is because it means nothing. That's never enough for Michael. It's a great thing to play. He's looking for love, not just a physical connection.

"The point of a date—or so it's been explained to me by those who do that sort of thing—is that you actually get to know the other person before you fuck him."

episode 106

Written by: Jonathan Tolins
Directed by: Kari Skogland

Michael and David grow closer, much to Brian's chagrin. Ted's quest to find a more stable average guy results in a guy that's way too average, sending Ted back to Babylon where he runs into Blake. Justin meets up with Melanie and Lindsay, impressing them with his artwork and his youthful exuberance. Lindsay encourages him to enter his work in the Gay & Lesbian Center's art show.

SCOTT LOWELL: I would go on-line and read the fan response and everyone just loved Ted. It was all "Poor Ted, I hope he gets better" and "My heart goes out to him." Then, after the episode where he kicks Roger out of bed, all of a sudden there were all these postings on the Web saying, "I wish Ted would go back into his coma." That's when I said, "I love being on this show." One week they can think you're just the cutest little puppy dog, and then the next week they want to wring your neck.

"Just because I fuck guys does not mean I'm part of some community. And it doesn't mean I have anything in common with someone else who does."

"There's a whole world outside Liberty Avenue. I'd like to show it to you if you'd let me."

episode 107

Written by: Ron Cowen & Daniel Lipman
Directed by: David Wellington

Michael and David exhibit all the telltale signs of a "relationship," capped off with a weekend in the country. Brian interrupts the romantic weekend with a call to Michael to tell him about an accident that totaled his Jeep. But it was no accident. Justin's dad was driving the second car in a rage after finding out that his son was gay and presumably seduced into the life by an older man.

PETER PAIGE: What I love about this show is we're allowed to be complicated. We're allowed to be mean to each other. We're allowed to make mistakes in a way that most TV characters aren't. Most TV characters are perfect—particularly the leads. God knows that's not true on this show. I think that friendships are at the heart of the show. I like the fact that, like my group of friends, we make mistakes. We fuck each other up and we're allowed to betray each other, intentionally and unintentionally. I think that's really, really human and that's the part of friendship you don't see on television. Usually the friends are always there and always perfect. My friends aren't like that. Nobody knows how to hurt me more than my friends do.

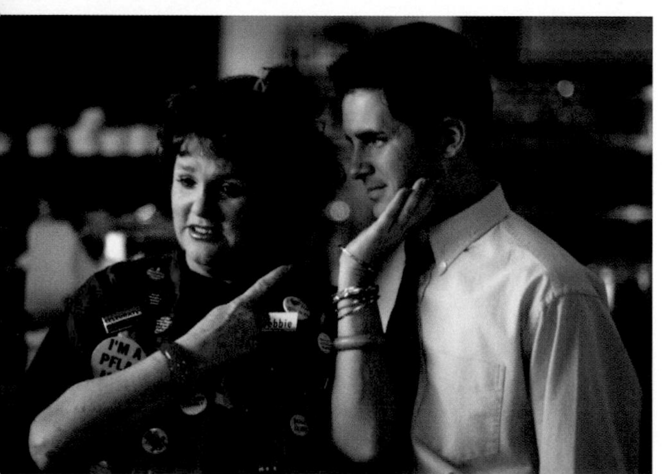

"It's not lying when they make you lie . . . when the only truth they can deal with is their own."

episode 108

Written by: Richard Kramer
Directed by: Steve Dimarco

Justin's father physically attacks Brian, then delivers his son the ultimatum to come home with him or never come home at all. Brian tries to do the right thing and return Justin home, but Mr. Taylor's impossible attitude sends his son out of the house for good. Debbie suffers from exhaustion at work and her financial stress is enough justification for Michael to play it straight at Big Q while angling for a promotion, even though he has to string Tracy along.

TONY JONAS: We have Sharon Gless doing this big larger-than-life thing and feeling pretty out there, and yet two minutes later she can make you cry. That's the kind of thing that really shows the range of the actress. She provided a tremendous anchor to all of these young actors in getting started because of her professionalism, but also because of her craft and being so wonderful. I think she helped elevate all of their acting at the very beginning. Almost everything she does is tremendous. She's a world-class actress who had the balls to say, "I want to be in this show."

episode 109

Written by: Jason Schafer & Jonathan Tolins
Directed by: John Greyson

Emmett takes "lessons" from the embodiment of his butch screen name. Michael meets Dr. David's friends at the dinner party from hell. Afterward, the doctor asks Michael to move in with him. Lindsay and Melanie rush Gus to the hospital but only the biological parents can go back to see the doctor, leaving Melanie out in the waiting room. Brian considers signing over his parental rights to her, but later refuses.

TONY JONAS: The British version was very working class and we decided to do the same thing. Our attitude was that we were trying to sell it as a reality. We were not doing the high end of New York or the flamboyance of San Francisco or even the L.A. scene. The whole idea was to say it's in everyone's backyard. What we were able to do was to make it real and make it bluecollar. We try and get flashy when it needs to be, but it's not like these guys are walking around with five hundred dollars in their pocket everyday. The idea was to underplay it with what they would have a budget for.

"I'd forgotten I was different—until I was so thoughtfully reminded."

episode 110

Written by: Doug Guinan
Directed by: John L'Ecuyer

After Brian kicks Justin out of the loft, the teen heads for New York City, forcing Brian and the guys to take a road trip to follow. They find Justin and return him to Pittsburgh, where he moves into Debbie's house. Conversely, Michael decides not to move in with David, causing the doctor to end the relationship. Lindsay tells Melanie that she wants to stay at home with the baby instead of returning to work, and Melanie makes a financial sacrifice to make the wish come true.

THEA GILL: I've been told by people in the business that the mom role is always so boring. I don't agree. I enjoy playing the mom. I think it's just because I love children. I'm not a mom myself so it gives me a way to express my maternal instincts through the role. But, there's a reason for Lindsay to be searching for something other than being a mom too. There's a reason for her to want to break out of being at home and staying at home and allowing Melanie to go to work. This gives the character a chance to break out when we get to season three.

"How do we find little boy lost?"

episode 111

Written by: Jason Schafer & Jonathan Tolins
Directed by: Michael DeCarlo

Events surrounding Michael's thirtieth birthday are far from celebratory as Melanie feels that she's growing distant from Lindsay, and Emmett has an HIV scare, forcing him to make a promise to God swearing off men. But the real drama comes after Debbie asks Brian to let Michael go so her son can have a chance at happiness with David. Brian throws a surprise birthday party where the biggest shock is delivered when Tracy arrives and finds out that Michael is gay.

"You can't do anything quietly, can you? Everything's got to be a spectacle . . . a drama. You couldn't have pushed him softly, you had to shove him off a fucking cliff."

PETER PAIGE: My favorite episode from the first season is the birthday party. I just think it is a masterpiece of writing. At that point in the story line there were ten of us all in one room, all coming to a head in these really interesting, complicated, emotional story lines. It all plays out in this one night at this party in such a complicated human way. I think that was the finest episode we did the entire first year.

episode 112

Story by: Richard Kramer & Ron Cowen & Daniel Lipman
Teleplay by: Richard Kramer
Directed by: John Greyson

After his HIV scare and subsequent promise to God, Emmett "sees the light" and joins a conversion-therapy group hoping to embrace the heterosexual lifestyle. Conversely, Ted reaps the sexual rewards of Brian's castoffs when temporarily filling the Michael void in his life. Lindsay and Melanie let Brian and finances get in the way of their relationship and continue to drift apart. Michael officially moves in with David, but Michael's stuff has a harder time getting into the house.

"When you spend your entire life keeping it a secret . . . who you really are. You learn to stop trusting people and it becomes second nature."

HAL SPARKS: Michael thinks of the other person he's with as a fountain of hope and he drinks with his eyes. It's the only way I can really describe it. If you look at him, he's just trying to get hope for the rest of his life from this person, to the point where the physical connection disappears for him. It's not about the groping and sex as much as making sure he can see the guy's face and see if he cares. It's the same when he's shying away from Brian the few times that Brian has come on to him. Michael can't make eye contact because he's afraid to get clicked into that. Because once he does, he's there for good because he does love Brian.

"Now I see the light."

episode 113

Written by: Drew Z. Greenberg
Directed by: Ron Oliver

Emmett continues to explore the straight lifestyle and finds that his gay friends will do anything to "corrupt him," including sending his favorite gay porn star to his door. Brian fucks a subordinate at work and winds up getting himself and his company sued for sexual harassment. Melanie meets another woman and has a fling that breaks up her committed relationship with Lindsay and forces her to move out of the house.

THEA GILL: One of the most creative scenes for me as an actor was the scene with Melanie and Lindsay in the hallway at the hospital when Melanie told Lindsay that she's had an affair. I liked the way that they cut that scene. I thought it was interesting that they used a wide shot for that whole scene. That had a strong effect. I remember shooting that and my legs were getting weak and giving out. I had never done a scene like that before.

"A leopard can't change his stripes and neither can a queer."

episode 114

Written by: Doug Guinan
Directed by: Michael DeCarlo

Brian asks Melanie to help in his sexual harassment suit, but Justin really lends a hand—and a dick—by scaring Kip straight. Emmett embraces the hetero world and starts dating a "former" lesbian who has also seen the light. They eventually give up on their quest to see someone else's light when Ted convinces them that God loves them no matter whom they fuck. Michael lies to David about seeing Brian because the doctor made him promise to stay away, until Brian convinces David he cannot keep a boyfriend through ultimatums.

PETER PAIGE: One of my favorite moments in the history of the series is Ted's speech to Emmett about "God loves you just the way you are." I think it's Scott's finest riff in the entire series, and it's just a phenomenal piece of writing. As a gay man, I came to believe that God loved me the way that I am later in my life. What I wouldn't have given to have heard that in a TV show when I was fifteen.

episode 115

Written by: Garth Wingfield
Directed by: Alex Chapple

Michael is uncomfortable playing the "stepmother" to David's visiting son until he realizes the boy's issues have more to do with his father's need to schedule every minute of their time together. Ted, feeling stuck in a rut, decides to explore the world of S&M. Brian is told that his father, Jack, is dying of cancer. In turn, Brian admits that he is gay to an unwelcome reception, but later introduces Jack to his grandson.

GALE HAROLD: As of yet, I don't think Brian has really learned the true meaning of love. And I mean love without conditions. He demonstrates lovelike qualities in crisis (Justin's attack) or when ulterior motives like control or self-preservation dictate. And although these are versions of loyalty and devotion, Brian has yet to initiate a genuinely selfless act. And to be fair, his friends, whatever their motivations, tend to enable him in this. I hope we can look forward to the moments when Brian Kinney finds himself compelled by nothing more than his heart.

"The thing about parenthood is you don't get anonymous-sex breaks twice a day."

episode 116

Written by: Jason Schafer
Directed by: Jeremy Podeswa

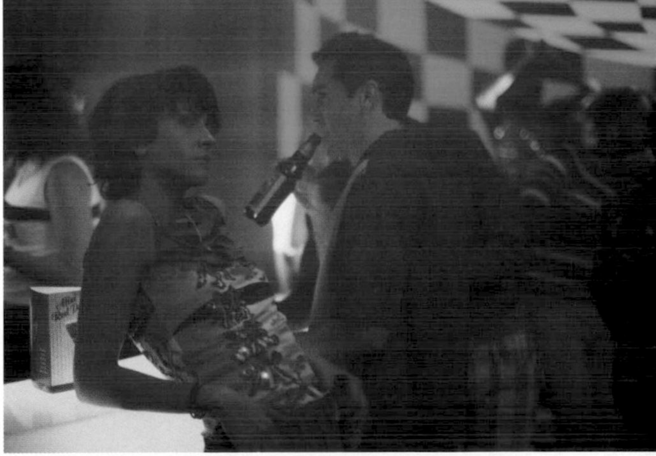

Michael rebels against being David's kept boy, until his friends convince him to get over it and accept a trip to Paris. Melanie seeks comfort from her friends when a mysterious Frenchman named Guillaume moves in with Lindsay and they announce their plan to marry so he can stay in the country. Justin tries—and fails—to form a Gay/Straight Student Alliance at school after suffering insults from Chris Hobbs. He gets his payback when Hobbs makes a trip to Liberty Avenue and Justin outs their secret locker-room handjob session.

MICHELLE CLUNIE: Ted and Melanie get each other. Of course Melanie's close with Emmett, but Ted was an accountant so they understand each other in a certain business level. I think with anyone that's in business, your mind works a certain way—it's very pragmatic and analytical. Ted has a mind like that so we get each other. Ted's like that one person that Melanie can talk to. You know those friendships you have where you can talk about anything and he'll always give you a nice sounding board or great advice. There's almost a brotherly love there that is a camaraderie among two peers and two friends. It's a really important relationship for Melanie because I don't think she has that with anyone else.

"I was rejected by everybody. It's good to be back."

episode 117

Written by: Jonathan Tolins
Directed by: Michael DeCarlo

Michael and David host a political fund-raiser for a senator, but Michael decides not to invite his friends and family. However, that doesn't stop them from coming and making the event a real party. Justin continues to be harassed at school, but even the principal refuses to let him start the Gay/Straight Student Alliance until Justin finds a new ally for his cause in the senator. Brian signs over his parental rights to Melanie under the condition that she and Lindsay reunite, thus putting an end to the fraudulent wedding.

"Mom, this isn't about me . . . or even what happened at school. This is about speaking out . . . demanding to be heard whether people want to hear you or not."

SCOTT LOWELL: I think the friendship between Ted and Melanie makes a lot of sense. They're probably the most conservative characters in a lot of ways. They both share somewhat of a disdain for Brian and his lifestyle, while Ted secretly desires it. I think Ted admires the way Melanie is not afraid to say what's on her mind. I think he admires her strength in that and I think they both have a very similar sarcastic sense of humor. It's a very interesting pairing in that way. Being the more business minded of the gang, I think it's a friendship that was kind of necessary.

episode 118

Teleplay by: Jason Schafer & Jonathan Tolins
Story by: Ron Cowen & Daniel Lipman
Directed by: Russell Mulcahy

Michael gets propositioned at Babylon on the same night Brian stumbles across David at the baths. At first Michael can't accept a relationship that open, but eventually he realizes that he's content with their loving partnership even though they both may slip up as men do. Ted reconnects with Blake, the cute guy who left him for dead from a drug overdose. Justin is accepted to Dartmouth for business and the Pittsburgh Institute of Fine Arts for his drawing. At first the decision between schools is easy until he finds out that his parents are getting a divorce.

"I know because I'm young you think I can just tumble out of bed and look like this."

THOM BEST (DIRECTOR OF PHOTOGRAPHY): When Russell Mulcahy came back to direct this episode, we were more prepared for him, knowing what his style was and what he wanted to do. He just hit the floor running and we got so many shots. We did somewhere in the neighborhood of seventy or eighty shots in a day. On a normal day we'd do like thirty shots. Some of my favorite stuff that we've done is the bathhouse scene with the underwater feel of the whole thing. There's an orgy going on that looks like this moving sculpture. I just love the energy of it. It's a great moment.

episode 119

Written by: Garth Wingfield
Directed by: David Wellington

Daphne asks Justin to be her "first" so she has some practice before sleeping with her boyfriend. Things quickly become weird between the two friends when the momentous occasion takes on more significance for Daphne than Justin. Ted continues to reconnect with Blake, over Emmett's strong objection. Brian's father dies, and Brian has a difficult time mourning for the man who hardly ever showed him love.

SHEILA HOCKIN: The morning that we were to shoot the funeral, there was just supposed to be a light dusting of snow on the ground, but when we got up, there was a massive snowstorm. David Wellington, who was directing the episode, phoned me and said, "This is just a disaster." The crew couldn't work. Everybody was soaking wet. It was a horrible situation to try to shoot in. He said, "We're thinking maybe we should relocate the scene into the cemetery's church." About ten minutes later he called me back and said, "No, no, we're going to do this. We're going to shoot outside." And the resulting scene is one of the most beautiful things that I've seen on television because you can't buy that kind of production value. It's just a blanket of snow falling on these people and this beautiful crane shot. After we delivered that episode to the network, they called and said, "My God, this is one of the most beautiful shots we've ever had on the airwaves."

"Gay men and straight girls sleeping together . . . isn't that one of the signs of the Apocalypse?"

episode 120

Written by: Jason Schafer & Jonathan Tolins
Directed by: Russell Mulcahy

Brian enters David in the contest for the King of Babylon. The good doctor plays along to prove to everyone that he's not as old as either he or Michael thinks he is. Emmett meets a guy and experiences all the stages of a romance in one night. The guys refuse to warm up to Blake, but that changes when he comes up with a contact to put up the money to bail Vic out of jail after he is picked up for indecent exposure in a mall rest room. Justin is tired of being Brian's backup plan and gets himself crowned King of Babylon.

PATRICK ANTOSH (COSTUMER): That fantastic actor hosting the King of Babylon contest is not a drag queen at all. We literally had to build his costume from scratch. I knew nothing. Now I do know everything about drag queens, but I had no previous exposure to that world at all. It was very intimidating for me to dress this guy in five or six different over-the-top outfits, one after the other. The thing that intimidated me most was that this act was going to be performed in front of two hundred extras who know a whole bunch of drag queens and know right from wrong. I wasn't worried about the audience and the producers, I was worried about the extras standing there judging my stuff. But I came out of that one with kudos.

"The next contestant loves the Powerpuff Girls, margaritas, and older men who take him for granted."

episode 121

Written by: Garth Wingfield
Directed by: Michael DeCarlo

Brian is chosen Ad Person of the Year and encouraged to try a job in New York. Ted finds a vial of crystal meth in Blake's jacket. Vic defends himself against the false charges of indecent exposure. David's ex-wife divorces her second husband, which sends David to Portland to help their son cope. When he returns, he decides that he wants to move there permanently and asks Michael to come along. After some thought, Michael agrees, without knowing that Brian's job in New York fell through.

"I'm not like you. I can't just wake up one morning and decide . . . boom . . . it's time to move on. No looking back, no regrets."

SHEILA HOCKIN: We got a lot of very poignant mail in season one. A lot of the cast got individual letters from people who felt connected to them. I know Thea and Michelle got a lot of very heartfelt feedback from the community of gay women who watch the show and were glad to see themselves represented. Quite a quantity of correspondence came in from older gay men who had struggled through their lifetime feeling completely unrepresented on television and who were overwhelmed to see some of their stories played out in an open way. We also got a lot of correspondence from straight women who had adopted the show wholeheartedly.

episode 122

Written by: Ron Cowen & Daniel Lipman
Directed by: Alex Chapple

It's Brian's thirtieth birthday and as far as he's concerned his life is over. Michael's plans to relocate to Portland fall through when David takes total control of the move, forcing Michael to reexamine his decision. Ted is forced to admit that Blake is a hopeless cause when he checks himself in and out of rehab. Justin and Daphne attend their prom together and Brian arrives and shares a romantic dance with Justin. The happiness is short-lived as a bat-wielding Chris Hobbs attacks Justin afterward. Brian rushes to Justin's aid and calls Michael for support, stopping him from getting on a plane with David.

"Don't you know that you still have your powers . . . *all* your powers and you always will. Whether you're eighteen or you're thirty or you're fifty or you're a hundred. You will always be young and you will always be beautiful. You're Brian Kinney for fuck's sake!"

DANIEL LIPMAN: I loved the end of the first season. I loved the whole "Save the Last Dance for Me." We hired someone to teach Gale and Randy to dance. Randy has done theater and musicals, so he's very agile—and Gale is less so. But they were great together. It was so romantic. I knew that people would look at that and swoon. That was a fantasy come true, taking a great-looking guy—your boyfriend—to the prom.

the writers' room

Outside "the industry," few people truly understand what goes on in this chamber where ideas are born . . . in which a team of artists come together to create the world of lives and stories that we enjoy. What is this hallowed hall? Where is this mythical place?

Well, it's simply a small, windowless room with a big table in the center and a dry-erase board on the wall.

Hopefully, knowing that doesn't take away from the magic that is performed in there.

Coordinating producer Adam Newman helps to pull together the talented voices that come together in that room. Following a working relationship and friendship with Ron and Dan that began during *Sisters*, Adam came back into the fold of Cowlip Productions for the second season of *Queer as Folk* to help the executive producers expand the writing staff.

Even though the critically acclaimed first season had already aired, he found the task to be just as difficult as the producers had with the original casting of the series. Writers didn't want to be associated with the "gay show," fearing it would pigeonhole their careers. But the show's uniqueness proved to be the largest stumbling block.

Adam explains, "Because the show has such a specific voice and it's written in such a stylistic manner, it's hard for me to find samples that are good to read to consider writers for. Since there's not another show on TV that has the same voice, it's very tough to find a sample that's applicable." Once Adam does find those unique voices, he takes the names to Ron and Dan, and together they assemble the staff.

The writing team gets to work fairly early on the new season in that understated, yet magical writers' room. The focal point of this room is that large dry-erase board on the wall. Here they will set the agenda for the new season. With filming scheduled to begin in late September, the writers meet

```
                MICHAEL
        Mom! I'm going home, what do you
        think? It's late.

                DEBBIE
        Or early. I mean for a young man on
        the make.
             (then, suddenly upset)
        God, Why are all the lights on?
        Something must be wrong with Vic --

She quickly gets out of the car, runs to the house.
Michael turns off the car and follows her into:

INT. DEBBIE'S HOUSE - KITCHEN - NIGHT
```

for two weeks in July to throw out ideas and possible story arcs for the characters. Ron and Dan start the process by coming to the table with stories that they want to tell, and the team elaborates from there. Once the framework of the season is created, the team settles into the work of shaping the episodes one by one.

"At the top of each week we talk about where we left all the characters off the previous week," Adam explains. "The stories here have to make emotional sense to Ron and Dan before we move on to tell another story, and the best way to do that is to connect from the previous week. So we talk about where we left characters and what makes sense for them to do next."

This is where the dry-erase board comes into play again. On the first couple days of the week, so many ideas float around the room and they change so often that it's more of a free-flowing brainstorming session. Usually by Wednesday the writers start to lock down basic ideas and something is written on the board. Each character gets a different color marker for his or her story line. By the end of the week the board is a rainbow of phrases as each element of the individual story lines is fleshed out. But not each of those story lines leads to a pot of gold.

After the "erase" function of the dry-erase board comes into play, the team gets to work on what's left among the plot elements. "Then we order them," Adam says, "and figure out within each act where the scenes in each story are going to fall so they make sense. That usually happens on Thursday or Friday." Then on Friday, the writer assigned to write that script develops a loose outline based on what was written on the board in the room, and then they're given notes on that outline. Once the outline is approved, the writer begins working on the script.

Ron and Dan are very hands-on every step of the way as the story goes from the board to the page. Under their guidance, stories evolve and grow, the episodes take shape, and the show comes to life. A simple phrase that starts on the dry-erase board as "Justin visits Liberty Avenue," "Michael quits his job," or "Brian joins Stockwell's campaign" will have far-reaching consequences for both the characters and the writers. The exciting thing is that, just like the audience, the writers don't always know where that simple phrase could ultimately lead them in the years to come.

TOP: Dan, Adam, and Ron

ABOVE: Left to right: co-producer Brad Fraser, executive story editor Shawn Postoff, script coordinator Rod Kavanagh (in white shirt), executive producer Ron Cowen, supervising producer Michael MacLennan (in tank top), writer's assistant Justin Spitzer, consulting producer Del Shores and executive producer Daniel Lipman.

He wears tight leather pants in a shade of orange slightly brighter than the sun. He can dress a table, a room, or a fabulous party platter and still have time for a manicure. He will fight to the death and play as dirty as need be to protect a friend. He is Emmett Honeycutt: Nelly Queen.

"It's not just that Emmett is a queen," Daniel Lipman is quick to assert. "His attitude is 'I will be a queen and I will be proud of it.'" And it's an important distinction to make. Emmett is not so one-dimensional a character as the stereotype could imply. Over the three seasons, Emmett has been shown to possess many levels beyond that simple description.

Dan attributes Emmett's well-rounded characterization to Peter Paige's portrayal as much as to the writing. "Peter knows who Emmett is physiologically, emotionally, and politically, and he brings that knowledge to the character. When Emmett becomes queeny, there's a real reason for it. There's not that kind of cringing embarrassment that someone is just being effeminate. It's a choice. It's Emmett's way of saying, 'I'm in charge, I'm in control, and if people have a problem with it—fuck 'em all!' "

That attitude comes across as both a positive and a negative for the character. Ron Cowen notes, "It's much harder for Emmett to be a 'man' than guys

emmett

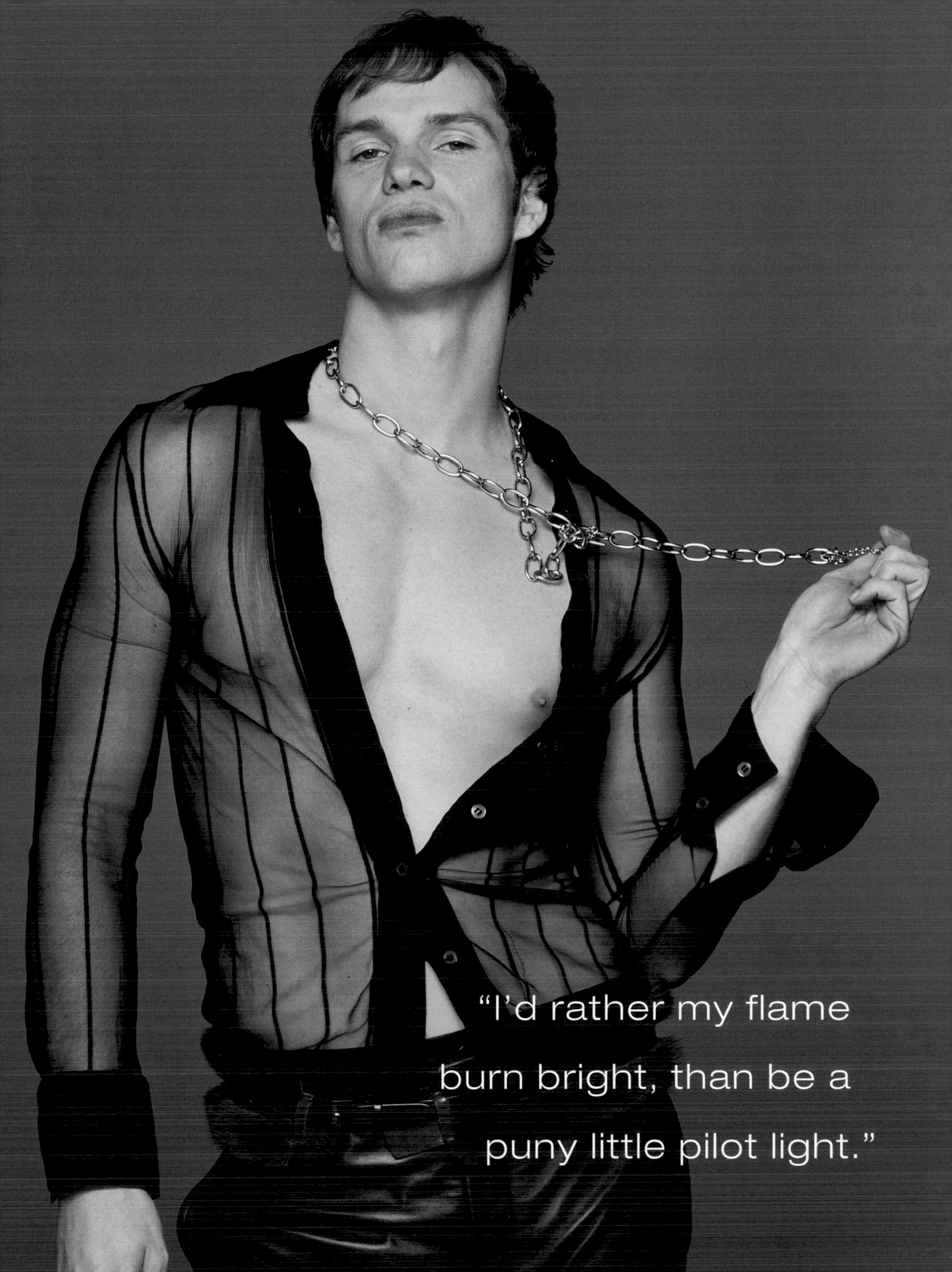
"I'd rather my flame
burn bright, than be a
puny little pilot light."

who play football just because of the way he speaks and the way he is. It's harder for him to be perceived as a man, and therefore I think he's more courageous because it doesn't come so easily. Everybody thinks a jock is a guy, but they don't know what it's like to have to deal with people thinking you're a sissy and overcoming that."

Growing up dirt-poor in a town where being trailer trash was much easier than being a sissy boy, Emmett eventually got out and then came out in Pittsburgh. "For me, Emmett is very brave," Ron says. "He knows who he is and he knows what he is. For people like Emmett to truly be themselves, they have to overcome a lot of prejudice—not just from straight people but from other gay people who look at him as a stereotypic queen. But I think he's a very strong character who can defend himself and stand up to anyone and will."

Not only does Emmett stand up to people, but he stands up *for* people as well. He's a fighter who defends not only himself, but his friends and his lovers. He helped George Shickel come out into the world and continued to fight for their love even after the man's death. Similarly, Emmett fought for Ted's freedom from prosecution over his website by pleading the case to Brian and not taking no for an answer. He even defended Ted when everyone was worried that the former accountant was addicted to drugs. Though misguided, Emmett's ability to stand up for Ted was a testament to his love, and even more telling when he knew that it was time to stop the fight.

At the core of Emmett, there is a basic tenet to which Ron says the writers remain faithful. "I think there are three characters in the show—Brian, Emmett, and Melanie—who tell the truth. They're honest characters. They're noble." It is that truth that allows Emmett to speak his mind and "fuck 'em all," though it may not be the most politically correct thing to do.

emmett and peter: face-to-face

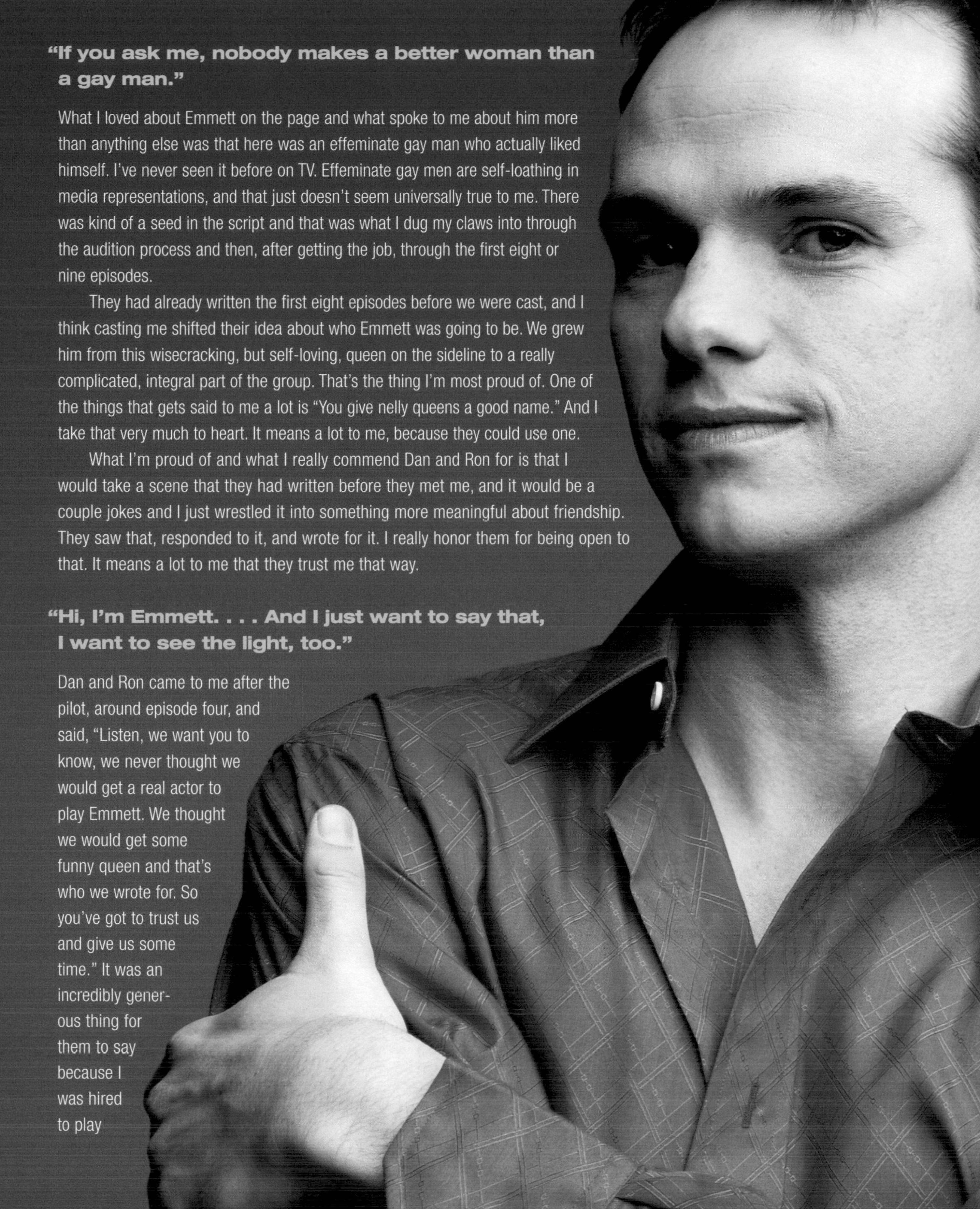

"If you ask me, nobody makes a better woman than a gay man."

What I loved about Emmett on the page and what spoke to me about him more than anything else was that here was an effeminate gay man who actually liked himself. I've never seen it before on TV. Effeminate gay men are self-loathing in media representations, and that just doesn't seem universally true to me. There was kind of a seed in the script and that was what I dug my claws into through the audition process and then, after getting the job, through the first eight or nine episodes.

They had already written the first eight episodes before we were cast, and I think casting me shifted their idea about who Emmett was going to be. We grew him from this wisecracking, but self-loving, queen on the sideline to a really complicated, integral part of the group. That's the thing I'm most proud of. One of the things that gets said to me a lot is "You give nelly queens a good name." And I take that very much to heart. It means a lot to me, because they could use one.

What I'm proud of and what I really commend Dan and Ron for is that I would take a scene that they had written before they met me, and it would be a couple jokes and I just wrestled it into something more meaningful about friendship. They saw that, responded to it, and wrote for it. I really honor them for being open to that. It means a lot to me that they trust me that way.

"Hi, I'm Emmett. . . . And I just want to say that, I want to see the light, too."

Dan and Ron came to me after the pilot, around episode four, and said, "Listen, we want you to know, we never thought we would get a real actor to play Emmett. We thought we would get some funny queen and that's who we wrote for. So you've got to trust us and give us some time." It was an incredibly generous thing for them to say because I was hired to play the wisecracking queen, and if they wanted to keep me in that box, they certainly could have. I was really grateful with that because by the end of episode eight, I was going a little bit crazy. I was ready to bite into something more. And then nine appeared, and I had this funny, odd cybersex story line, which I find quite a charming episode, and then eleven came and that's the HIV scare, and then the whole "see the light" thing happened.

It's a story that fans have always asked about. Emmett's the self-loving one and they wanted to know why he fell into that. But Emmett is an innocent in the sense that he is easily led down a path. I describe him often as like a kitten, because whatever is shiny and bright, you put it in front of him and he'll play with. This guy comes to him at the right moment and asks him the right questions and draws him to the *wrong* conclusion. Then what he embarks upon is the most soul-sucking, horrifying experience he can ever have.

"I prefer to think of them as lunatics. Except for Aunt Lulah, who was supposed to be the crazy one. She was my only friend."

I have a picture of Aunt Lulah in my head, but she is nobody I actually know. She's the one who made Emmett who he is and taught him that he was okay, because it's pretty clear that it wasn't his parents. We don't know much about his parents since he almost never talks about them, so I've made decisions about who they are.

Aunt Lulah is the kooky Southern woman. Among a million other places I've lived, I went to junior high in Alabama and high school in North Carolina, so I have a real relationship to and affection for the kooky Southerners. And that's who Aunt Lulah is. She probably didn't get dressed quite right and her hair is probably always a mess. She was just a crazy old Southern woman who saw the light in Emmett and just said, "Shine, baby, shine!"

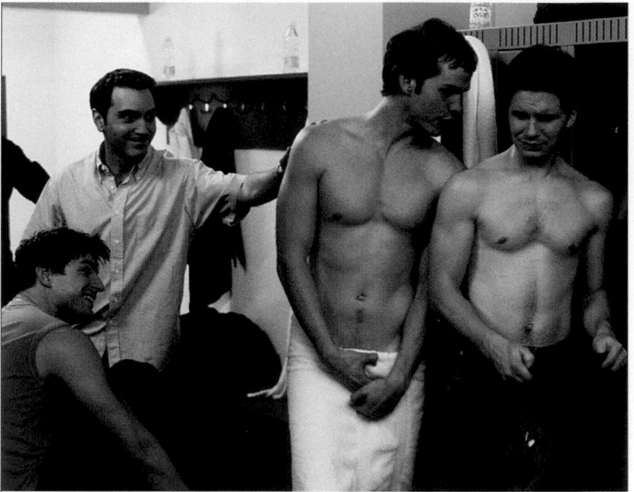

"'Fuck 'em all.' That was my motto. Still is."

Since I was cast on the show, everyone says, "God, your life must have changed so much." And it has, but not in the ways people may think. Yes, I can pay my bills and that's a very, very, very big change for me because God knows I couldn't before. And, yes, I get to go to big parties and dinners and that's great fun. But the way that it has changed me is throughout my life—I've been out for a long, long time—but there's always been this silent apology in how I conducted myself in the world predominantly about the fact that I was gay. And this show changed that in me. This show is "no apologies, no regrets." It taught me that I don't have anything to apologize for and that other people need to get over it.

I love the fact that this show has normalized the idea of two men or two women having sex or being in love. Almost every time I'm in an airport, some straight guy comes up to me and says, "My wife and I watch your show all the time. We love it so much." And if you asked them why, they say, "Well, we like the stories." They just like the show and are completely inured to the fact that it's two guys. When I was coming out, I had RuPaul. There wasn't anybody else. And I would have given anything to see these people.

"Sex is never the right thing to do. Feeding the poor is the right thing to do. Hiring the handicapped is the right thing to do . . . donating blood is the right . . ."

Because I'm openly gay and I have the big comeback voice of the show, I definitely get targeted with the politically correct side. They're the people who say, "My boyfriend and I aren't like that. We stay home and watch movies every night. Why aren't we on your show?" Well, first of all because that's boring. I'm sure these people have a great life and they're very happy, but would you want to watch yourself on TV? I wouldn't want to watch me on TV. My life is not that interesting and I'm someone who's on TV.

What I have found is that most of the people who have political issues with the show aren't actually watching the show, they're watching the hype. But the truth is it's a show about people trying to grow up. It's no different than what's happening on *Sex and the City.* It's no different than what happens on a lot of shows. Straight people are always trying to get laid. It's a part of life.

"You know how people always say how much smaller movie stars are when you see them in real life? But you're actually . . . not."

I did full frontal on the show first season. I rolled over on my back and there's my dick, in a rubber that no one could see apparently. I got several emails complaining, "Where's the fucking rubber?" And I'm like, "It was *orange.* It was an *orange rubber,* what do you think my dick looks like?"

That sex scene wasn't in the episode when I got it. I ended up fighting really, really hard to get it added. Not because I wanted to do full frontal—because I didn't—but because I felt like this whole story turns on Emmett having sex with this woman. It's a profound experience for him. Our show's about the fact that life is complicated and particularly that sex is complicated. Emmett has sex with a girl. That is huge!

I love that sex scene. When Emmett's trying so hard and he gets to the end and then . . . finally! The nudity thing came out of a conversation with the director where we were like, "They're so vulnerable at that moment and they're so naked," and I wanted the audience to feel that. I wanted the audience to be a little bit uncomfortable. And I think you are when you see it because it's so startling. And I have to tell you, that's the smallest my dick has ever been. That night, I was like, "Come on! I'm dry-humping on top of this girl. Do you know the last time I did that?"

"Honey, my flame has been rekindled and is burning brighter than ever."

Every year about a week before we start shooting, I get incredibly depressed. Not because I'm dreading coming back to work. I love my job and feel very privileged. I worked very hard to get here, so I know not to take it for granted, not even one day. But I get depressed because I know I'm about to turn my life over to Emmett. I'm about to spend more of my time as Emmett than as Peter. It's a really different thing than how I live my life when I'm at home hanging out with my friends. I'm a different person with different values and different priorities. And I actually go through this weird depression. I sound like total fucking psychobabble actor-speak—and it is—but imagine turning your life over to somebody else, giving control of your life to something else.

EMM

Peter Paige: The clothes are hugely important to me because I'm not Emmett. I don't put myself out in the world as Emmett. I don't really behave like him in real life. Going in and putting on those clothes makes me move differently. It makes me feel differently. It gives me a different sense of my body and what's important to Emmett. And it puts me in character for the day. I'm half in character once I'm on set just because I'm getting into these clothes.

Patrick Antosh: There was a note about Emmett's outfit being more outrageous and fabulous than ever. That's all it said. So I thought that if he's going to upset anybody, he's going to go in drag. I went to the producers and told them that I wanted to put him in drag, and since it was a political fund-raiser, I thought we should do it without sex and just do it with Jackie Kennedy's pink outfit.

Peter Paige: We put the suit on me, we put the wig on, we put a little extra eyeliner on, and that was it. It's like I have her face. I'm not kidding. The makeup artist pulled up a picture of her and she had the same slightly wide, deep-set eyes, big mouth, kind of a broad nose, and the same fairly high cheekbones. It's freaky. I look just like Jackie O. I wear practically more makeup on a Babylon day than I did in that freakin' scene, but I loved it.

Peter Paige: I loved the geisha outfit. It was so politically incorrect and everything I did with it was so . . . as the director said to me, "Strong and wrong. Strong and wrong." The way I justify it is that Emmett . . . (a) wouldn't know better . . . and (b) would do it with great gusto. So, he did.

Peter Paige: The costume designer on the pilot had found these orange leather pants and told me about them. But they weren't here yet. That night I dreamt of these orange leather pants with this hot-pink, see-through T-shirt. I went to her and I said, "How about a hot-pink T-shirt with the orange pants?" And she said, "The pants aren't going to be here in time. They're not coming out until the fall." And I was like, "What?!" So she called the designer, who gave her his pair off his body. They were already molded to the shape of his ass and legs, which fortunately is about the same shape as mine.

emmett's fabulous fashions

let's talk about sets

In the first season of *Queer as Folk* there were seventeen sets in one soundstage. The production team had to take the walls of Dr. David's apartment down to put the walls of Ted's condo up. When they added Babylon in the second season, they had to fly out the whole wall of the club to put the front wall on Michael and Emmett's place. Fire regulations required them to have four feet in between any two structures, and that's exactly what they had, creating a little rabbit run of four-foot tunnels through the studio.

Toward the end of season two the production team had to build Ben and Ethan's apartments and simply couldn't fit them in. So they rented a small "swing" studio to build the new sets. It wasn't a particularly good studio for long-term use and at the beginning of season three they found another, larger studio for their second space . . . about a half hour away from the main soundstage. The situation still wasn't perfect, but it gave the art department the space it needed to design new sets and add rooms and halls to existing ones, thus opening up the filming opportunities.

Production designer Ingrid Jurek and set decorator Megan Less now have a much easier time walking through the sets.

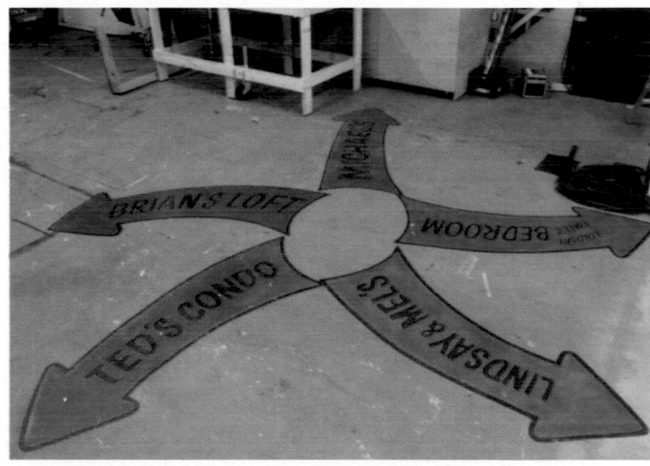

Ingrid: Brian's loft was the first set we ever put together. It was on a really tight deadline the first year because of actor availability. Suddenly the scenes in the loft came to the forefront and we just rushed like crazy. Megan got the set to decorate at about 9 P.M. the night before for a 6 A.M. call for the first day of shooting. We were still pouring concrete in the back when they were filming in the shower.

Megan: In the beginning it was a lot of brown and a lot of white. Brian was darker in the first season. His "softer" side developed with Justin and his relationship with Michael. All that hadn't happened when we were originally dressing the set. The drapes we picked looked like metal and chain mail because that was the way we saw Brian. This was his fortress. This was his space. And now they're made of softer linen.

Ingrid: Ted's condo has changed a few times. As other sets would infringe, the layout would change. It's basically been like this for the past season and a half.

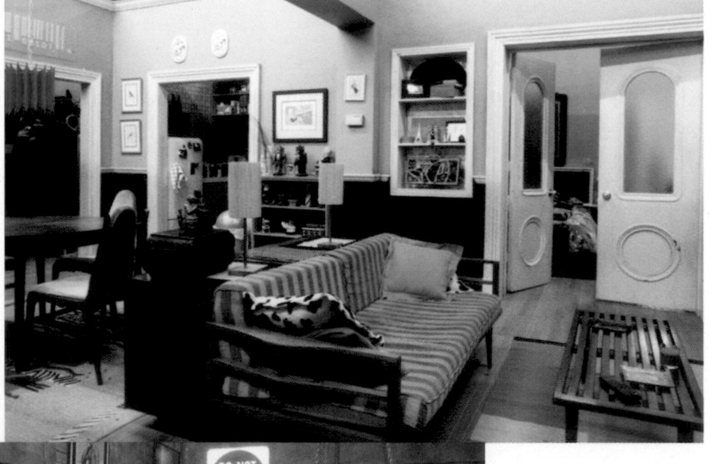

Megan: It was a little hard to instill Emmett in Ted's condo. We looked at a lot of pieces and tried desperately to make it work. The thing is you watch Ted and Emmett together and they're really good as a couple. They actually work really well, and I think we took a lot of our cues from them. It came easier once we thought of it that way.

Megan: In the beginning we made these comp boards for Dan and Ron—who were in Los Angeles—so we could have these conference calls to discuss everything. It wasn't what we originally intended to do, but in the photo there was a model in the picture wearing blue jeans and there was a vase with yellow tulips. And the lesbians became the blue-and-yellow set. There's blue and yellow in the kitchen.

Ingrid: In the first season Melanie and Lindsay's bedroom was crammed in between everything else and then taken down in two or three days. Last year we built a second-floor set and put it on risers. All of a sudden it was like their house came to life. It had a hallway. It went from a little box that was their bedroom that you saw so much to being able to carry people up the stairs and around the house. It's nice because people can transition and walk through the spaces, and the camera can follow them to give the show a bit more flow.

Ingrid: Megan and I talked about the characters at the beginning and how they interrelated. I had a bit of a thing going with Michael and Deb still being very close to each other, so some of the colors in his apartment reflect what she has. She has olive green in hers, and the green came in here. The diner was orange in the beginning and we brought it into Debbie's house in the kitchen. Michael's bedroom is the same blue that's in his childhood bedroom. The interesting thing is that that blue is also the color of Brian's back wall. It's very close to it since they were linked together in their childhood.

Ingrid on Debbie's couch

Ingrid: At the beginning we were going pretty close to what the real Woody's Bar in Toronto looked like. Ron, Dan, and Tony came into town and said, "This is it." And every season we would try to add more to it by adding more neons and more lighting sources. It was a challenging set just in the way that we wanted it to look very worn and very real. Architecturally we went into a real history as well. Some of the windows were boarded up because we were pretending the building was once something else and then one thing was added and another thing was taken down. That's why we've got brick on one side and then another finish on the other side. It's really been through quite a metamorphosis.

Megan: If Deb and Vic's set had been ready at nine o'clock [to dress] the day before we shot it at 6 A.M., I would have been ripping my hair out. With this space you want to bring in a first layer and then you want to come back and you want to look at it again. Then you want to move some things around and put in another layer. Then you want to age it so it has much more personality. My favorite find is Deb and Vic's sofa and two chairs. Original upholstery: 1976, banana velvet. Two matching chairs and a sofa: $140.

Ingrid: We have the most wonderful person doing our legal clearances. We could not have done the comic-book store without Mara McSweeny. She's gotten us everything we used to decorate the store and she was able to get Marvel to sign off on it all.

Megan: She's gotten us independent comic-book people from around the world, too.

Ingrid: It started out as Buzzy's Comix and then we gave it a really sixties/early-seventies look with all the colors. That's why we have the acid yellow and the purple. They're very psychedelic colors. Then we brought more of Michael in and painted the bins blue at Megan's suggestion.

Ingrid: We thought that Michael didn't have a lot of money because opening a new business you can't really redecorate and renovate. We said that he'd pull up the carpets and paint the bins because that was something he could do himself.

Ingrid: The diner set started out as a location. After the pilot we built a set and we were able to make various improvements to what we saw at the location to make it more dinerish by putting the stainless trim onto things. Every year we've just done a little more.

Megan: It seems to be a challenge every time they come in here. It's always hard to shoot the diner because it's often the whole cast. It's always big things. There are no small, little vignettes. Every table is a vignette and I think it's very hard for them to shoot.

Ingrid: And they're in the booths, too. The booths are all wild; you can pull them out. Generally you do end up with people against a wall, but that is the structure of a diner.

babylon

Its name comes from the ancient city renowned for its great luxury. The club Babylon is also a mythical place where people are forever young, bodies are perfect, and sex is free to almost anyone who enters. To capture this gay Shangri-la, the production team moved from locations around Toronto and finally into their own soundstage to re-create a world of luxury and pleasure.

In the first season, Babylon was a couple of Toronto clubs: The Government was used in the pilot and later episodes were filmed in a club known as Fly. But the problems with working on location were many, especially considering the number of scenes set in Babylon throughout the season. The production was always dependent on the club's schedule, and shooting could never run over since the place would have to open for business. The crew also had to work with the space provided no matter what the physical limitations may have been.

KING of BABYLON contest
March 31, 2001
doors open at 9pm
Complimentary Admission
Before 10pm
with DJ
Danny G
sponsored by
OLD PITT
TORSO
BABYLON

Before production began on the second season, a conversation took place about building the club in the studio. However, that studio space was already incredibly tight. But once production designer Ingrid Jurek came up with a plan to make the new set fit into the existing space, it was agreed that Babylon would become a permanent set and the design team could get to work. "The preliminary designs were more clubby," Ingrid explains. "But then Ron and Dan reminded us that this is Pittsburgh, so they wanted it to be more on the industrial side. That's why it ended up essentially being a concrete and steel box . . . with some chains."

The designer gave one of the walls a simple, yet dramatic accent with the addition of rows of metal slats running from floor to ceiling. "The wall was a fun thing to add," Ingrid notes. "Everybody was hesitant about this idea of having all the metal slats, but our DP, Thom Best, really liked it. You can backlight it with all these colors to get the slats to really come out and create a wild space. With all our nightclub stuff, it's really the lighting that makes it."

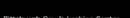

"And it's always changing," Thom adds. "The light's always moving. So we can block where people don't have to stand still. There's a lot more freedom in that set than the others. It's fairly easy to shoot in Babylon because we've just lit it in such a way that you can shoot in pretty much any angle. It's not that big a set when you stand in it, but it shoots big. And when it's packed full of people and we use wide lenses on the camera, that really sells it."

Considering the aforementioned lack of studio space, it helps to have a set that's basically a big empty room that can easily be reconfigured. The side walls were moved back for the Carnal Carnivale in the third season, and the space was enlarged for the party celebrating the release of issue number one of *Rage* at the end of season two. Depending on the requirements of the schedule, other sets for smaller scenes have actually been built within the walls of Babylon, bringing true meaning to the phrase "form follows function."

"So many men,
so little body hair."

—Brian Kinney

sharon gless as debbie novotny

Drag queens look up to her. Twinks confide in her. Debbie Novotny is the most popular fag hag on Liberty Avenue, and yet her son often tries to avoid being seen with her. It's understandable considering the likelihood of his stepping out of the back room at Babylon some night and running right into her.

"Debbie is a character everyone loves," Daniel Lipman says proudly. "She doesn't have any boundaries, but to be Debbie's son must be difficult at times. She had Michael when she was very young and they're more like pals. Even in the pilot she's at Woody's having a drink and she's always intruding upon him. Some might even say she's a fag hag, but so what. I mean, every good gay community needs a fag hag."

"I think Debbie is a very complicated character," Ron Cowen adds. "Interestingly enough, a lot of gay men love Debbie. I think that's because a lot of gay men love their own mothers and have a very deep bond with them. When I talk to certain gay men, they say, 'Oh, my mom's my best friend.' I'm not saying that straight men don't have that, too, but I think on the whole, gay men have a more complex relationship with their mothers."

Debbie is not just Michael's mother; she's also the matriarch of this Liberty Avenue family. Aside from taking Justin in, it's clear that on many occasions she

"This is still my house.
And in my house
you still say
'Mother, May I?'"

LOVE ME LOVE MY T-SHIRT

Just because I'm a Mom doesn't mean I care

I ♥ MY PENIS

I'm not as vanilla as I look

NEVER WASTE AN ERECTION

Pussy Power

YOU SAY TOMATO, I SAY FUCK OFF.

Need Head?

AS LONG AS I HAVE A FACE YOU'VE GOT A PLACE TO SIT.

was more of a mom to Brian than his own mother ever tried to be. She also has wonderfully touching moments with each of her other children—Ted, Emmett, Melanie, and Lindsay. And they give back to her as well (although none more intimately than Emmett with his oral tutorial).

As the mother, she is also often the voice of reason—or for what passes as reason in Debbie's mind. The things that come out of her mouth are often surprising, but always true. "She's very lovable and she's honest," Dan says. "I think that is a very redeeming quality in any character and any person. People respect honesty. And I think that's why they respect Debbie."

She has a close bond with her brother, but it's clear that Debbie often mothers him as well. The relationship between Debbie and Vic runs the emotional spectrum from fun banter to heartbreaking drama. It also goes to show what a fighter Debbie can be and how far she will go to protect a loved one.

For all the bravado and the shocking behavior, Debbie can also be insecure and gentle. She carried a lie for decades so that her son wouldn't know the complicated truth about his father. Her uncharacteristic response to finding out Michael was dating an HIV-positive man revealed that her maternal instincts took control in spite of any politically correct leanings. But it was her attempt at romance that allowed her to drop her guard and allow her real beauty to shine through.

debbie and sharon: face-to-face

"Article fourteen of the Super Mom handbook says no kicking assholes when they're down. They'd take away my halo."

Debbie functions from the fifth chakra. She functions totally from the heart chakra. That's where she comes from and she's got a mouth on her. Before getting the role or even talking to the producers, I did this whole backstory on Debbie. I thought, "This is a woman who had gotten knocked up when she was very young. I think she wanted to go to beauty school. She had saved her money to go to beauty school to get her own beauty parlor, and that's why she's so outrageous." I assumed the father had deserted her so she had to start waiting tables. That's what she did and she just never left that post. I think she's been in that diner forever.

"They talk big and they act tough. But the truth is, the thing that they're most afraid of—even more than his dad finding out and beating the shit out of him—is that you will stop loving him."

Debbie and Justin's relationship has grown as he's become a man. She honors that he's grown. She sort of helped to raise him that first year of his being out—with the permission of his mother, of course. That was nice. She got the permission from his mother to take in another boy that she loved. I think that relationship will always stay. I think he will always have the gratitude of that first year, being out and being with her. He knows she's wacko, but no matter how old he gets, he still takes shit off her if she thinks he needs it.

"Well, no need to worry . . . Michael can do it. He's a red-blooded all-American gay boy, which means he gets a whack attack three, four times a day!"

I am sure Melanie and Lindsay are going to rue the day they picked Michael as the father because Debbie comes with the dinner. You know she'll be over there with every piece of clothing she can make for the child. Can you imagine the awful things that she's going to sew for that little kid?

"I want you here sick and I want you here well. I'll take you any way I can get you."

I love Jack. I think it's a real honor to have a man of his background on the show. My favorite scene was when they brought a dance instructor in and taught us the hustle. It was so free and so loving. We weren't dealing with Vic's illness or whatever Debbie would be going through with Michael. We were just having fun folding laundry and "The Hustle" comes on the radio. It was like being brother and sister from years ago when life was simpler. I loved it because even when Michael came in and interrupted us with the bad news that he had, I just kept doing the hustle. I was talking to Michael and dancing around the table while I'm talking to him. It was a fun, freedom scene.

"Holy shit, I look . . . nice."

It was huge for me when Debbie first got kissed. They took Peter MacNeill and me in for a sex meeting and they asked, "Would you like to try the kiss here?" And we were like, "No, we don't want to try it here!" But it was very exciting for me. I really respond to that moment of waiting and waiting and putting Horvath off, and then finally she lets him kiss her. Even though it's a show about the gay community, it's nice for Debbie to get a chance with somebody.

"All right, I'm going to make you very, very happy. You always wanted a normal mother? Okay, you got one. I don't want you dating that guy."

We were invited to the Museum of Television & Radio in Los Angeles for a panel on the show, and they opened it up to audience discussion. There was one guy in the audience who said, "I'm appalled at this show. I'm with someone who's HIV-positive and I'm disgusted by Debbie's response to Michael and Ben being together. Debbie of all people to treat him like that and not have the compassion." Everyone in the cast grabbed the mike and

everyone wanted to talk. I waited until the end and I said, "May I speak for a moment?" And they said, "Sure," and handed me the mike. I said, "Please understand, I know Debbie is everybody's champion, but this time, her response is not fair. Michael is going with a man who is HIV-positive and going to be—excuse me—boinking her son, and all she sees is a killer. This man is going to kill her boy. 'If the rubber breaks, if my kid is infected, he may die. So, when it comes to my son, all bets are off.'" When it comes to Debbie's son, all bets are off. All this wonderful human being that she is, if she thinks his life is being threatened, she will kill anyone in his path.

"Come and give your mother a hug."

Several times a week since I've started this show, men will come up to me and ask if they can be hugged or held. It's a real nice perk for me, because I'm not the one that people write to. They don't have any passion for Debbie or love affair with Debbie. But it's nice to have people come up who want to hold me or hug me or, more importantly, be held by me.

On a couple of occasions, two men—one in New York and one in Connecticut—just started sobbing in my arms. I could feel it as I was holding them because they were shaking. All I could think was "Damn, what has been done to this boy, that someone who plays this mother, if she holds him, he just dissolves?" I'm learning so much about how fragile we all are and what kindness like that can do. They don't understand that I'm getting a gift when they come and ask me to hug them. It validates that I'm doing my job.

Keep your pants on. At least until dinner. • **You should try to eat some of your protein off a plate.** • I never forget a butt . . . especially a cute one. • **I've always said it's not who you love, it's how you love. Genitalia is just God's way of accessorizing.** • You get my tits in a knot, Sunshine, and you're gonna be in deep shit. • **You smother a pork chop, not a son.** • I want you to hear what I say on an empty stomach, so maybe you'll digest it. • **I know you're uncomfortable hanging out in gay bars with your mother. But look at it this way: if you meet somebody nice, you won't have to take him home to meet me because I'm already here.** • You're not lost. You're just full of shit. You're only lost if you're alone. You are surrounded by people who love you. You'll find your way. • **Keep it up, Sunshine . . . the good work, I mean.** • I'm biting my tongue so hard I'm tasting blood. • **After a healthy breakfast, the best way to start the day is by telling me what the fuck's going on.** • Who says that love's an easy ride? General Motors? Michael's used to bumps. He grew up with me.

debbie's words of wisdom

jack wetherall as vic grassi

In the British version of *Queer as Folk*, an older gentleman named Bernard was a boarder in the mother's home. For the American version, Ron and Dan felt there needed to be more of a family connection on the show, especially for Michael. In creating Uncle Vic they took an idea that had its genesis in a project they had written almost twenty years earlier: the groundbreaking AIDS television movie *An Early Frost.*

"When we did *An Early Frost,* people said we should do a sort of *Early Frost Two: The Son of Early Frost,*" Dan explains. "And I wondered, 'What would that be?' Because the character didn't die at the end of the TV movie, we realized that the *Son of Early Frost* would be a person who thinks he's going to die, maxed out all his credit cards, sold everything, and then all of a sudden has a new lease on life. And that's what happened with Vic."

vic

"When I look in the mirror, I see someone I barely recognize. I still imagine I'm like Brian . . . able to walk in a bar and have practically anyone I want. And I had plenty, too. But now, in his place I see this tired, somewhat faded old gentleman who measures his life from a pill bottle and who nobody wants."

"Sex isn't careful. And if it is, you're doing it wrong. It's messy and it's human and it's mixed up with other things. It's a genie who won't stay in a bottle. If you think you made a mistake, move on and accept it like a man."

Vic's at an age where he's lived a hard, fast life and had his fun and sowed his oats. I think that distinguishes him from the others. It's terrific that he's not a prude. I think he's very connected to Brian, for instance. I think he understands Brian. There's something in the isolation of Brian that he understands . . . the wildness of Brian. He's gone through that himself and I think what he's really looking for is a way to take back his life from having been sick.

Essentially he came home to die. Now, I think he's trying to reclaim his life. He's like many of the people I know that are stuck on disability and trying to reclaim their life and their reason for living. It's not so much sexuality that he's interested in, it's companionship and friendship and a real connection to somebody. I think there is a terrific opportunity to explore a quieter side of what it is to be a gay man and a gay man living with AIDS.

"It's a nasty world out there. If he doesn't have the guts to be gay, then I say fuck him."

Michael's as close to a son as Vic has, and as a consequence I think there are certain frustrations. I think I can love Michael, but I don't always have to like him. Often I think Vic is ready to take Brian's point, whereas Debbie immediately defends the son. I have enough perspective to say, "You know what? Michael puts himself in that situation. What the hell is he doing still mooning over Brian?" Michael has a tendency to complicate other people's lives when he should just be getting on with his own. Vic can be tougher with him than Debbie. I often just do it with a look or I can do it with the way that I respond to Brian as opposed to Michael.

There's obviously a great deal of love for Michael, and I feel a great deal of love back from Hal and from Michael. There's a physical closeness that we all have on this show. It's a great cast and there are no inhibitions. When you do all that other physical stuff, it's easy for us to touch. So we're a touchy family. Debbie and I are very physical with each other, and that's the same with Michael, which is true of an Italian family and very different from my own family. There's a great deal of love in my family, but it's expressed differently. That's why one likes being an actor, because you get to live other people's lives.

"That was the worst part . . . even worse than being arrested, or put in jail, or having to go to court. It's that I believed him."

The tantalizing thought that a younger man would be interested in Vic and then to realize that it was entrapment . . . he started to beat himself up wondering how he could have allowed himself to believe it. When Vic decided to defend himself, I thought of Proctor in *The Crucible* and the value of the name and the reputation. It's a long-standing theme that goes back to Shakespeare: reputation, reputation, reputation. The victory in the court really does spark Vic to get past this place he was stuck in. From then on there's a real change in Vic and a desire to really get him mobilized and back into life and into the flow of things.

In the entrapment scene I got to open up to Debbie because it's the first time Vic really got to express what he's feeling, and the fact that he is so lonely, isolated, and yearning for touch. The director got very excited by that scene, too, and would feed little directions that we'd do and it would bring in new information. So that scene was very much about the acting, which was very exciting, because sometimes in television we've got a lot of stuff to cover so once we got a good take, we have to move on. It was really nice because we really took time and it had intimacy. One felt that we had really accomplished something by the end of it.

"If I go, it looks a little . . . Fagin and Oliver Twist."

I've played Cyrano and I've played Henry V and Richard II and Macbeth. These are intense characters, but you play them for a certain amount of time onstage and then they're gone. I've lived with Vic in my psyche for three seasons. Even though the seasons are short and I don't work that much, he stays with me. He sort of walks with me. I have to be careful because there's a tremendous weight because of the stuff he has to play. He has been isolated and there's a darkness to Vic that I have to make sure doesn't creep into my own worldview. Friends have seen the role impact on me. It's caused some disruption in my own personal life. Vic gets in the way sometimes. So that's been interesting to explore.

Six weeks have passed since the attack and much has happened while the audience was away. The early episodes of the second season serve to tie up some loose ends, including Justin's rehabilitation and Michael's offscreen breakup with Dr. David. They also serve as a launching point for a season that provides considerable transition in the lives of all of the characters as they continue to grow from boys to men.

Due to the attack, Justin will never again be the innocent boy he was that first night he visited Liberty Avenue. Emmett finds love in a May/December romance that makes the age difference between Brian and Justin seem almost nonexistent by comparison. Ted's entire world is turned upside down, and both he and Michael discover their true callings in life. But Michael goes a step further by falling in love with Ben Bruckner and embarking on a relationship never truly explored on series television before. Brian's growth is subtler, but it is seen in glimpses throughout the second season up to the moment he lets Justin go.

But it's not just the boys who are changing. This season, Melanie and Lindsay tie the knot in a ceremony made possible by their family of friends. And Debbie makes a romantic connection following a unique set of circumstances that will continue to play out through the end of the third season in unexpected ways.

Through it all, *Queer as Folk* continues to explore taboo subjects of sex and love among the lives of this group of friends. As the season progresses, their bonds grow stronger as the world continues to throw its harsh realities with a light punishment for Chris Hobbs, an anonymous body found in a Dumpster, and a brush with death for the newest character on the show.

And it all ends with a celebration of newfound success . . . and loss.

season two

“Things change a lot.
And if you don’t
change with them,
you’ll get left behind.”

episode 201

Written by: Ron Cowen & Daniel Lipman
Directed by: Alex Chapple

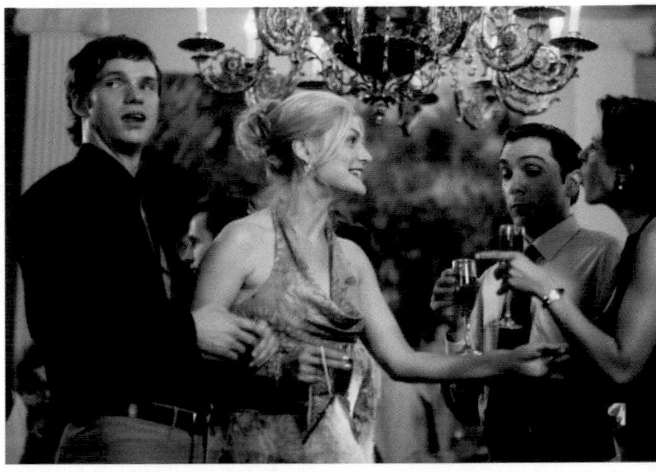

While Justin recuperates in the hospital from the attack, Brian makes secret nightly visits to watch over him. Jennifer tells Brian to stay away, echoing his own guilt by blaming him for having made her son a target. Chris Hobbs pleads guilty to assault and gets a light sentence. Michael comes back from Portland for a visit that turns out to be a return as he and Dr. David have broken up. Lindsay takes Melanie, Ted, and Emmett to her sister's wedding, where she suppresses her lesbian self for her family. But, when the charade proves too difficult to keep up, she proposes marriage to Melanie while toasting the bride.

"I've read Miss Manners, cover to cover. And nowhere does it state one must subjugate one's own sexuality. Even at the bride's request."

RON COWEN: There's the person who suffers the attack and the posttraumatic stress that they have to deal with in recovering from their attack, but there's also the witness. The person who witnesses the attack feels a tremendous amount of helplessness and guilt. There was nothing they could do to stop it and they feel a sense of responsibility because of that. Witnessing an act of violence can often be as devastating as being the victim. I feel that that was what Brian's situation was at the beginning of the second season; that he felt incredibly guilty.

episode 202

Written by: Ron Cowen & Daniel Lipman
Directed by: John Greyson

Jennifer realizes what her son really needs to heal emotionally, and she asks Brian to take Justin in. Melanie finally accepts Lindsay's marriage proposal. Michael's been partying a lot since he got back to Pittsburgh, and due to financial constraints, he's forced to go back to work as assistant manager at Big Q. Ted is fired for watching on-line gay porn while at work. Emmett considers a butt lift and gets a job as a nude waiter to pay for it.

". . . then you turned around and smiled . . . then I knew why Debbie calls you Sunshine."

SCOTT LOWELL: Season two was all about Ted coming into his own. Accounting had been this guy's life. It was something that he could count on, because it was reliable and safe and he tends to go with what's safe. He took a big step going down in the dungeon with leather master Dale in season one. That was a huge growth moment for him, but it wasn't really complete until he started the website. It was all part of the evolution. As an actor you don't always know where these growth moments are going to come in as part of the arc, but it's nice to look back and see how nicely they progressed.

“I’m the snake in the Garden of Eden.”

episode 203

Teleplay by: Karen Walton
Story by: Ron Cowen & Daniel Lipman and Karen Walton
Directed by: Michael DeCarlo

Emmett becomes the sexual plaything for a gay couple who claim to have the perfect monogamous life. Brian receives the Outstanding Gay Hero award for saving Justin, but when a hypocritical gay author complains about the hero’s lifestyle, they try to take the award back. Michael is excited about the annual ComiCon, until Brian blows him off as well—but he eventually makes up for it.

DANIEL LIPMAN: Gay as Blazes came about because I wanted to do this politically correct gay drama that all the very proper, politically correct people felt Queer as Folk should be. People were outraged by the little scene we did and I love when people are outraged by the show. As our production executive, Pancho Mansfield, says, “The purpose of the show is to be outrageous. It’s not to offend or be outrageous solely for the sake of being outrageous, but to tell the truth. And the truth is outrageous, so we created this show within a show. I thought it was just hilarious, but people were out of their minds. They were thinking we were giving a big ‘fuck you’ to them. That wasn’t true at all. It was just a really fun show to do.”

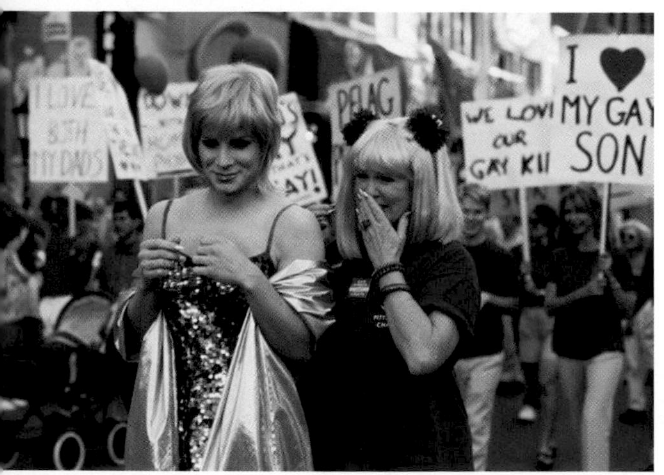

“I’ll be glad when pride’s over so we can all go back to being ashamed.”

episode 204

Teleplay by: Michael MacLennan
Story by: Ron Cowen & Daniel Lipman and Michael MacLennan
Directed by: Kevin Inch

Pride weekend starts off with tragedy when Pittsburgh’s greatest drag queen, Godiva, dies, and only Emmett seems to mourn the loss. Justin runs into Chris Hobbs, working his community service. Brian decides that a homophobic client has the perfect wine coolers to market to gays. Ted gets a pity fuck from a really hot guy, but he doesn’t realize that’s all it is. Melanie’s ex-girlfriend Leda comes to town to shake things up for Mel and Linz. Michael backs out of agreeing to march in his first pride parade when he learns that coworkers will be watching. But he does show up, wearing Godiva’s clothing so he won’t be recognized.

HAL SPARKS: The scene called for me to go up to my own boss in drag and kiss him and have him not know it’s me. There were a lot of things we had to do to make sure that you could not tell it was me right away, because it would have been really annoying if it had just looked like me with a wig on. We put this wrap on my head and pulled all my skin up tighter and tighter and tighter until it held my eyebrows up, held my jawline tighter, and changed the shape of my face. Then we put the hair and makeup on and bleached my eyebrows—and then we secretly dyed them back to black at the end of the night so we wouldn’t get into trouble with the producers for doing it in the first place. The bandage was giving me a migraine and nausea. My vision was so blurry that I couldn’t see much beyond Sharon. After about five minutes with it on, I could literally feel my pulse in my temples like someone knocking on a door with a hammer. But I was like, “If that’s what it takes, let’s do it.”

episode 205

Teleplay by: Efrem Seeger
Story by: Ron Cowen & Daniel Lipman & Efrem Seeger
Directed by: David Wellington

Melanie and Lindsay announce their plans to marry. Justin attends his first day of classes at art school, but his hand shakes uncontrollably as he tries to draw. Ted's being unemployed leads him into depression and marathon jack-off sessions in which he won't leave his condo. After almost getting into another rut job, he realizes that his true mission in life is to produce on-line porn. And Michael finally discovers his dream after quitting the Big Q and buying a comic-book store.

"My dream is . . . to one day know what my dream is."

PETER PAIGE: There's a trio on this show of Brian, Emmett, and Melanie—and sometimes Debbie is in that slot—but they're the characters who live their lives by some credo. They're out there saying what they think. Everyone else is stuck in the middle somewhere trying to get to one side or the other, and they kind of vacillate back and forth, but the trio stands their ground.

episode 206

Teleplay by: Matt Pyken & Michael Berns
Story by: Ron Cowen & Daniel Lipman & Matt Pyken & Michael Berns
Directed by: Bruce McDonald

Michael meets Professor Ben Bruckner, who is HIV-positive. Ted opens his porn site and it immediately starts losing money until he convinces Emmett to lend a hand (and a dick). Lindsay has issues with Ted's porn site, which bothers Melanie, because she has her own soft-core past, having posed for a girlie magazine in college. Justin wants to be more in a monogamous partnership with Brian, but they reach a mutual agreement for an open relationship.

***To Michael, Beneath whose mild-mannered appearance beats the heart of a superhero.*—Ben**

RON COWEN: We were looking for someone who came from a different world from our Liberty Avenue guys—that he was more academic and not like the rest of them. So we weren't really thinking of somebody who looked like Bobby Gant, but luckily he showed up and we realized we could use that to feed into Michael's superhero fixation.

episode 207

Teleplay by: Blair Fell
Story by: Ron Cowen & Daniel Lipman & Blair Fell
Directed by: Michael DeCarlo

Emmett embraces his role as Fetch Dixon, Internet porn star, until Ted gets very demanding on Emmett's time and sex life. The rising star is forced to strike until they realize their friendship is more important and Ted gives in to Emmett's request for perks. Lindsay asks her parents for financial help with her wedding, but they decline. Michael and Ben grow closer, even though Michael's friends and his mom have issues with Ben's positive status. Michael believes he's fine with it, too, until it comes time for sex and he's not as comfortable as he had thought.

"I'm ready for my close-up, Mr. Schmidt."

ROBERT GANT: The bathroom scene was really hard to do because Hal and I were supposed to be looking at each other in the mirror. In reality, they pulled the wall out, brought the camera right into our faces, and stuck a little piece of tape on it. We had to look at the piece of tape like we were looking at each other. We were acting to a piece of tape, so the scene had to be about what was going on inside ourselves. And this relationship was so new. We hardly knew each other. Acting is such a weird thing on camera. It's much easier onstage or on a sitcom—which is essentially stage—because you're in the experience. In drama there's so much technical stuff when you're cutting and pasting and moving the camera right in your face.

episode 208

Teleplay by: Michael MacLennan
Story by: Ron Cowen & Daniel Lipman & Michael MacLennan
Directed by: Alex Chapple

After breaking up with Ben, Michael can't stop thinking about the professor, and a series of dating disasters certainly doesn't help. Fetch Dixon gets a secret admirer, but Emmett's dreams of Prince Charming are initially dashed when he meets George Shickel. He quickly learns that appearances can be deceiving. Brian and Justin's new arrangement seems to be working on the surface, but both guys are a little jealous over the other's extracurricular activities, especially when Justin breaks the "no kissing" rule.

"Real love, when it comes, doesn't look anything like what you expect."

PETER PAIGE: Emmett as a porn star was not my favorite thing, because I hated doing it. Like any reasonably attractive young actor, there were opportunities to do porn. I made very conscious decisions not to do that despite the fact that I was starving. So to come into a set with a few video cameras set up around a dirty warehouse and it's freezing cold and to strip down and pretend to fucking whack off—I was like, "I am a hard-on away from making porn." That's a big difference. I looked at Dan and Ron at one point and was like, "How much longer? How much longer?" They were like, "One more. You have one more." And I was thanking God. I was so happy to see that go, even though it was an interesting story point.

episode 209

Teleplay by: Efrem Seeger
Story by: Ron Cowen & Daniel Lipman & Efrem Seeger
Directed by: Bruce McDonald

Brian's sister insists that he take more of an active role in their mom's life and tricks him into taking her to a church service that's coincidentally led by a guy he fucked at the baths. Ted is exhausted from work and takes some Viagra to help when he has the potential for action, but gets the boner that won't die. Much to Debbie's chagrin, Michael and Ben reunite and partake in some safe sex.

SCOTT LOWELL: I know some fans got upset when Michael started dating Ben and Ted was very much against it—very much against him dating a person who was HIV-positive. People got up in arms: "How dare he? Who is he to say?" But it totally came out of the fact that Ted loves this guy. He didn't want to see him hurt in any way, physically or emotionally. It's why I think Ted kind of tangles with Brian so much. There's that little bit of seeing the manipulation that Brian puts Michael through and wanting to protect Michael, and also being jealous of the fact that Michael's attentions are more on Brian than on Ted.

"Now, if you'll excuse me, I'm going to hell."

episode 210

Teleplay by: Matt Pyken & Michael Berns
Story by: Ron Cowen & Daniel Lipman & Matt Pyken & Michael Berns
Directed by: Michael DeCarlo

It's a sad day for Michael when his favorite superhero makes his last appearance on the comic-book page. In the real world an actual death rocks Liberty Avenue when Debbie finds the body of a young club kid in the trash behind the diner, but it's a homophobic cop and the general indifference of the gay community that really pisses Debbie off. Emmett introduces his new old beau, George, to his friends. While searching for her granny's wedding dress, Lindsay finds a not-so-dirty little secret—letters from her granny Faye's female lover.

DANIEL LIPMAN: When you do a network show, there are commercials making the show take place in four acts. Films are usually three acts. When we started the first season of *Queer as Folk,* we were writing in four acts, since it was something we were used to. Now we've changed to the three-act structure, but there are no breaks. You don't see it, but you feel it. Internally there's a structure. You know that you have to build to a certain point, get to a point. There is a structure to storytelling. And I believe very strongly in good storytelling.

"If it's true they killed Captain Astro because he's gay, that makes his death a hate crime."

episode 211

Teleplay by: Karen Walton
Story by: Ron Cowen & Daniel Lipman & Karen Walton
Directed by: Kevin Inch

Lindsay and Melanie's wedding plans fall apart due to the alignment of the planets, but their friends come to the rescue. Emmett finds George's house to be the perfect place to hold the ceremony and puts up the money for his new butt to pay for decor. Vic and Debbie get past the stress of having temporarily worked together at the diner to make the cake and the dress respectively. Michael and Ted manage to put aside their argument over the wedding gift when they see the beautiful brides so happy. And Justin decides to stay for the wedding instead of going with Brian to the White Party in Miami.

"If you ask me, somebody up there doesn't think we should get married. Maybe there's a reason. Maybe that's because people like us aren't supposed to get married."

MICHELLE CLUNIE: People write to me and send pictures of their and their lover's child saying how they look up to us. When I went to work and shot the wedding episode, I was thinking about all the people that would see it and who it would affect and what it meant to people. I've always been able to get married to the love of my life, but I get letters every day about what's going on politically in different states. Then you go to work and you shoot this episode that you know may have an impact on that and it means a lot. You can't help but have a tear in your eye when you're saying your vows because you're not just saying vows for Melanie and Lindsay, you're saying vows in the name of love and in the name of freedom.

episode 212

Teleplay by: Michael MacLennan
Story by: Ron Cowen & Daniel Lipman & Michael MacLennan
Directed by: Thom Best

In the small world of Liberty Avenue it comes as a bit of a shock for Michael to learn that Brian and Ben had a one-night stand in the past. Although Michael tries to act nonchalant, he is jealous of both Brian *and* Ben. Ted mingles with an upscale gay crowd that is only interested in him as a pimp for the men on his site. After the cops fail to find out the identity of the body found in the Dumpster several weeks ago, Debbie puts on her investigator hat and gets to work identifying the boy.

"It's Pittsburgh. No degrees of separation."

PETER PAIGE: I think Emmett's the only character in this show—except Debbie—who is not afraid of Brian on some level. Even Melanie is afraid of him because of Lindsay and Gus. Emmett is really just, "Fuck off! You overfucked idiot!" He's willing to call Brian on his shit and that does not intimidate him. There was a line in the script that had Emmett saying, "Wow, if Brian had fucked my boyfriend, I would have to break up with him. That would be game over." And when I saw it, I was like, "No!" Emmett just doesn't feel this way. I just don't believe that Emmett thinks that there's anybody who is so much better than him that somebody couldn't love him, too. And Ron and Dan were like, "You're totally right. That's Ted." And of course Scotty had to get the line.

episode 213

Teleplay by: Efrem Seeger
Story by: Ron Cowen & Daniel Lipman & Efrem Seeger
Directed by: John Greyson

Ted and Michael manage to get the famous drag queen Devina Devore to perform at the Angel Ball because she used to date Debbie back in high school, back when she was a he named Danny. After seeing a photo of Danny, Michael realizes his mom has been lying to him about his father and that his real dad is the drag queen. Melanie and Lindsay try to get Gus into the best preschool and mistakenly think they have problems because of their being same-sex parents. Justin's dad announces that he is not paying for school anymore, forcing Justin to get a job dancing at Babylon.

SHARON GLESS: It wasn't a show just about Michael finding out about his father. It was also about the end of a lie Debbie's had to live with so long. It was a lovely script. The obvious was to just go with the story of "Oh, Michael meets his father." But it became about so much more. For Debbie it was also about the pain and the lie this woman's had to live for so many years and she's suddenly found out. It was the one lie she kept and it was to protect her son.

"His last words were 'Tell my son I love him more than life itself . . . and I'll always be proud of him.'"

episode 214

Teleplay by: Matt Pyken & Michael Berns
Story by: Ron Cowen & Daniel Lipman & Matt Pyken & Michael Berns
Directed by: John Fawcett

George springs for a trip around the world for himself and Emmett, but dies in the midst of applying for membership in the mile-high club. Debbie continues to take out her frustration over Michael's new relationship on Ben. But when the homophobic Detective Horvath asks Debbie out, Michael behaves just as irrationally toward his mom. Justin's new job as a go-go boy is affecting his life, but things take a real turn when he is drugged and almost raped at his boss's party. Justin quits the job and accepts financial help from Brian.

"Holy shit . . . I look nice."

PETER PAIGE: My favorite scene from season two is the scene where George dies. I truly believe that is something you will never ever see anywhere else on television ever. It is uniquely *Queer as Folk.* It starts off as this fun, naughty, mischievous, sexy scene in an airplane bathroom that just goes terribly, terribly wrong. As an actor I love how it turned. I love how this great thing went from this moment of wonder and then the terror and then the horror of being trapped. We had done a few takes, and in each one they cut a moment after one or two bangs on the door. In that last take they let me bang forever. The director just let me get crazier and crazier, and freak and freak and freak. They used a lot of that in the final take. I just love how genuine it was.

episode 215

Teleplay by: Karen Walton
Story by: Ron Cowen & Daniel Lipman & Karen Walton
Directed by: Jeremy Podeswa

Michael and Justin team up to create the new gay comic-book hero *Rage.* Even though their work is patterned after Brian, he is jealous over Michael and Justin's new bond. Fetch Dixon is nominated for the Gay Porn Awards as New Cummer of the Year, and Emmett uses the opportunity to speak on behalf of his love for George after being removed from the man's funeral. Lindsay wants to turn the attic into a studio and reluctantly allows Leda to move into the house and do the work.

HAL SPARKS: The root emotion of the Michael/Justin relationship is jealousy because Michael finds Justin replacing him in Brian's heart. Once that passes, they have a lot more in common. Through Debbie teaching Jennifer to be more supportive and loving, Michael's family situation is a window for Justin's acceptance and happiness. To Michael, the jury is still out on Justin's ultimate reality and motivations. Michael knows Justin's an unformed person and he could go in any direction. He could end up like Michael or he could end up like Brian.

"There's nothing as sexual as the act of creation. When I'm writing, and it's pouring out of me, I swear to God, I'm completely turned on."

episode 216

Teleplay by: Michael MacLennan
Story by: Ron Cowen & Daniel Lipman & Michael MacLennan
Directed by: Bruce McDonald

Justin and Ben share a birthday, but their boyfriends have very different plans for marking the occasion. Michael plans a surprise party that blows up in his face when Ben lashes out in front of all the guests after learning his infection has become resistant to the cocktail. Brian decides to ignore Justin's birthday entirely, so Justin goes to a violin recital and meets a cute violinist. Meanwhile, Ted attends a gay-celebration church, meets a really great guy, and lies about his job.

THOM BEST (DIRECTOR OF PHOTOGRAPHY): I'm really proud of the work that everybody's done. Everybody's risen to the challenge. We all have our own personal reasons for why we've done the show. It was just important to me. For good or bad or however you feel about gay lifestyle, it provides a dialogue for people. If you don't like it, at least it gives you something to talk about and that's what I liked. Gay or straight, it opens things up for discussion. That's what I've always liked about this show. A lot of things are in-your-face and it's intended to be.

"Maybe it's time you exposed yourself to a higher form of cultural expression than the *thumpa-thumpa* at Babylon."

episode 217

Teleplay by: Efrem Seeger
Story by: Ron Cowen & Daniel Lipman & Efrem Seeger
Directed by: David Wellington

Brian has to cancel plans for a weekend away with Justin when his boss sells the agency and Brian has to prove himself to the new owner to keep his job. Justin goes to Vermont anyway while Brian saves his job and gets himself named partner. Lindsay and Melanie suffer lesbian bed death and nothing they do can reawaken their sexual urges until Leda joins them in a threesome. Emmett finds out that George has left him his fortune, but the Shickel family intercedes.

"I generally don't like discussing kink on an empty stomach."

THEA GILL: Around the time we shot this episode, there was an assistant hairstylist who was going to have a baby, so we all got together and raised some money to give her as a gift. We were doing the scene where Emmett's handing out all the gifts, and Peter does a great improvisational turn while we're shooting and says, "Oh, and we would also like to give this present to Helen." The look on her face was absolute shock. Tears poured down her face. There was this moment of pure joy that we had come together and done this for her and did it in a special way. We didn't just hand her money. That was a beautiful moment.

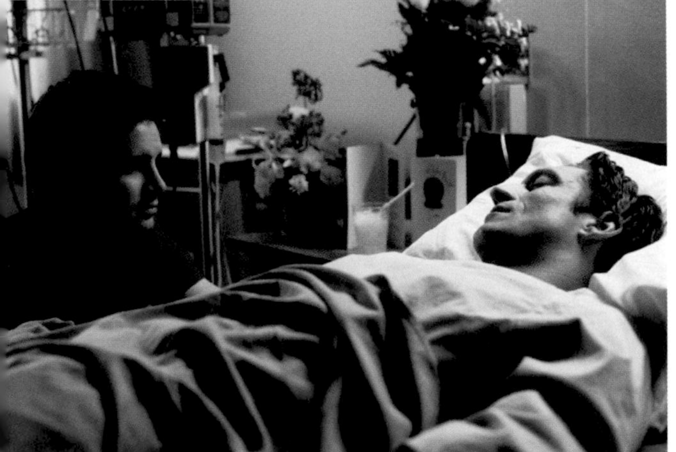

episode 218

Teleplay by: Matt Pyken & Michael Berns
Story by: Ron Cowen & Daniel Lipman & Matt Pyken & Michael Berns
Directed by: Alex Chapple

Emmett fights to keep the money George left him. Fearing scandal, the Shickel family offers to settle and give Emmett a million dollars so long as he disavows his relationship with George. He refuses. Ben collapses while teaching class, suffering a near fatal reaction to his new meds. Debbie makes peace with Ben in the hospital. Justin runs into Ethan, the violinist he met on his birthday. When Brian continues to refuse Justin's romantic gestures, Justin finds himself in Ethan's arms.

"How about staying in the 'now'"

HAL SPARKS: Michael won't accept help from anyone, and finally he calls Brian to come to him. When Brian shows up and the script has me say a few lines, and then it says, "Michael breaks down quickly." On one line it just switches emotional gears. Well, since everything's shot out of order, we had already shot a scene with Ben where he was leaving the hospital. So I would go into the room and there was a fresh pillow there. I would touch the pillow and imagine that I had come to see a sick friend who had died, and when I had come up to get his things, they had already changed the sheets. That's what I used for my emotional place. I would put my hand on the pillow and feel that, and I would walk out to do the scene while trying to hold it together.

episode 219

Teleplay by: Efrem Seeger & Michael MacLennan & Matt Pyken & Michael Berns
Story by: Ron Cowen & Daniel Lipman
Directed by: Michael DeCarlo

Leda wants to continue her affair with Melanie and Lindsay, and the girls have trouble letting her down gently. Ted hits a dry spell when porn no longer affects him, until a new distraction arrives when he realizes he has feelings for Emmett. Debbie challenges Horvath and his friends to a gay versus straight bowling match and manages to lose gracefully, while she grows distant from the cop. Michael sees Justin with Ethan and tells Brian.

SCOTT LOWELL: As far as Ted and Emmett go, they're such opposites in so many ways, but they are the best of friends and they kind of complement each other in so many ways as well. It's kind of telling that with Ted's lack of luck in the marketplace that he tends to throw his attention on those who are his best friends. The crush that he's had on Michael since the beginning of the series predates what we see in the show. That's one of the things that really, really attracted me to the character when I first read him in the pilot. I related to the sadness of that. It was a terrific thing.

"Love comes at the strangest times in the strangest ways."

episode 220

Written by: Ron Cowen & Daniel Lipman
Directed by: David Wellington

It's time for the *Rage* release party, but few people feel like celebrating. Justin apologizes to Brian about Ethan, but then gets into a fight with Michael over the situation. Ben announces that he's leaving for Tibet, but he will only go if Michael's okay with it. Michael reluctantly gives his blessing, but Debbie convinces Ben to stay. Ted admits feelings to an unreceptive Emmett. However, upon further consideration, Emmett changes his mind and locks lips with his friend. And in the end, Justin makes his choice to go with the romantic Ethan, leaving Brian behind.

RON COWEN: Brian was starting to realize how much he cared about Justin, but he could not fully give up his own needs and his own life to become a monogamous couple because it was taking away his own independence. Brian grew up in an extremely dysfunctional family with a very cruel and abusive father and an alcoholic, ice-cold mother who was very judgmental and punishing. I don't think he found any love in his family at all. Debbie probably showed him more love than anyone in his own family. I think Brian has a lot of trouble with love because he didn't have a very good example of it at home. If that's what he saw growing up every day, then of course he doesn't want to get married or be in a relationship. It was a nightmare in his house, and I think he's very afraid of that and very suspicious and mistrustful of what goes under the name of love. Brian couldn't really give Justin what he wanted because he was too afraid.

"I tried to forget about you but I can't. You're all I think about."

gale harold as **brian kinney**

It's safe to say that no other character in the history of North American television has been introduced to the audience while getting a blow job in the back room of a gay club. But it's also safe to say that very few characters on television are like Brian Kinney. He claims that at eighteen he was fucking anything that moved. His balls-to-the-wall approach to business made him one of the most successful advertising executives in Pittsburgh. He treats people the way he feels they deserve to be treated without fear of repercussions, and his friends have an almost unrelenting loyalty toward him.

"Brian, to me, is a very heroic character," Daniel Lipman says, explaining the dichotomy of the seemingly heartless hero. "He's very Ayn Randian in his individualism. In many ways I think he's the most moral person on the show, because he lives by his code. And that's the definition of what makes a man moral. Brian is very much the proponent of the so-called queer life." And he defines that life by simply noting that in Brian's mind gay men should not spend their lives trying to imitate straight people. It may not be a popular opinion, and certainly not one shared by most of the other characters, but it is what motivates Brian and is the cause for many of the things he does.

brian

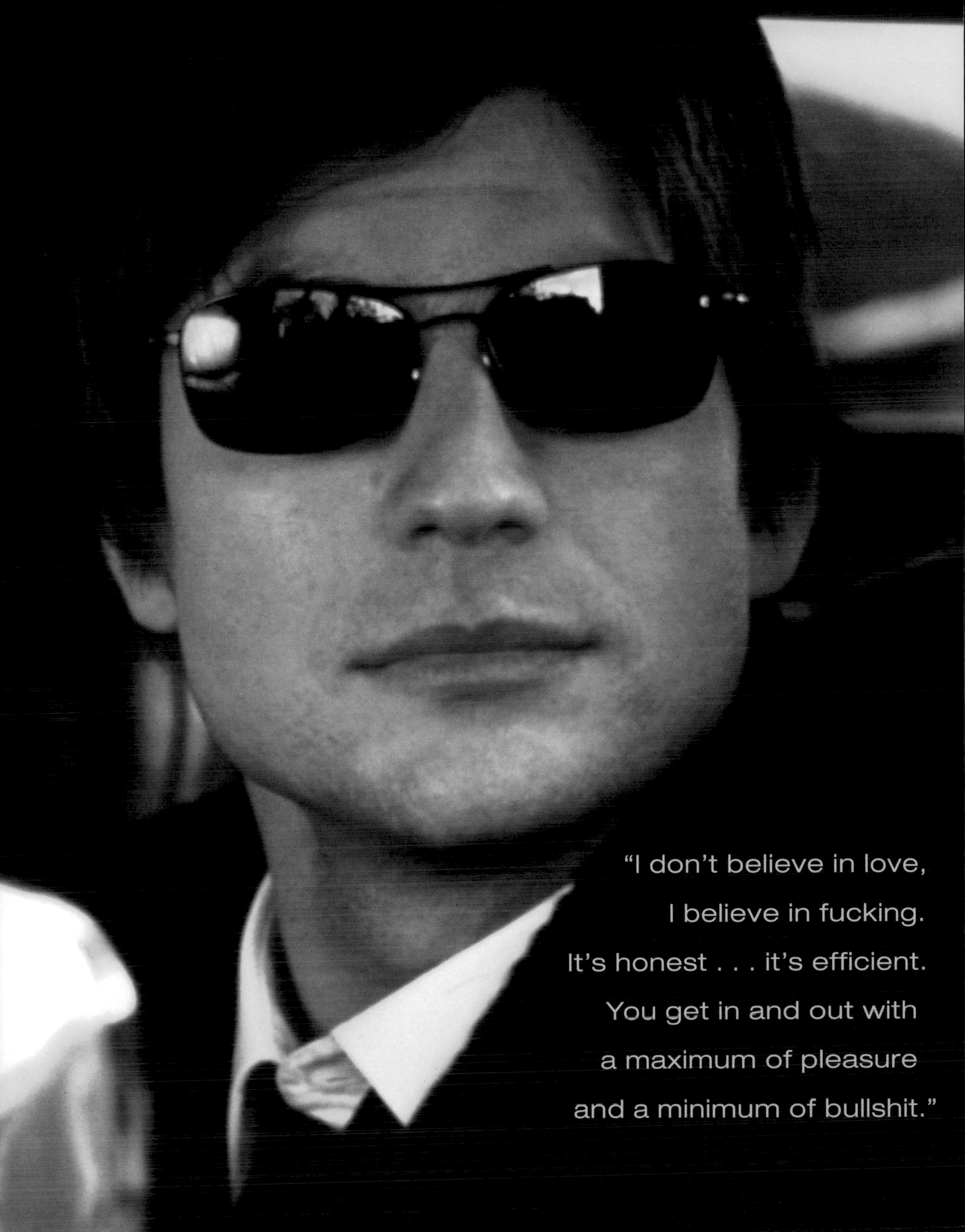
"I don't believe in love,
I believe in fucking.
It's honest . . . it's efficient.
You get in and out with
a maximum of pleasure
and a minimum of bullshit."

"Brian is a highly evolved character," Dan continues. "I think part of the criticism of the show is based on the Brian character. Here we have this very masculine center that is gay and very sexual. I always felt that if he were a straight character, he'd be applauded. You see stories about young straight males who fuck everything that moves and nobody complains. They're hailed. They're cheered. Brian is not that. If Michael is the emotional center of this show, Brian is the sexual. All the energy of this show comes from Brian."

The energy provided by Brian gives the show its edge—its drive. He keeps the action moving in the only way he knows how. "Brian is not a man of words," according to Ron Cowen. "He's a man of deeds and actions. What he does speaks louder than his words. He doesn't really say that much. I would imagine out of all the characters his dialogue is the most sparse."

It's what he does with those words and those actions that prove the kind of man he is. Ron continues, "He doesn't make false promises. Brian's way of showing love for someone is to be loyal, to be there for them when they need help. I think he's a very loyal and very generous friend, and there have been a million examples in the course of the show where Brian has come through for everyone in his life. But he is selfish, too. And I don't mean selfish like 'No you can't play with my toys.' I mean he looks after himself first, and out of looking after himself he can then take care of other people. But I do not think he's an altruist. I think the dirtiest word in his dictionary is *sacrifice*."

These "selfish sacrifices" don't hide the true self that is buried deep beneath the hardened exterior. His childhood gives great insight into why he has become the man he is today. He helped Justin through the attack, aided Michael in getting the funds to buy his store, and had given of himself to provide Lindsay and Melanie with a child. He's been there on scales large and small, both anonymously and in the spotlight for all of his friends and even his family. But the one person he is there for the least—even as selfish as he is—would have to be himself.

brian and gale: face-to-face

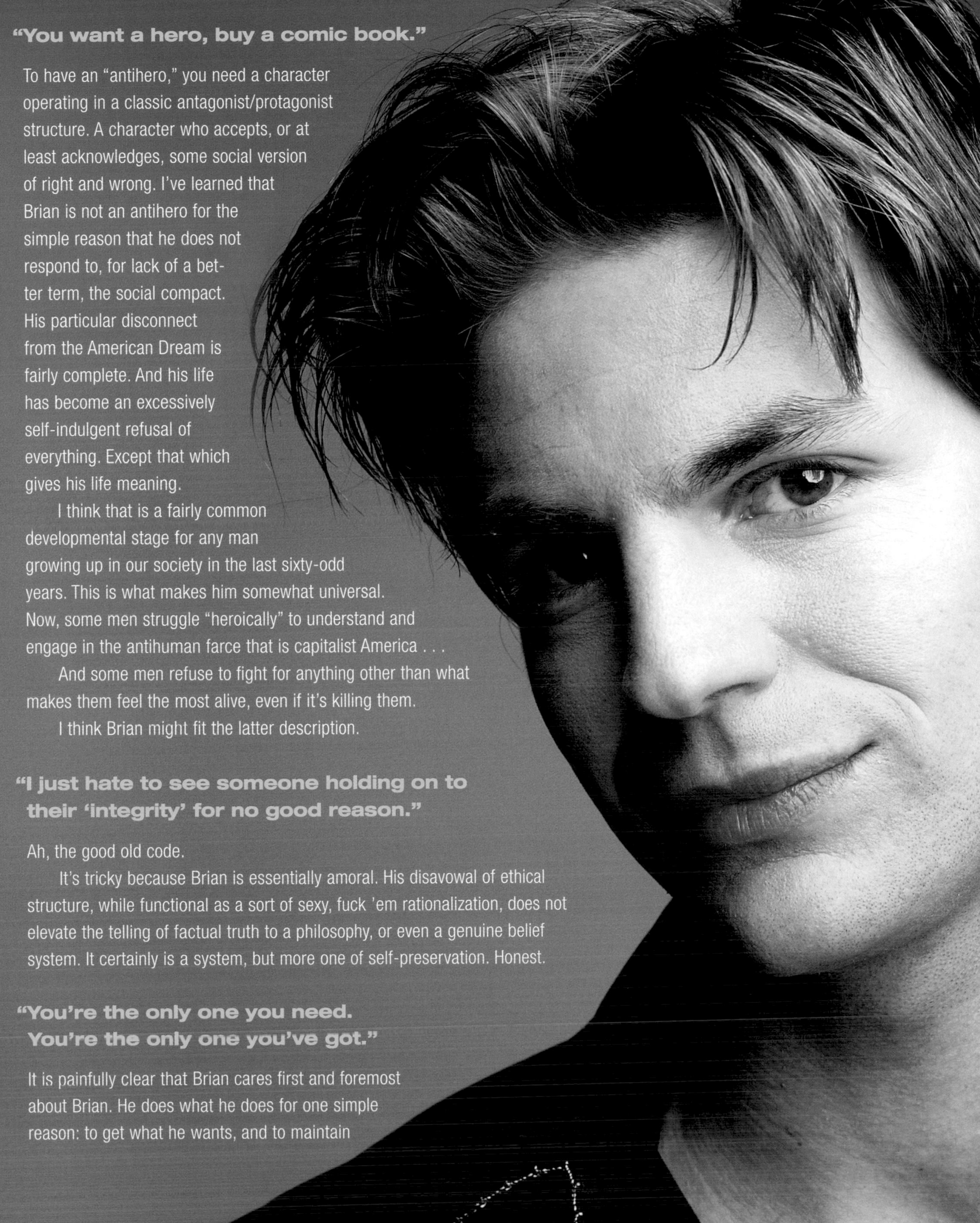

"You want a hero, buy a comic book."

To have an "antihero," you need a character operating in a classic antagonist/protagonist structure. A character who accepts, or at least acknowledges, some social version of right and wrong. I've learned that Brian is not an antihero for the simple reason that he does not respond to, for lack of a better term, the social compact. His particular disconnect from the American Dream is fairly complete. And his life has become an excessively self-indulgent refusal of everything. Except that which gives his life meaning.

I think that is a fairly common developmental stage for any man growing up in our society in the last sixty-odd years. This is what makes him somewhat universal. Now, some men struggle "heroically" to understand and engage in the antihuman farce that is capitalist America . . .

And some men refuse to fight for anything other than what makes them feel the most alive, even if it's killing them.

I think Brian might fit the latter description.

"I just hate to see someone holding on to their 'integrity' for no good reason."

Ah, the good old code.

It's tricky because Brian is essentially amoral. His disavowal of ethical structure, while functional as a sort of sexy, fuck 'em rationalization, does not elevate the telling of factual truth to a philosophy, or even a genuine belief system. It certainly is a system, but more one of self-preservation. Honest.

"You're the only one you need. You're the only one you've got."

It is painfully clear that Brian cares first and foremost about Brian. He does what he does for one simple reason: to get what he wants, and to maintain

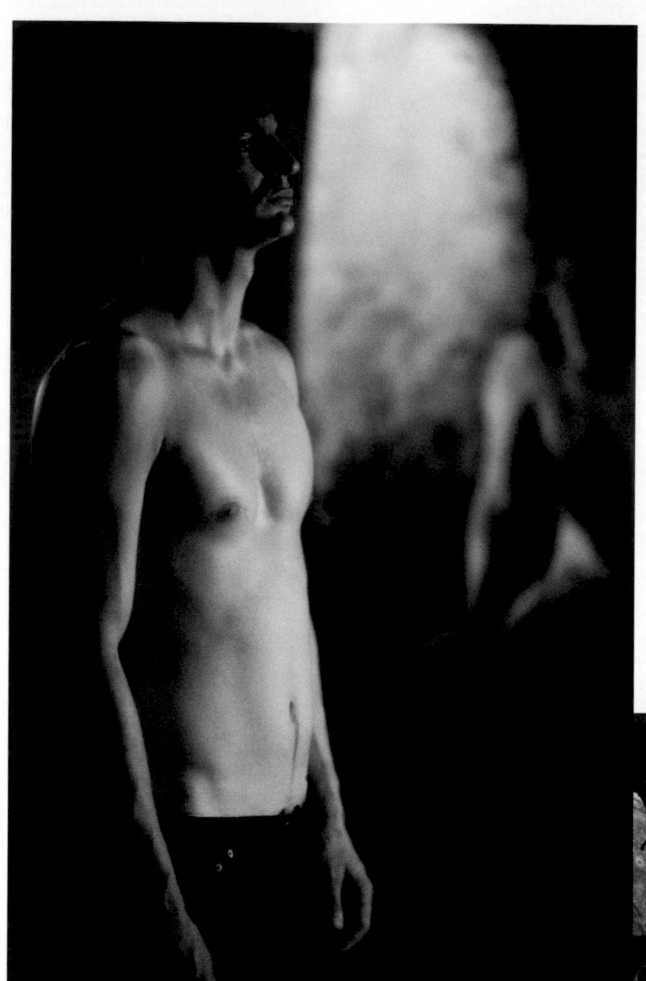

"Not every boy is lucky enough to have a mother who's equally at home in the kitchen as she is in a gay bar."

If you consider the idealized concept of "family" as people who accept and understand you for who you really are, then it would make sense for Brian to have found some version of that "ideal" in his relationship with Michael and Debbie.

That said, I think the structure is tenuous at best. And most dramatically resonant when Brian's unbearable self-absorption is rendered down by Debbie's and Michael's stubborn will to keep loving the brother/son they should have sent to hell long ago. . . .

what he perceives to be a state of control. At times, the best choices for Brian have benevolent side effects.

My desire, above all else, is for Brian to be as realistic and human as possible. So, I try, within the constraints I am given, to find a way. How, for instance, do I show the effect of the genuine, heartfelt response of Ted (episode 307) to Brian's intervening on Ted's behalf legally? After the old "It's just bizness, pal" scene, does Brian feel some inkling of self-worth? Or is he too wrapped up in his, uh, code?

I try to let something get through. And I hope that if enough gets through, there will be significant growth for Brian at least to become more self-aware. And hopefully some self-awareness will lead to deeper accessibility to his feelings toward his friends and lovers.

the covenant

BRIAN: Don't get the idea that we're some married couple, because we're not. We're not like fucking straight people. We're not like your parents. And we're not a pair of dykes marching down the aisle in matching Vera Wangs. . . . We're queers. And if we're together, it's because we want to be, not because there are locks on our doors. So if I'm out late, assume I'm doing exactly what I want to be doing. I'm fucking. And when I come home, I'll also be doing exactly what I want to do . . . coming home to you.

JUSTIN: Okay. I want some things, too. You can fuck whoever you want, as long as it's not twice. Same for me. And no names or numbers exchanged. And no matter where you are, no matter what you're doing, you always come home. By two.

BRIAN: Four.

JUSTIN: Three. One more thing . . . You don't kiss anyone on the mouth but me.

DANIEL LIPMAN: We call the scene where Justin and Brian are on the floor of Babylon coming up with the rules for their relationship "the covenant scene." That was based on the play *The Way of the World,* when the two characters Mirabell and Millamant declare that they're going to get married, "but this is what the rules are." Everybody around them was silly. There were fops and silly dames trying to comprehend how their world operates. Mirabell and Millamant knew how to maneuver through their world and so do Brian and Justin.

BRIAN

You like to rim?

JUSTIN

Oh, sure. I love it.

BRIAN

Good. Then do it.

JUSTIN

Do it?

BRIAN

Do it.

JUSTIN

Okay.

(a beat, then)

What exactly do you mean?

the anatomy of a sex scene

INT. BRIAN'S LOFT—BEDROOM—NIGHT

Brian and Justin are naked on the bed. Justin is lying on his stomach. Brian kneels over him, licking his back, going lower and lower, moving with masterful precision and expertise. He spreads Justin's legs apart, lowers his head between them.

ON JUSTIN'S FACE

As his head pops up, grinning.

BRIAN

Now you know what rimming is.

As Brian's head submerges and Justin's eyes practically roll back in his head, his back arching, fingers clutching the pillow.

It starts with the writing. Every sex scene or love scene begins on the page, and that's the first place *Queer as Folk*'s graphic sexuality had its impact on the production staff. "What we've learned is that showing sex is very much like opera," Daniel Lipman explains. "In opera, the reason people sing and go into their aria is because language can only take you so far in terms of expressing emotion. When you sing, it's expansive and that's how you express your emotion. It's the same thing with sex. We have sex for many reasons, whether it's anger, vengeance, joy, celebration, or despair."

Since the start of the series, the graphic displays of sexuality seen on *Queer as Folk* have been unlike anything else seen on TV. Sheila Hockin explains that it wasn't just the writers who needed to learn a new approach to sex. "One of the things we realized a few episodes into the first season was that a sex scene on the written page could be interpreted in many different ways. For the sake of the directors and the cast involved, we needed to be really clear about what was expected."

The realization was partially a result of bringing in day players for sexual scenes. The producers felt that in the casting they were clear with the actors about what would physically be involved. "But an awful lot of people filtered that through an understanding of what's acceptable in mainstream television in North America," Sheila admits. "They would get to set and be a little surprised at how graphic cable can be. So we'd have some nervous actors who felt that they had committed to something larger than they had really understood."

Sheila also notes the production was concerned about the comfort levels of more than just the day players. "For our lead cast who stepped into the show so bravely and have been extraordinarily courageous, we also felt that we needed to equip them with pragmatics before we went to set. So we started doing sex charts." The charts are episode breakdowns that list any kind of sexual activity. For each sex scene listed on the chart, the producers hold a meeting with the episode's director and the cast members involved in the scene.

"We first talk about what the intention of the scene is emotionally," Sheila explains. "Because that is always important and there always is an emotional intention. There's never really been a scene that was sex for the sake of sex. Then we get the director to describe how they want to shoot the scene, some of which involves interpreting from the written page. If the script says two people are making love, there are many ways that can be interpreted. There's a lot of very pragmatic considerations. So that the actors can go from 'Brian and Justin are making love' to an understanding of 'Are they in the bed? Who's on top? Who's on bottom?'"

Following the basic choreographing of the actors, the meeting moves on to the choreography of the camera. Camera positioning and angles are discussed. "The wider the camera angles, obviously, the more physically exposed the actor is," Sheila notes. Then the meeting talks about the coverage, which, generally speaking, is alternative angles and reaction shots. These are usually more comfortable for the actors because oftentimes they can put on underwear or some piece of clothing.

"Basically we treat them like stunts," Sheila explains. "If you were shooting a stunt, you'd have a meeting where everyone involved would work through it to know exactly how the stunt was going to work so that nobody would come to harm. We basically do the same thing with the sex."

Although the sex scenes are performed on a closed set with as few crew members as necessary, the entire production usually helps prep them as if they were any other scene. Surprisingly, one of the most important components is costume, and the most important wardrobe piece on *Queer as Folk* is known as the cock sock.

Costume designer Patrick Antosh explains that the birth of the cock sock came from his work on the film *American Psycho.* "There was a scene with Christian Bale running around entirely naked covered in blood. He didn't want to do full frontal nudity, so I developed a spandex pouch that fits over the entire genitalia. Then you can run around and do whatever. It also gives you courtesy if you're rubbing up against somebody or you have to do something friction-oriented, because there's just that difference between you."

The costume designer also came in handy with something one wouldn't typically associate with clothing. In a sex shop, he purchased a phalanx of soft penises that conveniently came in three sizes. "It's like a dildo except that it's not erect at all," Patrick says. "It's completely flaccid and soft and looks and feels absolutely real. We use those quite often inside of underwear and tight pants, because if somebody has to grope somebody, you don't really want to do that in a professional atmosphere. So now they're groping a piece of rubber instead."

Usually in the sex scenes, the only costumes worn by the actors—besides the cock sock—is body makeup. Considering the amount of flesh exposed in the series, this is the area where the greatest amount of trust needs to be established between the actors and the crew. "For actors' comfort we had a privacy curtain installed in the makeup trailer," key makeup artist Stephen Lynch explains. "One of us is usually there during carnal scenes. You have to approach it as professionally as possible. If they have an obvious bruising or tattoos, we have to get rid of those and cover them up. We just try to be gentle with them."

The makeup artists are not just there to cover up. They also work to enhance the look of the scene by adding a little faux sweat or perspiration for the hot and heavy scenes or maybe a glisten of oil. Stephen also relies on a product called body butter to give the bodies an unusual sheen that almost makes the skin glow. Once the makeup is applied, one of the makeup artists, often Stephen himself, is on set by the monitors to do touch-ups. The makeup artist, like the rest of the crew, tries to stay out of the actors' sight lines so as not to make the actors uncomfortable.

Hair is also a concern during the sex scenes. In many cases the hairstylists have to develop a structured but methodically placed freshly fucked bed head to look natural on the screen. Key hairstylist Clara Dinunzio explains that the amount of work that goes into hair for these scenes "depends on the sex. Love scenes will be softer, sweeter. If it's a heavy scene that would be more than twenty minutes, I would just go in and mess it up and make it look very real—not like soap opera hair, but messy. Real sex with a hot, sweaty, big fuck-knot in the back."

As the actors are being physically prepared, the director is working with the director of photography (DP) to set the scene. This is where the realities of filming are addressed while creating unique sex scenes every week. "For obvious reasons we can't show an erect penis," explains DP Thom Best. "The sex scenes are highly choreographed because of what you can't see and what we want to allude to and what we want you to see. You always try to make it as visually interesting as possible. You want to whet people's appetite and leave them wanting more."

Once everything is prepped, the set is closed and the actors take their places. Each actor approaches the sex scenes and love scenes differently, but with *Queer as Folk* it's not just the male actors who are expected to perform. "To me what always makes a great love scene, or just a great acting scene, is to have specific choices attached to it," Michelle Clunie explains. "It's never a love scene that's just a love scene. To me it's always 'What kind of lovemaking is it?' Once I figure that out, I can start to work on how that psychology manifests itself into behavior. To me it's always about the specific choices. The more work you do on a scene as an actress—especially a love scene—the less self-conscious you'll be. If you're so consumed with all these different choices to make that you're spinning five different plates, you don't have time to be self-conscious. The last thing I'm thinking of is that somebody just saw up my snatch, because I can't. I don't have time."

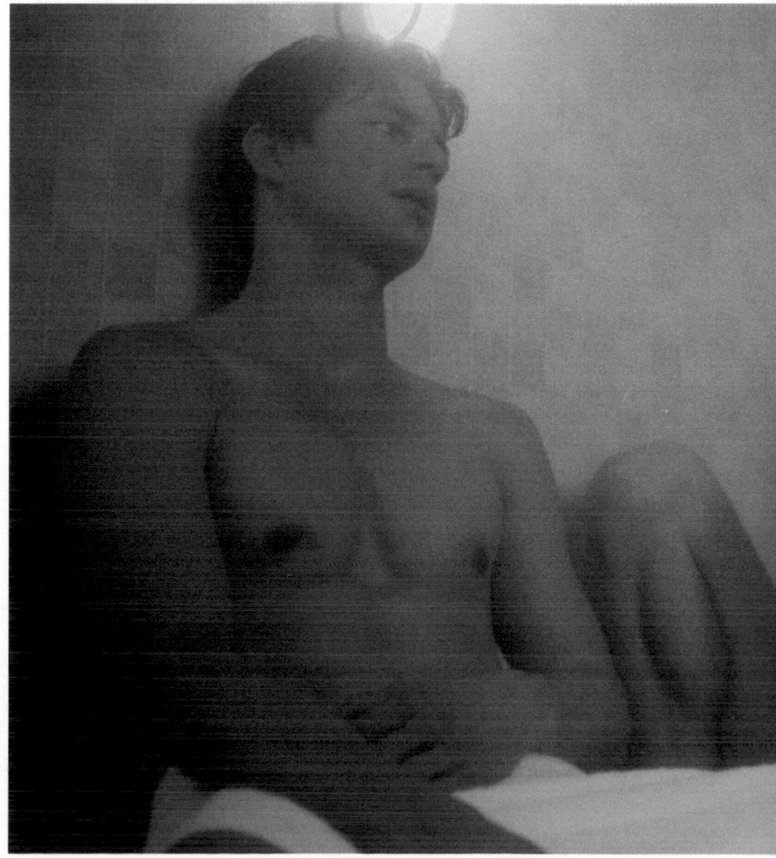

michelle clunie as melanie marcus

"I always talk about Lindsay and Melanie together," Daniel Lipman says. "Not to marginalize the women on the show, but because they were always conceived as equals. Once again we're in a situation where we're dealing with a different kind of gay relationship from the others on the show. It doesn't matter that Lindsay stayed at home with Gus for the first two years. Lindsay and Melanie are very much emotional equals." Yet, that same equality has been most problematic for Melanie when it comes to their relationship.

It would be easy to cast Melanie as the stronger of the two in the pairing, but that would be far from the case. Throughout the series, Melanie struggled to assert her equal role in their family, beginning with losing the opportunity to name her own son. This eventually led her to seek refuge in the bed of another woman to make up for what she had been missing. But only when she and Lindsay realized that they both needed to give a little to maintain that equality (aside from what Brian had to give, too) could they reconcile.

In addition to being part of a couple, Melanie is also a unique individual. She's a professional businesswoman with strong ties to her religion and her family. Melanie is a fighter who tries to stay within the letter of the law, but admits that the legal system has its failings. One of the most active voices on the show when it

melanie

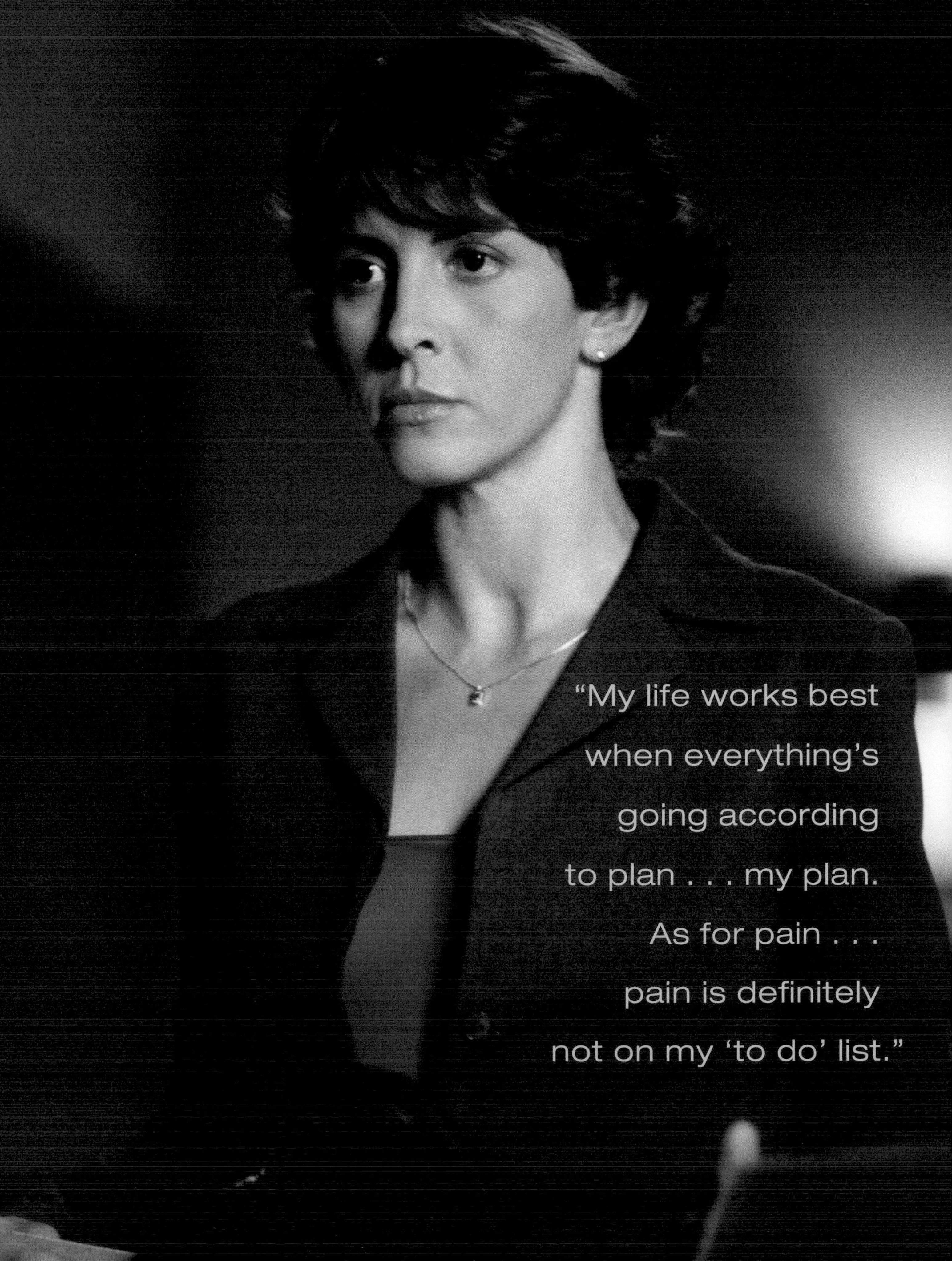
"My life works best
when everything's
going according
to plan . . . my plan.
As for pain . . .
pain is definitely
not on my 'to do' list."

comes to gay rights, she avoids speechifying to make her point, instead relying more on a velvet-fist approach.

"Melanie is a very strong woman," Ron Cowen says. "But, I don't think of her as butch. I just don't see her that way. She's not trying to be an imitation man. I find her a strong but womanly woman who simply defines herself by being an independent person."

In the third season, Melanie rounds out that strength by making the surprising decision to carry their next child, proving that she can both bring home the bacon and fry it up in a pan. But she handles her bun in the oven in true Melanie fashion, at first fighting against relaxing one part of her life before relenting to find the perfect balance. In that respect, she is the true embodiment of the modern woman.

melanie and michelle: face-to-face

"Well, I'm Jewish, and after neo-Nazis there's nothing that Jews fear more than silence."

I come from theater and I love taking a big bite out of stuff. I love playing Antigone and I love playing Maggie in *After the Fall.* When I saw this role, I recognized it as an amazing role. This was a revolutionary character that you don't get to see on television all the time. I love to act, but it's more that just being an actress. I've always wanted to be a revolutionary spirit. I want to be a "first." I want to do things that are first, that are pioneering, that are going where no man has gone before. That's what drew me to it. I like that spirit in people. I like people that push the envelope and take things to a place where it's not safe. And this show is not safe at all.

I don't even know what I connected with in Melanie. Maybe it was that she had to be a fighter her whole life. When you think of a Jewish lesbian lawyer, this is not a woman that has had the road paved before her. She has had to pioneer in her own way. I definitely relate to that. I think I've tried to act very tough when in reality I'm such a softy on the inside it's pathetic. I see that in Melanie. That's what I connected with. She's so tough, but it's almost put on in a way because underneath she covers up how deeply she feels for her family and how things mean so much to her. It's very much how I am, so I understand how much people mean to me and how seriously I take my relationships and my friendships.

When something does happen, I take it very personally and I get very hurt, but I always put on this tough act. I liked that about the character a lot because I thought what a beautiful, complex, interesting character filled with so much humanity in this interesting package. It's revolutionary to see this character on television and it's an honor to play her. I love Melanie.

"Don't fuck with Mother Nature, huh? Well, I'm here to tell her . . . don't fuck with me!"

At first I couldn't believe Melanie was going to get pregnant. When the producers first told me, I was a bit shocked. They had hinted the previous season that it might happen, so I wasn't completely shocked, but I couldn't believe when they really said they were going to go through with it. I could almost not wrap my head around it, but then I allowed it to sink in. After the first minute, I thought, "Okay . . . okay . . . oh, wow, that's really fascinating. That's a great choice to take a character and turn her inside out and make her do something that no one would ever think that she would really do." Then, of course, I had to fill it with my own personal feelings about it.

I came up with this take that there's a part of her that has to win. There's that lawyer part of her that has to be right and has to win every argument. She will go to any length not to lose, whether it's in love or losing face or losing an argument or losing her son. So she's a fighter. She couldn't raise her first son the way she wanted to raise him. She couldn't raise him Jewish and she was pushed around quite a bit and told how to raise the son—she was even told what to name him.

There's a part of me that thinks this is Melanie's way of saying, "I will have a son, goddammit, and I will raise him my fucking way by my fucking religion and no one will stop me because *I will win!"* I know that's an almost pathological choice, but in real life we make these choices all the time. People often have babies because of some egotistical reason and not just for the fact that they want to raise a great human being and contribute to the world. They want to see a little version of themselves walking around. I think for Melanie there's a part of her that wants to raise a child and have more control over the raising of that child.

"Not that I give a shit about saving your ass, but it might be amusing to have you indebted to me for the rest of your life."

The relationship with Brian is complex. Sometimes I make fun of the relationship between Melanie and Brian because it's comical. These people hate each other so much, but on some level—I can't speak for Gale's character—but Melanie has respect for Brian. I think it's just having respect for someone who makes bold choices in his life. Whether it's right or wrong, he makes a choice and knows who he is, and that's admirable. So I think there's definitely a certain level where she respects him, but she would never let anyone know that.

I remember going over one of the scripts first season with someone whose opinion I admire very much and he said to me, "These two characters—you and this Brian character—are the two monoliths in a way. They are very strong characters that clash. It's a very important dynamic." I've always felt so. I've felt like that clash was strongest in the first season and then it became softer in the second season, but I think it's always there rumbling beneath the surface.

"I wanted a fuck and boy did I get fucked."

I thought the affair story line was great and it was right on. I think Melanie felt as though Lindsay had shut her out so much and so she had that justification on top of the justification that Brian was not treating her with respect. She was feeling absolutely no love, unappreciated, and really questioning why she was really in the relationship. She felt that she was with a woman that doesn't even respect her enough to ask her feelings on something as simple as what to name the baby.

I think Melanie is a giver and she gave and gave and gave, and then she just snapped. She didn't stand up for herself as she should have because when in love you bend and get mushy and even the strongest of us

fall in the face of love. So it wasn't necessarily ethical what she did, but it was inevitable. I think that she almost had to do that. She had to give up the relationship in a sense to get it back. I think the relationship still has problems, but no relationship is perfect.

"It made me realize that despite our ups and downs—and the occasional dry spell—you're the only one I ever want to be with."

The great thing about Melanie and Lindsay is that I see their relationship as one big playground for them to both learn. That's the beauty of it. They may scream at each other, they may get mad at each other, they may screw around on each other, but through that they will always come out wiser. I think the sad part about relationships nowadays is that no one is willing to work through anything. They give up. I think the great thing about Melanie and Lindsay is that they're not perfect as people. If you're given the chance to evolve and you have someone that loves you, it's a great gift. I think they give that to each other. They give each other that room to figure out their own journeys.

"Wait. We need to experience this moment, recognize the magnitude of it all."

The first season felt like a bunch of theater actors getting together and doing this Equity-waiver play. We're all running around in our jeans and tennis shoes running lines in the back alley someplace, getting together for

dinner and talking about our characters. It wasn't like we were showing up to memorize our lines and then going to The Ivy for lunch. We were in Toronto on location. The first season all we had was each other, so the work was very intimate.

The show sent us to a gay and lesbian expo in New York for three days after we finished the first season. We went to a press conference and this had been the first time we had all been somewhere together since the show had been on the air in the States. We had no idea what was going on—if people liked it, if people hated it. We walked into this room and there were three hundred people there. As soon as the cast and producers walked up on the platform, everyone stood up and started cheering—and it was the press, not specifically our fans. All of our mouths dropped. We were absolutely shocked by the reception.

Afterwards security took us to this booth in the Javits Center where we were going to sign autographs. When we went inside this booth, hundreds of people lined up. This was the first time we had ever experienced anything like this. This woman was standing six people out from me and she had tears rolling down her face and she was screaming, "Melanie! Melanie!" I'm sitting there going, "Oh my God, I can't believe this is happening. It's too surreal."

After that they rushed us into a van. And there were people all around the van waving and saying, "Hi!" Then we were driving back to the hotel and I remember it was dead silent. We were all shaken to the core. We were all staring forward and no one said a word because I think we were all in shock.

the wedding

MELANIE: **Honey, I wasn't sure we'd make it here today. But thanks to our friends—I should say, family—not even the stars or the planets could keep us from exchanging our vows. I love you, Lindsay Peterson. I will fight for you. I will protect you. You are my *beshert*.**

LINDSAY: **Melanie, with so much love and support around us, I really do believe that there is no obstacle, no problem, we can't overcome. Together, in friendship and in love, our hearts will be eternally united. I love you, Melanie Marcus.**

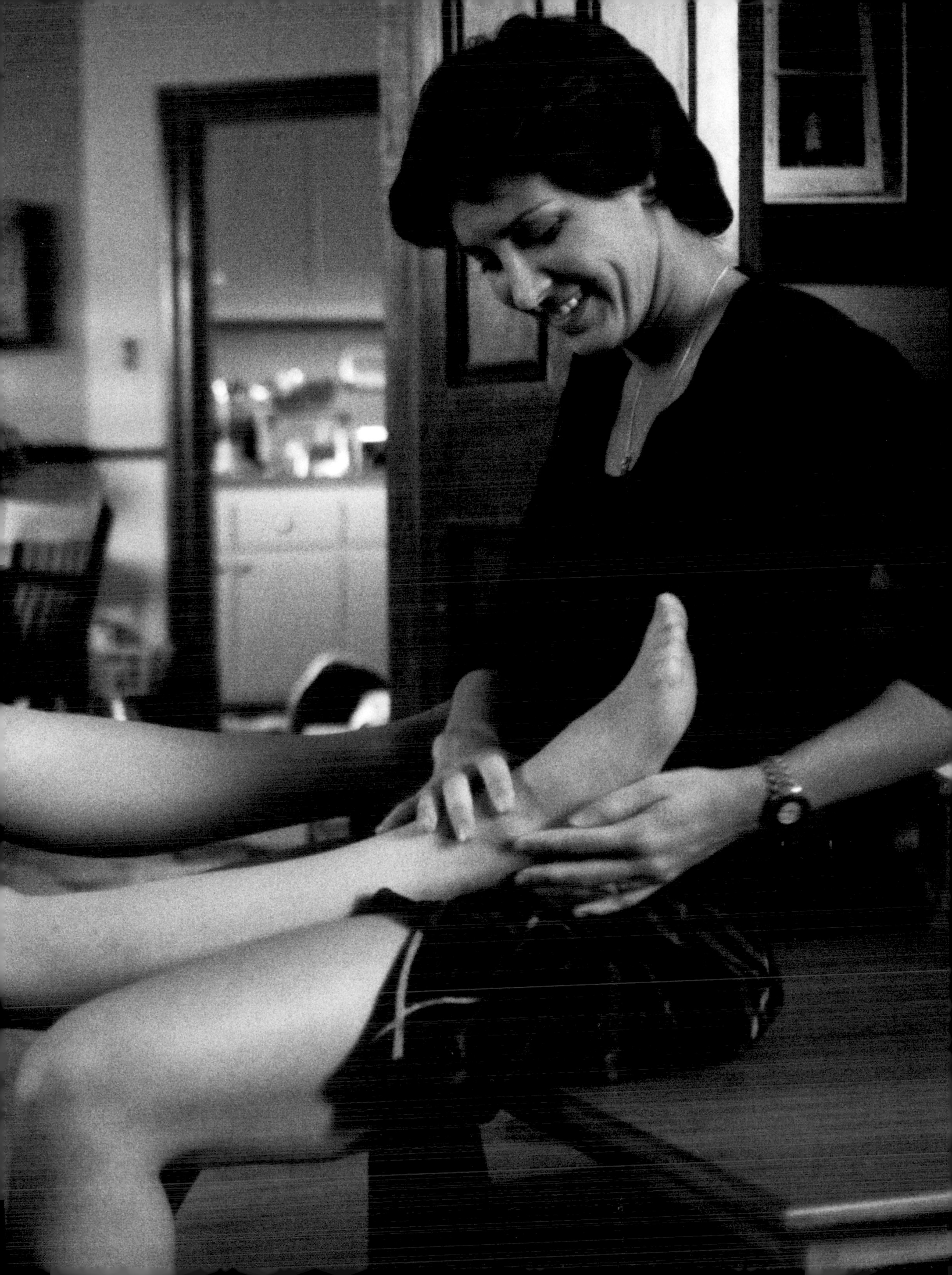

thea gill as **lindsay peterson**

Lindsay Peterson is easily one of the most deceptive characters on *Queer as Folk.* On the surface, she's the harmless mom who wants nothing more than to keep the peace, but she's also got the heart of a rebel who's not afraid to grab life—and Brian—by the balls when she has to.

"Lindsay is like the earth mother," Ron Cowen says. "She is warm and generous and good-hearted. But I also think she really understands Brian and part of her yearns for that outrageous behavior. She doesn't really express it so much in her own life, but I think she lives through him in a way. She's the one who reminds him, 'No apologies, no regrets,' like she did in the wedding episode." It's an interesting contradiction in that she can be the buttoned-up daughter of a conservative couple in the morning, the half-naked party girl in the afternoon, and a mom throughout the day.

One of the most important facets of Lindsay's character is obviously her relationship with Melanie. From their first scene on-screen together, Melanie is holding Lindsay, who, in turn, is holding their child. Without words, they painted a picture of the happy couple and defined their roles in the relationship in that moment. But that was also a deception. Although it would be easy to write them off as Melanie being the masculine one in the relationship while Lindsay is the feminine, over the three

lindsay

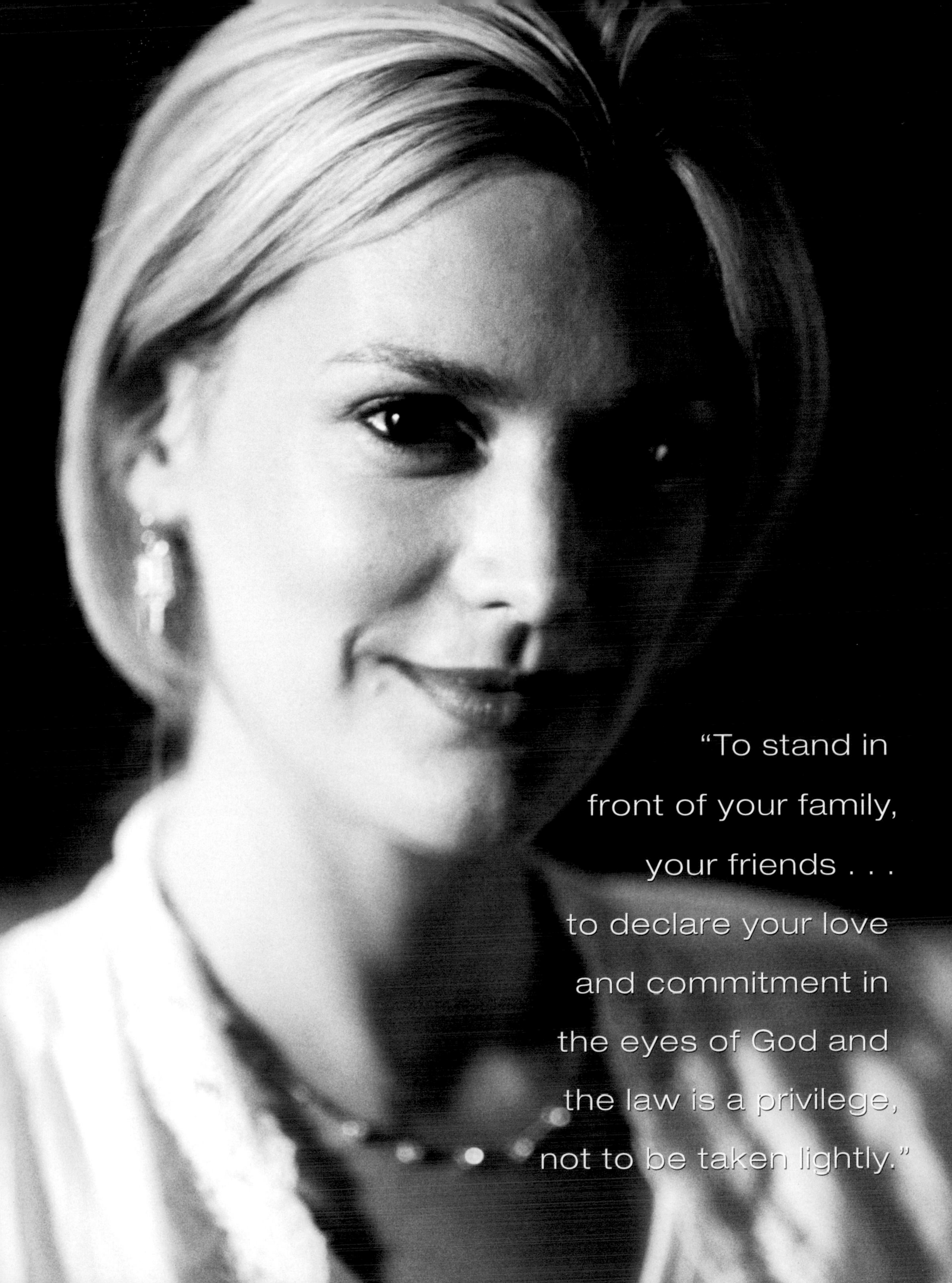
"To stand in
front of your family,
your friends . . .
to declare your love
and commitment in
the eyes of God and
the law is a privilege,
not to be taken lightly."

seasons it has become quite obvious that they do not fall into such simple parameters.

"We always try to calibrate Thea and Michelle in their performances to make sure they remain equal," Daniel Lipman explains. "Because the baby is often in their scenes, you would always see Lindsay in a chair with Gus while Melanie is walking around. Visually, that gives Melanie more power and it makes Lindsay appear subservient because she's always sitting. So we changed it in the third season. We put her in a stronger wardrobe and we got her walking around. We got the two of them really confronting each other. This is not about butch and femme. It's about two women who are equals. And we're very fortunate that the two actresses adore each other."

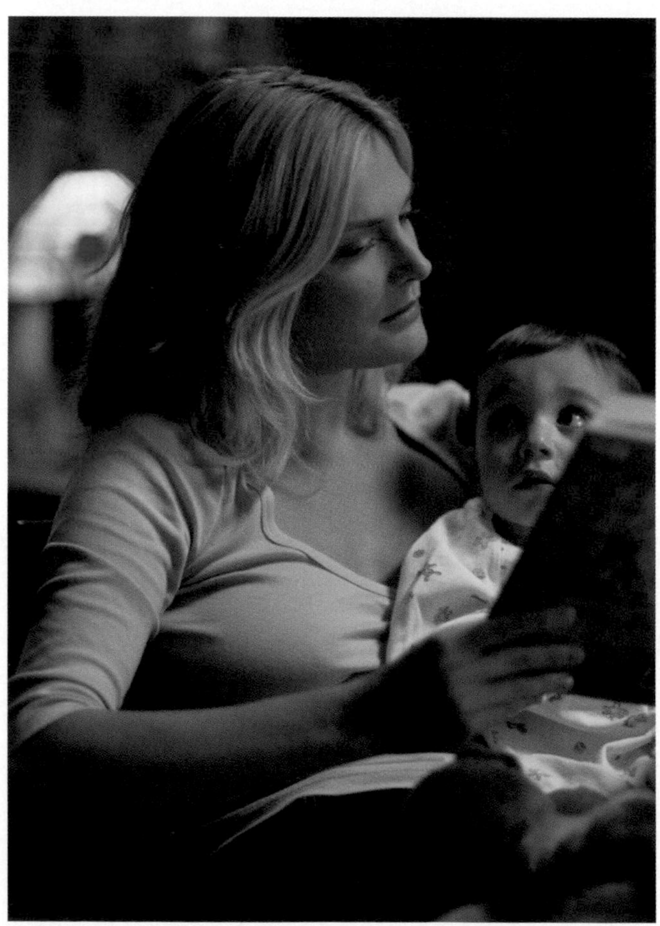

The lipstick this lesbian wears is muted and meant to accessorize, not accentuate. She doesn't fall into the neat little stereotype often seen in Hollywood representations of girl-on-girl love. Lindsay is equal parts mom, lover, mentor, friend, and fighter. She is redefining the role of the modern family as well as modern love.

lindsay and thea: face-to-face

"All I know is, if I talk, I may say something I regret."

Lindsay's gone through little minichanges and growths. At the beginning of season one, we see Lindsay as very much a compassionate, empathetic, instinctive kind of person. She's always trying to keep things under control and trying to keep appearances up to a certain degree. I think that as we go along, that starts to unravel for her. She doesn't know how to deal with the triangle of Melanie, Brian, and herself. In the second season she breaks that down a bit and starts to find her backbone so she sticks up for herself and can grab Brian by the balls.

I think some people wondered where that came from. To a lot of viewers it may have come out of the blue, but there's a reason why she likes Brian and there's a reason why she likes Melanie. She has difficulty expressing that a lot. Lindsay has difficulty because she comes from a very traditional, conservative background and she needs to fight that. She does fight it in the second season, especially with her mother and father.

The proposal at her sister's wedding was a big pronouncement for Lindsay to make. It was a big step in terms of finding her strength and her self-respect. And in the third season she becomes even stronger. She even becomes a bit of a bitch. There's this moment where I'm doing the scene where I'm firing someone and I thought, "I can't believe I've come this way. Lindsay's actually firing someone." It was weird to play that out, but very liberating. To actually fire someone and cause someone to lose their job. You look at her in that scene and then go back to seeing her in the hospital with Brian and Melanie. It's like, "Whoa, what a one-hundred-eighty-degree turn."

"When are you going to figure out that Justin really loves you? He's young, but at your age, that's a good thing. And Michael would give up his life for you. . . . And I love you, too. You think you're going to find that on Madison Avenue?"

I think the friendships are one of the most beautiful aspects of the show. In a sense I think that is the show. Yeah, it's about sex, too, but I think the show wouldn't be as successful if it didn't have the underlying bond of friendship between all our characters. That's what ties us all together and it's a genuine friendship. Peter once told us that someone had said to him, "Oh, I can't believe all you guys would be friends. You guys are all such different characters. That doesn't seem real." I think the fact that we're all very different and unique is the reason we bond together and what makes such a complementary group.

Every season we see a different friendship develop. In the third season, suddenly there's a friendship developing between Melanie, Lindsay, and Michael, which we never really saw before. We knew that Lindsay particularly knew Michael because of the friendship she has with Brian, but we never saw that happening onscreen. So, in a way every year the different friendships have been fleshed out and carried on.

"Brian Kinney sacrificing for others? Trapped in a hideous display of sentimentality? I'd lose all faith, all hope. What kind of gift is that?"

On the message boards and on all the forums, there are times when the women viewers of the show are highly critical of the relationship between Brian and Lindsay. I find it interesting that they're very upset about it. A lot of viewers on the forum think that Lindsay wants to be with Brian, but I've never interpreted it that way. I saw that relationship right from the start as a purely platonic love. I think it's nice to see that they have moments of intimacy, but it's always based on an emotional, deeper connection. In real life we find those people and we don't have sexual relationships with them, but we love them for how they make us feel and what they give us. There's a very big gift that Brian gives Lindsay and hopefully Lindsay gives back to Brian.

I think what makes that relationship special is that they won't be that couple that the audience is used to seeing. They have something other than that. It comes and it goes, but when Brian and Lindsay do have scenes together, they say a lot in little ways. I like it that it's not a sexual relationship; of course, Melanie thinks it is and will never be able to know for sure. Her character's always insecure of that relationship and very suspicious—and rightly so because it's a tough one to understand for a lot of people, especially since there has been a history. Brian and Lindsay have done something, and because they have done something at a time when they were younger, it sort of bonded them. They came out together, essentially, and that's how we've been playing it. I think when you discover your sexuality and you experience your first love, you'll always remember the friend you discovered it with. No matter how many years down the road, whether or not you keep in touch, that is the person who will bring you back to that place and time where your life changed.

"It was just a spontaneous, I-don't-know-how-the-hell-it-happened-but-there-you-are-doing-it sort of thing."

Yes, the love scenes are technical, and, yes, we map them out, and there's a closed set and everything's very orchestrated and organized, but there was no doubt of the fact that you're making love with another person. It is acting and you are in your role, but your bodies are intermingling in some way. That is something that actors do, but most people who don't act wouldn't do that. The beauty of being a performer is that you get to go into realms of places that are completely erotic or exotic. You have to do it professionally in a systematic way, but at the same time lend yourself over to the moment. That can be weird at first. Then you just throw yourself into the moment when you shoot the scene and surrender. You have to surrender so there is a moment of real intimacy.

As the years go along, not only do Melanie and Lindsay have more of a history together and get closer together, but Thea and Michelle have gotten closer together. It's funny how both our lives mirror our characters' lives in a way. We definitely bring a lot of our characters to our real friendship. Sometimes it's hard to draw the line between our characters and ourselves, but in a way, that has deepened our marriage onscreen as well as our marriage as friends offscreen. I like the relationship a lot.

I think the most difficult part about love scenes is the anticipation, especially with someone you don't know very well. Because Michelle and I have known each other for so long now, that anticipation is not as strong as it was in the beginning or when we had to stage the threesome with Leda. That was the most difficult love scene for me. I didn't know what to do with it. I had questions about why it was happening and why Lindsay would choose to do it. For the first time in the show I felt stuck over how I was going to act something. Now, in hindsight, I wonder why I got stuck. We had a good director on it and we spent a lot of time shooting it, even though the scene came down to a few seconds' worth. It was definitely a very difficult scene.

"Our wedding's been methodically and systematically deconstructed. If you ask me, somebody up there doesn't think we should get married. Maybe there's a reason. Maybe that's because people like us aren't supposed to get married."

A show like ours is either going to be viewed positively with open arms or it's going to be viewed negatively and critically. I know we were all prepared for a bit of a

backlash and sometimes comments are pretty vicious, but I don't know why.

The most vicious reaction I got was when we were on our *Queer as Folk* float at the New York Pride Parade. I remember we were dancing and having a great time when I saw this man give me the finger and he would not stop. As our float kept on going along, he kept on following us and giving us the finger the whole time. I kind of lost it and was screaming to him, "Don't do that! Don't do that!" I was stunned. I had never had such a direct hate. He was looking me in the eyes. I felt like it was directed right at me.

A lot of the letters I get are letters of thanks for taking the role. When they were trying to cast the show, a lot of actors didn't audition. I guess I have always been fortunate enough to be in a community of friends who have been liberal and open-minded. I've never encountered such hatred until I started to work on the show. Then I started to realize what it felt like. It was shocking. But then there's the wonderful response, the loving response, the intelligent and supportive response. Those are much more important. Those are the ones that are going to stay with me. And hopefully that's eventually what will last and be the overall memory of the show.

the look

Characters start with the writing. Then the actors get the script and assume the roles with the help of the directors and producers. But they are not the only ones with input. The artists involved in dressing and making up the actors also help create their characters. If it's true that "the clothes make the man," then much can be said for the artisans who make the characters. Key makeup artist Stephen Lynch, costume designer Patrick Antosh (above, left), first-season key hairstylist Michael Pfister, and third-season key hairstylist Clara Dinunzio discuss "The Look" of the Liberty Avenue gang.

emmett

STEPHEN LYNCH: With most of the guys I like to make it look like they're not wearing makeup. I like to take a little bit more of a filmic approach to it as if their faces are going to be blown up forty feet. The exception is probably Emmett. If he's at a club, Emmett would absolutely wear gloss and put shimmer on his cheeks occasionally or smudge out his eyes or wear some neon colors. I took my cue on that from our background performers, because a lot of them came made up. I asked if that was just for the show and they said, "No, I always carry this base and this lip gloss."

ted

MICHAEL PFISTER: We started off with something a little more like a Caesar cut on Scott, but it was so hot in the summer and it just wasn't lasting through the shoots. So I changed a little bit and he started wearing a bit of a mock crew cut or a little bit of a mock flattop on him. We gave him a little point in front and kept the sides and back really tight and clean. The thing with gay men is that they always seem to look like they've had a fresh haircut.

CLARA DINUNZIO: Emmett and Ted have changed a lot. They've gotten a lot funkier. Ted has come out a lot, too. It depends on who you're going out with. When you're dating someone, you end up dressing like him a lot because you're influenced by that person. So he's gotten a little bit funkier since he's been dating Emmett and we reflect that with his hair, too.

melanie and lindsay

STEPHEN LYNCH: I try to keep Melanie and Lindsay more grounded. It's very popular to be lipstick lesbian in Hollywood, but I think in Pittsburgh it's different. Most of the lesbians are pretty down-to-earth about how they look, so we're trying to keep that reality-based. They wear makeup, but we don't want it to look like makeup. Personally, I don't think makeup is a big part of their arsenal. They don't think that way. It's not a war paint. That's not how they're going to win this war. They'll do it with their brains and their personalities and not have to rely on that. I don't think a lot of actresses would go for that, but Thea and Michelle do.

MICHAEL PFISTER: When Michelle arrived from Los Angeles, her hair was very long. It was down past her shoulders with blond highlights. She looked like the quintessential girlfriend on any show. We needed to turn her into something a lot more powerful than that and ended up cutting off most of her hair. I think we spent about three hours and it was traumatic for both of us. We went through a couple different looks as we gradually got to where we wanted to be. As we left the trailer, we started to walk and then we turned around and said, "God, we have to have a cigarette before we show everybody." It was such a dramatic change for her, but it was perfect for her and the character, and everyone fell in love with it right away. It was the most dramatic change out of all the actors in terms of developing the character for them.

PATRICK ANTOSH: There's a big fashion change midseason in year three when the dynamic in their family changes. Lindsay gets a real new look that I'm thrilled with and Thea's thrilled with. We're all happy with that. Over all three years as their relationship goes through highs and lows, they dress very similar when things are going very well. When there's a crux in their relationship and they're not on the same level is when I divert their clothing so that visually you see a break in the relationship. I try to use harsher colors if there's a conflict and mellow tones if there's not.

ben

PATRICK ANTOSH: Bobby is the easiest person to dress. I mean, the guy's built like a horse. He's just got a perfect body, so anything off the rack fits. There's a conscious effort to cover up his body a lot of the times to keep the scene from turning sexual. When Michael and Ben go to bed at night, somebody's got a shirt on if there's a serious matter going on in their life. That's so that you don't feel a sexual tension. There are other times when things are very smooth and you'll see them walking around in Jockey shorts or whatever.

justin

STEPHEN LYNCH: Justin we've simplified a little more because he's actually changing quite a lot. His face is changing so much every year and he's getting a bit more of a tougher look in a really positive way. He's getting a little toughened up so we've laid off a little of the makeup, especially a product which I call "flush of youth." We don't use it anymore. He doesn't need that natural flush that kids get when they're embarrassed or shy. Now his face sort of says it all. He doesn't need much help from us.

PATRICK ANTOSH: I definitely tried to play up the dynamic and the controversy between him and Brian. I put him in tight T-shirts. Then there was a maturity that came after the horrible bashing. So I've matured him up and I'm not going back because you can't take his innocence back. Once it's gone, it's gone.

michael

MICHAEL PFISTER: Hal basically maintained the same look he arrived with. His hair was already conservative like the character. The only thing we tried to do in the beginning was to tweak a piece at the crown to make him look just a little bit offbeat and a little bit corny. He's always the guy that's just not making the grade from being hip.

PATRICK ANTOSH: Michael is a child inside a man's body, and that's part of the reason he's so popular. It's almost like a Marilyn Monroe quality. There's a sexuality that comes of being that innocent. So his clothes actually play on the juvenile side. He's in primary colors a lot, with short-sleeved shirts and bigger pants that make his demeanor look smaller. He doesn't have a small body, but it keeps him innocent looking, though not in a naive way, because Michael's not stupid. He looks at the world through rose-colored glasses.

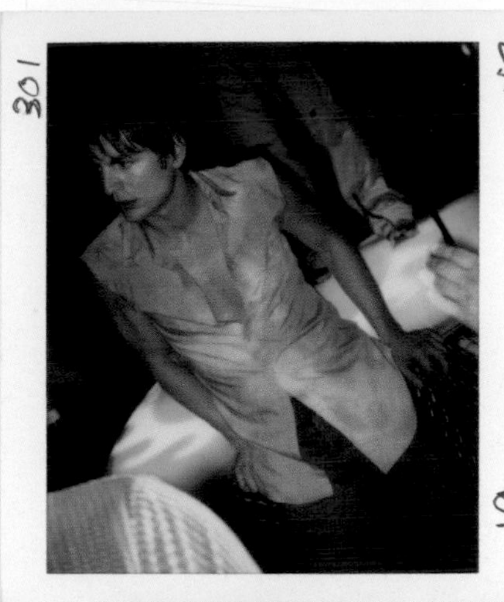

brian

STEPHEN LYNCH: If you think of Brian, he likes to be low maintenance. He doesn't want to look like he spends an inordinate amount of time on himself and sort of pulls it all together with a minimum of fuss, although privately he's more into it. He doesn't like to have a heavily styled look so we keep that very simple. We keep him clean and great looking, which isn't difficult, and we do the same for Hal with Mikey.

MICHAEL PFISTER: Gale and Hal were probably closest to what they were going to look like. Gale's personality lent itself a great deal to the character of Brian in terms of having that bit of rebel feel about him with a bit of a James Dean thing going on. His hair was a bit longer and sort of unkempt, and we just wanted to go with something that was long on top and something that could be messed around. Brian needed to look like he was just freshly fucked and out of bed all the time.

debbie

STEPHEN LYNCH (below): I get to have a bit of fun with Debbie. She's so great . . . the colors that she wears, the outrageous outfits. Sharon Gless is a very beautiful woman. I think of the things we do to her and people must think we're just horrible. She'll have bra straps showing, there's something hanging over the back, and she'll have tights that she shouldn't wear. This is her statement and her armor to a degree. I think she'd go further if we let her. But I think she likes to play and I think she's got lots of queens for friends.

PATRICK ANTOSH: There are times when Debbie has a T-shirt on that says nothing, and that will be because of the dramatic essence of the scene. I don't want it to be taken away from by a snappy one-liner. I also don't ask the directors to focus on the T-shirt so it actually becomes a bit of a game for the people watching the show to try to figure out what that one said. She's a hard one to dress. It's a way-larger-than-life character. I question myself all the time thinking, "Is it too much?" But honest to God, I'll go into a mall and then see a person that I know if I brought them to a producer, they'd say, "Nope, that's not real."

scott lowell as **ted schmidt**

"Poor Ted."

It's the one constant on *Queer as Folk.* Almost every episode has a moment where the viewer is thinking those very words. Ted Schmidt may eke his way to the top of the heap and finally find happiness with a successful porn site or true love with a close friend, but soon enough it's guaranteed to come crashing down around him. But the biggest problem is that the self-abusive character was doomed from the start.

"I was a big proponent of Ted dying," Daniel Lipman admits. In the British series the "Ted" character died of a similar drug overdose that *only* sends Ted into a coma in the current incarnation of the show. Of course, in the British series the equivalent characters of Emmett, Melanie, and Lindsay were also quite minor, so there was definitely precedent for making a change, but Dan wasn't too keen on that particular alteration.

Dan remembers: "There was some character in the pilot of *Hill Street Blues* that was killed and we were shocked to see it, because when you first introduce characters, you're presenting what your world is going to be on this series." And Dan wanted to have that same kind of shock value with this show. "Then, of course,

"Oh, I think God appreciates it even more . . . because He created you in His image. At least that's what I was always taught. And since God is love and God doesn't make mistakes, then you must be exactly the way He wants you to be . . . the way He intended you to be. And that goes for every person, every planet, every mountain, every grain of sand, every song, every tear, and every faggot. We're *all* His, Emmett. And He loves us all."

we met Scott Lowell," he goes on to say. "And we fell in love with him. So when you fall in love with Scott, you can't just toss him away."

Pretty soon, Ted proved to be a useful character for the writers. He and Emmett made a wonderful team to comment on the action. They were the Greek chorus. In the first season, he was more of a grounding force compared to some of the more outrageous things happening around him. But he also provided a lovable loser for the audience to cheer for, knowing that they never really wanted to see him succeed, because it's always nice to see someone who is worse off than you.

Ron Cowen describes Ted's appeal as being "that aspect of a lot of people who have a lot of insecurity and lack of self-confidence in terms of their lives and their sexuality. Until the third season, Ted had been going after the wrong people. Club boys and gym bunnies and muscle guys aren't going to be interested in Ted, but that's what Ted was interested in. He set himself up to be rejected, and in some ways he thrived on that rejection as an affirmation of his own lack of self-worth the way a lot of people do. To me Ted's journey from boy to man is finding the self-respect or confidence in himself, appreciating the many good qualities he does have as a person."

His most interesting arc has to be his descent into the addiction to crystal meth. Though it would seem unlikely that, after surviving a drug-induced coma, he would ever touch another drug again, it actually makes perfect sense. When his series of failures finally led him to what seemed to be rock bottom, he made the one decision that would allow him to go even further into despair. But, in the end of the third season, that story line allowed him to experience the one thing he never truly felt before: hope.

ted and scott: face-to-face

"Everything we do—even the clothes we wear—is a conscious or, worse yet, unconscious attempt to get laid."

The difficulty about a character like Ted is that he is the guy who—more than anybody else—is constantly searching for something. Everyone else seems to be able to find their way or at least know somewhat where they're going. When you're that kind of person, especially in a dramatic television series, invariably you can never get fully what you want or the story's done. That's something I've had to make peace with, because it can be tough.

The difficult part is the initial connection I had with Ted and still continue to have with him. I really love the guy and it is sometimes very hard for me to watch the tapes of this show. I have enough of a separation between him and me to watch it, and I just feel terrible for him and it really makes me sad. He's a guy who wears his heart on his sleeve so it's going to get sneezed on a lot. The trick with him is that you want to see him happy, but take some pleasure in seeing him fail.

"I saw you . . . fucking. When I woke up. And I thought, 'I'm in hell and this is my punishment . . . watching Brian Kinney fucking for all eternity.'"

Even with the sexual nature of the show, I think what's more groundbreaking and what's going to have the lasting effect is that it's showing characters—regardless of whether they're gay or straight—as fully three-dimensional and sexual people. What scared me about the show is that who we are sexually is as much a part of who we are as people. If you really want people to see these characters, understand these characters, you need to see what they're like.

It hit me when we finally got to see the pilot, which wasn't until we were seven episodes into shooting the first season. When I saw that first scene between Brian and Justin, I had the exact same response as anyone else who watched the show. It was shocking. It was hot. It was amazing. But it really clicked in with me and I really got it at that point. Then you see where this obsession starts. Without that, I don't think it would be as strong. That goes for all the other characters as well.

Ted likes his porn, and that speaks volumes about who this guy is. A guy who spends the majority of his time feeling safer at home whacking off—that's very telling. If you don't see it, you don't get to see, in some ways, how sad it is.

Oven

"Look, let's not pretend there's not a moose in the middle of the room. I know you're using again."

The Blake story line was wonderful for me. It also ended up being very personal. I went through a long phase in my life where I was attracted to wounded birds, as if I could just fix that person up to be mine. And those things never ever work out. So when that story line popped up with Blake coming back into Ted's life in that way, it touched me deeply and I just knew what needed to be done and what I wanted to show.

"Any other night I'd go home, log on to cumquick.com, and get it over with. But no, it's *Pride*. You actually want to experience some of this 'sexual freedom' we supposedly fought so hard for."

The majority of the response has been positive and amazing. We get wonderful letters from people in places like Nebraska that say, "I don't know any other gay people here, but I feel like I have a family now." And that's amazing. The thing about doing a television show is coming into people's houses once a week creates a very odd bond where they feel like they know you, so they tell you a lot about themselves right off the bat. They've seen me naked so they figure they can spill. But because of that, you get amazing stories of people coming out or feeling that they could come out because of this show. Those stories are truly what stick with me the most.

Almost every single person comes up and thanks you for doing the show, rather than just, "That's a great show, I love the show." They actually thank you for doing it, which I can't imagine happening with any other television program. I think that's what makes me feel so fortunate to be a part of it all.

haven't i seen you somewhere before?

One of the first steps in creating a fictional world is to populate it with people. In some cases the people are merely atmosphere to color the background, but certain personalities come in and affect the lives of the main characters and then keep coming back. These guest stars are an important part of the story and the family created within the series (clockwise from top right).

Dr. David Cameron (Chris Potter)

He readjusted more than Michael's back when he provided the man-child with his first truly adult relationship. Unfortunately, the love could not last as their conflicting lifestyles eventually led to the end of their partnering.

Detective Carl Horvath (Peter MacNeill)

The straitlaced detective started out as the diametric opposite to Debbie and her flamboyant ways, but the pair was able to meet in the middle to find love. Regretfully, their differences proved too many and pulled them apart every step of the way.

Ethan Gold (Fabrizio Filippo)

The violinist with the magic touch threw Justin and Brian's arrangement into discord. But his romantic promises proved too empty once he met his first adoring admirer.

George Schickel (Bruce Gray)

Emmett's elderly love went from being a closeted social recluse to an out and proud member of the community again. If only his heart would have had the same strength as his will.

Leda (Nancy Anne Sakovich)

Melanie's ex-girlfriend certainly shook things up for her and Lindsay when the motorcycle dyke came riding back into town. But Leda also offered them a solution for their sexual rut in a well-timed threesome that helped put the girls back on track.

It starts off with a bang—or more specifically, a punch in the face. And the third season of *Queer as Folk* is off and running.

This is the year that all manner of friendship is put to the test and relationships are rewritten when friends like Michael and the girls literally become family. Though the season has shortened to fourteen episodes, that does not infringe on the powerful stories yet to be told. What happens between Michael and Brian following that punch? Can best friends Ted and Emmett make a go of it as lovers? And what will happen when Ted secretly makes an ultimate betrayal of Melanie and Lindsay?

The family of friends will experience tremendous highs and lows in their lives and loves as each continues to grow and change as they follow the initial edict of the series. There will be a shift in dynamic between Lindsay and Melanie, a reunion between Brian and Justin, and a struggling relationship for Debbie. But the most powerful story arc of the season will come when politics starts to affect the lives of the Liberty Avenue gang. A mayoral candidate on a mission shakes things up, follows through on that promise, and a plot from the past returns for a final resolution.

season three

"Mourn the losses
because they're many.
But celebrate the victories
because they're few."

episode 301

Written by: Ron Cowen & Daniel Lipman
Directed by: Jeremy Podeswa

When Justin walks out on Brian at the *Rage* release party, he thinks that he's walked out on all his friends. But Michael is the only one glad that Justin is out of their lives entirely. While one relationship has ended, others are beginning, moving forward, and celebrating milestones. Ted and Emmett have intimacy issues, but move past the emotional obstacles for a night of uninhibited sex. Ben moves in with Michael after subletting his apartment for his canceled trip to Tibet. And Lindsay and Melanie celebrate eight years of mostly monogamous love.

THEA GILL: We've been fortunate enough to remain supportive of each other as a cast. I think it's unusual—maybe by the third season on a lot of shows the star turns start to happen. That hasn't happened with us. We have remained as an ensemble. I think that whenever anything comes up that is something that disturbs us, it's always brought to attention and discussion. It's always worked out and worked through. I think that's reflected and it shows in the series.

"A lot of thanks you get for saving his life. If you ask me, it wasn't worth it. You might as well have left him lying there—"

episode 302

Teleplay by: Michael MacLennan
Story by: Ron Cowen & Daniel Lipman & Michael MacLennan
Directed by: Bruce McDonald

Melanie considers a second child, but Lindsay considers it out of the question. Brian is fucking young blonds with visions of Justin in his head and starts monopolizing Michael's time. Justin considers dropping out of school due to cash-flow problems until Brian insists on honoring their original financial agreement. Justin goes back to working with Michael on *Rage* to pay Brian back. Emmett has a quickie with a pre-Ted arrangement named Dijon . . . like the mustard.

SCOTT LOWELL: Ted almost goes through a *Chinatown* kind of moment there of "My mother, my sister, my mother *and* my sister." Where it's "Who am I? Am I your best friend or your lover?" I love that scene. It was challenging to play to get those gearshifts back and forth. It was terrific that it happened that early on in the process of adjusting from best friends into lovers.

"They say in the vast emptiness of space, the faster you move, the slower you age. Figure same holds true of Pittsburgh."

episode 303

Teleplay by: Efrem Seeger
Story by: Ron Cowen & Daniel Lipman & Efrem Seeger
Directed by: Laurie Lynd

Melanie decides that *she* wants to be pregnant, so long as Brian's not the father. Debbie's concerned about her first time with Horvath and turns to Emmett and Ted for a little oral education that is both a success and a failure. Ben finds out his former lover died and he starts taking steroids to combat his own possible wasting. Brian helps plan the Gay and Lesbian Center carnival for a fee and turns it into a *Carnal* Carnivale. The party's a huge success and Justin bails out on a night with Ethan to attend.

"There's no fucking way Brian Kinney's fucking sperm are doing the breaststroke up my fallopian tube."

SHARON GLESS: First of all, they pay me to keep my clothes on. I'm on this show with all these young, beautiful people who take their clothes off at the drop of a hat. I did a lot of bed scenes in my youth, but I felt funny doing this one. It was fun to do because I got to go so many places within a short period of time. So many emotional things happen to her in that little bitty period. "Was I horrible? Was he happy? He says he was." I went through all of that. "And he said I was great." And then the realization that he thinks she's a tramp. It's not Debbie. Especially since she knows people probably see her as a common waitress, then to be called a whore. I think Debbie has great dignity within herself. She knocks on herself, she dresses funny, because it's all that she can afford, but I think there's a dignity to her about certain things.

episode 304

Teleplay by: Del Shores
Story by: Ron Cowen & Daniel Lipman & Del Shores
Directed by: Kari Skogland

Melanie and Lindsay choose Michael to be a "sperm donor" and later broaden the title to "father." Ben is spending more and more time at the gym. Brian's nephew accuses him of molestation, but Justin saves the day. Ted asks Emmett to move in, but is quickly overwhelmed by his new boyfriend and they split, until Ted suggests they get a brand-new place of their own.

"I say we get a genius from the sperm bank. It's easier."

MICHELLE CLUNIE: At first I was shocked because I thought, "Wouldn't it be Ted's sperm?" because they're so close. But then I realized that she would choose Michael because she gets instant grandmother who will always be around to baby-sit. And then my second thought after that was "Oh my God, you *do* get instant grandmother. What if she never leaves the house?" Then I thought Michael would be a great father. When he came over for the bris, I remember hugging him and saying, "Hi, Mikey!" There is a strong friendship there that's never been explored. We've never really had an opportunity to explore it. We have fun doing scenes together because it's a new energy.

episode 305

Teleplay by: Shawn Postoff
Story by: Ron Cowen & Daniel Lipman & Shawn Postoff
Directed by: Kelly Makin

Police Chief Stockwell's campaign for mayor heats up with Brian joining the team. Michael has some difficulty making a deposit at the sperm bank. Ethan performs in a competition in New York and comes in second, but his looks attract a first-rate talent representative who expects Ethan to sacrifice more than he's prepared to. Ted and Emmett can't agree on the perfect house, until Ted gives in to his new lover. Michael sees Ben shooting steroids, and dancing boys are dropping at Babylon.

"It never changes. Someone drops—we don't know if he's dead or alive—but nobody misses a beat. The *thumpa-thumpa* goes on."

BILL "POOCH" GODDARD (POST SUPERVISOR AND COPRODUCER): We try to get songs that we know will be timely, but also to work story-wise. We used the "Barbie" song in this episode. If you listen to the lyrics in the background with what's going on with the drug boys that are passing out, it's "It's a plastic world . . . life is plastic, it's fantastic." And these guys are going down, boom, boom, boom. So it's happy, happy, happy on a musical level, tragedy in the background, and then our guys are in the foreground with their problems as well. So you've got three layers going and it's all contextual to the music.

episode 306

Teleplay by: Brad Fraser
Story by: Ron Cowen & Daniel Lipman & Brad Fraser
Directed by: Bruce McDonald

Liberty Avenue sees a heavy police presence during Stockwell's campaign. Ethan is invited to fill in at the Harrisburg Symphony, but is told not to bring his boyfriend. Justin goes to surprise Ethan and gets his own surprise when he sees the fiddler go off, presumably to fiddle around with an admirer. Michael confronts Ben about the steroids, but gets nowhere. Ted and Emmett's move seems to be working out, until Ted is arrested for employing an underage worker at his website.

"Back in Hazelhurst, I used to look up at those houses on the hill . . . you know, where all the good people lived. And dream that someday I'd live there, too."

ROBERT GANT: I'm really glad that they came up with the steroids story line. I think it was absolutely the right way to go on so many levels. The obsession with looks permeates all of gay culture, and all of society to be honest. In many people's cases it's because they want to be perceived as strong or healthy whether they're battling HIV or not. To that end, it's had such broad reach. Personally, I think it will really hit home in the gay community where there's so much focus on trying to be beautiful and the beauty myth that runs rampant.

episode 307

Teleplay by: Michael MacLennan
Story by: Ron Cowen & Daniel Lipman & Michael MacLennan
Directed by: Kevin Inch

Ted goes to court as Stockwell enjoys a bump in his polls. Following a plea from Emmett, Brian convinces the mayoral candidate to let Ted go. Michael shocks Ben into quitting steroids by threatening to infect himself. When Ethan's cute fan from Harrisburg shows up, Justin realizes the romantic promises were just lies and leaves him. First time proves to be the charm when Melanie gets pregnant with Michael's sperm. And Uncle Vic gets a boyfriend.

"We all know your charming sense of humor. But we also know that deep down you care about us . . . even though you'd never admit it."

MICHELLE CLUNIE: I came out of the bathroom and was like, "It's blue!" And it's weird because when I was acting the scene, it all came together for me. It was not the sentimental "Oh, look, honey, it's blue . . . wheee!" It's more like, "It's blue, motherfucker! I am fucking pregnant! I beat Mother Nature! And I will beat everyone and I will have a Jewish child!" It's that. That's how I put it together in my mind. That's one reason why I could see Melanie deciding to have a baby.

episode 308

Teleplay by: Efrem Seeger
Story by: Ron Cowen & Daniel Lipman & Efrem Seeger
Directed by: Bruce McDonald

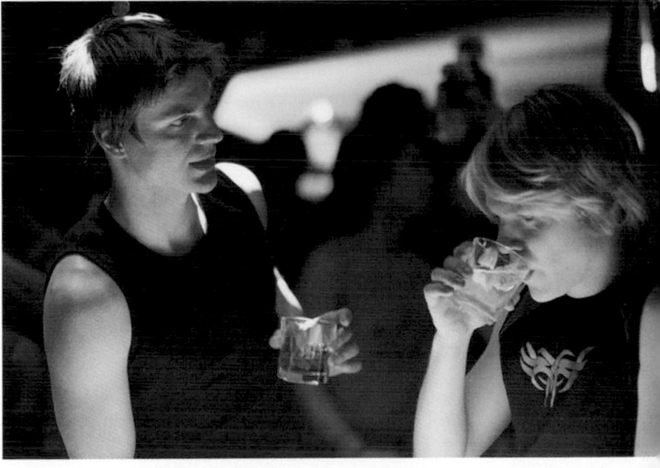

With Liberty Avenue being cleaned up, the hustlers are moving to other neighborhoods, namely Michael and Ben's, but the professor takes pity on one of the youngest call boys. Justin moves in with Daphne and resumes pursuing Brian. Lindsay goes to work in an art gallery and hires Emmett to throw a party for a show opening. The night is a huge success, but Ted can't be happy for his guy when a bad back and a general feeling of worthlessness settle in.

"Congratulations. You just made yourself a real enemy."

DANIEL LIPMAN: Candidates get elected for running a campaign like Stockwell's "defending family values." But from the viewpoint of Liberty Avenue, liberties are being taken away. If adults wish to indulge in sex or drugs, it's their choice. The minute you say, "Okay, that should be taken away," when does it start to affect your life in some way? Because it will. That's the danger of censorship.

episode 309

Teleplay by: Del Shores
Story by: Ron Cowen & Daniel Lipman & Del Shores
Directed by: Kelly Makin

Ted is in a jobless rut and can't even get work at Big Q. Brian and Justin return to their original agreement of a "relationship." Melanie starts cutting back at work, but doesn't like when work starts cutting back on her. Stockwell fires Brian for being gay, then rehires him for the same reason when the polls start to dip. Debbie gets to work against the politician and ends up losing Horvath. Justin designs a racy cover for the second issue of *Rage.*

"There's no shame in earning an honest day's pay for an honest day's work."

JACK WETHERALL: Vic is very concerned with Debbie's involvement with Horvath. As much as Vic's stuck in his life, so is she in hers. She's the classic caregiver and she looks after everybody but herself. As much as he's cautious for her and very protective with anyone she gets involved with, I think he recognizes in Horvath a genuine concern and love for Debbie. But she's been my main relationship and suddenly there's another man involved. There's jealousy that is a possibility. Then we get busted at Woody's and she's decided that Horvath is to blame and I actually end up defending him. I think Vic's trying to be very nurturing of her and give her back some of what she's given him in the years that she took care of him when he was sick.

episode 310

Teleplay by: Shawn Postoff
Story by: Ron Cowen & Dan Lipman & Shawn Postoff
Directed by: Kevin Inch

Bathhouses are closed up and down the avenue as Stockwell gets the endorsement of the fine, upstanding gay community members. Michael is overwhelmingly concerned about Melanie's health since she's carrying his child. Ted goes away for a weekend in the country, but detours at the Paradise Motel for a drug-filled sex party. Ben takes pity on hustler Hunter and is about to give up when he finds out the kid is HIV-positive. The back room at Babylon closes, pushing Justin to start an anti-Stockwell poster campaign.

"It's become a bona fide police state here at Loss-of-Liberty Avenue."

STEPHEN LYNCH (KEY MAKEUP ARTIST): We had to see the orgy through Ted's eyes, so we made everyone highly glistening. He's on crystal meth so everyone has to become so beautiful. So we quickly did makeup on them to take away the bad crystal meth look and give them the beautiful crystal meth look as seen through Ted's eyes. Then we covered him in a bronze shimmer powder so he would look so beautiful to himself.

episode 311

Teleplay by: Brad Fraser
Story by: Ron Cowen & Daniel Lipman & Brad Fraser
Directed by: Chris Grismer

Justin and the gang crash Stockwell's speech at the Gay and Lesbian Center. The mayoral candidate puts two and two together and finds Brian post-sex with the cause of many of the campaign's recent problems. Brian is fired due to the revelation. Ben and Michael open their home to the problematic Hunter. Melanie and Lindsay ask Ted to manage Gus's college fund, but he only manages to use it for an impromptu trip to Palm Springs for the White Party. And Brian forcibly reopens the back room of Babylon.

"The gay community bashes back."

RON COWEN: Michael has a very loving mother. His mother is probably the most important person in his life. So to see this kid who has been so abused by his mother, who—as we find out—actually wanted him to be a prostitute to bring extra money in, that's such a violation of a mother/son bond. The mother/son bond is so seminal to Michael's personality. To see a mother violate a son must be pretty horrifying for him.

episode 312

Teleplay by: Michael MacLennan
Story by: Ron Cowen & Daniel Lipman & Michael MacLennan
Directed by: David Wellington

Ted returns from Palm Springs and apologizes to the girls, even though Emmett has already replaced the money. Emmett refuses to admit there's a problem even when Ted "convinces" Emmett to join him in some crystal meth. Hunter reveals that he knew the "Dumpster boy," Jason Kemp, and saw the kid go off with the *cop* who could have killed him. Debbie goes to Horvath, but he tells her that Stockwell cold-cased it. Brian enlists Hunter and Justin's help to discover the identity of the cop, but Hunter changes the plan and goes off on his own with the guy.

"You want to have fun, fun, fun till your daddy takes your freedom away. Well, in case you haven't noticed, he already has."

SCOTT LOWELL: Ted's describing what it's like to be on the crystal meth and how it finally silences all those voices in his head that are always telling him that he's ugly and he's for shit and all this kind of stuff. He says that it finally makes him feel hot and sexy, the way that Brian must feel all the time. There's something very engaging about that for Ted, and very much something he desires for himself because it's so far from how he feels about himself that he almost can't imagine it. It's a grass-is-always-greener thing. His life would be perfect if he could have as much sex as Brian is having and have people look at him the same way people look at Brian. I think in the end that's the hold these drugs have on him.

episode 313

Teleplay by: Efrem Seeger
Story by: Ron Cowen & Daniel Lipman & Efrem Seeger
Directed by: Alex Chapple

Justin appears in front of a school disciplinary committee to apologize for his behavior at the ad agency, but he refuses to apologize to Stockwell and gets suspended. Hunter shows up with a condom full of cop sperm as well as the alleged murderer's name—who turns out to be Stockwell's former partner. Emmett caters Ted's orgy, but leaves before the festivities start, thus angering Ted and causing him to end the relationship. Melanie and Lindsay invite Emmett to stay with them after forgiving each other for Ted-inspired tensions.

"I'm not saying you should be sorry. I'm saying you should apologize."

RON COWEN: Everyone just thought we dumped the Dumpster boy, but we didn't. In reality, as opposed to television shows, there are a lot of crimes and even murders that go unsolved. Sometimes they get solved. Sometimes they never get solved. Sometimes five years later they arrest somebody. It doesn't happen three episodes later in real life. So we wanted to be more realistic in that they couldn't solve the murder. It did get shelved and forgotten about. Then a year and a half later something surfaces. That just seems so much more interesting than tidying it up. That story was good fortune smiling on us because we didn't know last year how it was going to come back.

episode 314

Written by: Ron Cowen & Daniel Lipman
Directed by: Kelly Makin

Liberty Avenue takes on a colorless existence under Stockwell's reign as Debbie continues to enlist voters. Brian sells off most of his possessions to pay for an anti-Stockwell TV ad campaign and voter turnout in the Liberty Avenue precinct leads to Stockwell's downfall. Melanie worries about miscarriage because of family history, but makes it through her first trimester. Emmett refuses to go back to Ted, who hits rock bottom and enters rehab, where he runs into Blake—one of the counselors. Hunter's horrible mom shows up with the cops to take him away, forcing Michael to take the kid on the run, stopping only to get Brian's last worldly possession, his car.

"This used to be such a magical kingdom full of sprites and fairies."

DANIEL LIPMAN: It always goes back to Michael and Brian in a way—the two friends. Michael has seen Brian funding this commercial so that it could possibly defeat Stockwell, or at least put the doubt in people's heads. This seems spontaneous and has a lot of consequences, and Michael doesn't understand it. Brian doesn't believe in sacrifice and he doesn't believe in love, but of course he is in love with Justin. So despite what he says, his actions don't always equate. Then Michael is faced with exactly the same kind of thing in doing something spontaneous, something that is sacrificing with consequences without thinking about it. The two of them are in the same place emotionally in the last episode.

robert gant as ben bruckner

When a character is brought into a series midrun, he is often used to shake things up a little and add a new level to the show. Ben Bruckner certainly fits that description. As arguably the first main character on a television series really *living* with HIV, Ben turned Michael's world upside down both romantically and socially. Suddenly the ultraliberal Debbie became a true mother in every sense of the word, worrying first and foremost about her son. But Ben was more than a plot device and much more three-dimensional than to be defined simply by his illness.

"We wanted someone who lived in a different world than the rest of our people," Ron Cowen explains. "We made him a professor and a writer because we wanted someone more intellectual and somewhat outside of the world of Liberty Avenue. Ben was conceived as someone who is perhaps more political and more thoughtful, but not someone who looked down on the world of Liberty Avenue. He likes to go there, too, but he doesn't do as much in that world as the other people do. He has a world outside of that."

"I already have what I need.
And I don't have to go to Tibet to find it."

Ben's initiation into the world of *Queer as Folk* was difficult on several relationship levels, but he eventually integrated himself into Michael's life. Now, like Melanie and Lindsay, it is difficult to talk about Ben without discussing him as part of a duo. "He's a good complement to Michael," says Daniel Lipman. "I think that the interesting place where Ben has led us is this neg-pos relationship, which you certainly don't see on ongoing shows. When you look at Justin and Brian, that's one kind of relationship, and when you look at Mel and Lindsay, that's another kind of gay relationship."

"Ben is a very stable, practical, principled person," Ron adds. "I think he's very much got his feet on the ground. He was originally conceived to be the Rock of Gibraltar for Michael. He has a spiritual side. I don't believe he's a Buddhist, but he believes in a lot of Buddhist thinking. He tries to find some peace of mind in that. I think he has a certain spirituality the other characters don't necessarily have. As the series progressed, we wanted to show that stability cracking."

Ben's comfortable world is shaken in some major ways. First, he has a reaction to his meds, then he deals with the death of his first lover, who infected him. These things shake him to the core, but the spiritual rock remains. He is there for Hunter when the boy needs him, but, more importantly, gives some of that strength and maturity to the man he loves, helping Michael grow.

ben and robert: face-to-face

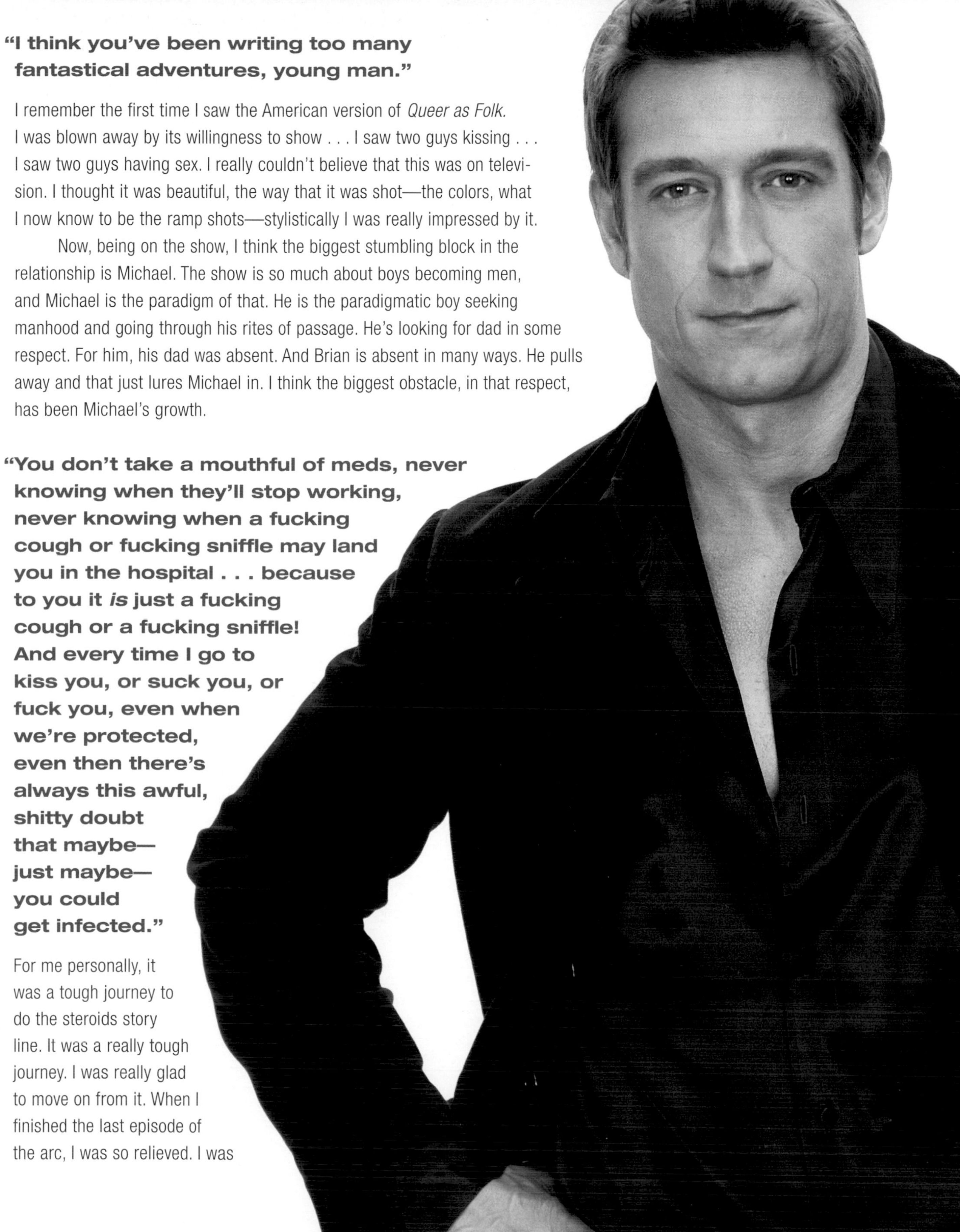

"I think you've been writing too many fantastical adventures, young man."

I remember the first time I saw the American version of *Queer as Folk.* I was blown away by its willingness to show . . . I saw two guys kissing . . . I saw two guys having sex. I really couldn't believe that this was on television. I thought it was beautiful, the way that it was shot—the colors, what I now know to be the ramp shots—stylistically I was really impressed by it.

Now, being on the show, I think the biggest stumbling block in the relationship is Michael. The show is so much about boys becoming men, and Michael is the paradigm of that. He is the paradigmatic boy seeking manhood and going through his rites of passage. He's looking for dad in some respect. For him, his dad was absent. And Brian is absent in many ways. He pulls away and that just lures Michael in. I think the biggest obstacle, in that respect, has been Michael's growth.

"You don't take a mouthful of meds, never knowing when they'll stop working, never knowing when a fucking cough or fucking sniffle may land you in the hospital . . . because to you it *is* just a fucking cough or a fucking sniffle! And every time I go to kiss you, or suck you, or fuck you, even when we're protected, even then there's always this awful, shitty doubt that maybe— just maybe— you could get infected."

For me personally, it was a tough journey to do the steroids story line. It was a really tough journey. I was really glad to move on from it. When I finished the last episode of the arc, I was so relieved. I was

exhausted. I really took the journey with Ben and it spilled over into my life. I remember feeling lots of anxiety and being very depressed. Ideally as actors our job is to walk in the shoes of the character and to really be there when that camera's rolling, going through whatever they're going through.

I remember doing scenes where I'm throwing up and everything—just putting myself into this state for the whole day. I remember Hal, after we did the needle scene where he's threatening to inject himself. We really worked hard and he broke down crying after that scene—he just broke down and wept. If you're really doing it as an actor, you're experiencing all of it as a person. I was experiencing all of this. I have never felt so glad to do a story line and then to move on from it.

I wasn't really pleasant to be around on set during those episodes because I was living the whole rage-at-any-moment kind of thing. I had to go apologize to two of the directors because I was a nightmare. I really was. I consider myself to be a pretty easygoing guy. But I worked myself into this state of anger at anything. I remember Kevin Inch in Episode 307. After I snapped at him about something, I said, "Kevin, you know I'm really sorry. Look, you gotta understand, please bear with me because I'm just in the middle of this crap." And he says, "Bobby, I can feel it radiating from you. It's great! It's really coming out of you." Which is exciting to hear on one level because it works, but on the other, more personal level . . .

"The secret is to stop regretting the past and fearing the future, and just live in the 'now.'"

I think that the lovemaking scenes are where I do the least preparation. I really try to let go and surrender to the fact that my partner in this is really straight—and he's wonderful, I have to say. He takes a little grief, but the truth is he shows up 100 percent. He is such a thespian when it comes to doing this. He would shock me because he really just throws himself into the middle of the experience, but I think that's the key.

I think I've started to do the same thing, which is to just hurl myself into it and whatever happens, happens. I think that makes it easier and I think it makes it more honest and organic. It's awkward because it is intimate, but it's the moments in between when you're just sitting there with virtually nothing on and just keeping things light and chatty. I think it's a lot easier for us now that we've become friends. There's trust, just like in any relationship. You're trusting your acting partner. It's nice that we have established that because we can translate that into the relationship between the characters and into the lovemaking.

The first time, I had a lot of trepidation about the nudity. I had a lot of issues around that as a kid and what I learned around my parents and whatnot. We all have our version of that. But I knew it was coming. So when in that second episode that I did, I really had to go for it. Hal had pants on. It was the bathroom scene where he tells me he can't do it, which is such a great scene. But that was the first time when I was butt naked, except for my sock, my armor. I was fine with it when I saw it on-screen. I was in good shape, so I was like, "Okay, good." I think if I had been out of shape at the time, that probably would have been more mortifying for me because I still carry some of that baggage of being a fat kid, but it's getting better.

"Hate wasting time. Life's too short. After all, who knows what could happen tomorrow . . . or even five minutes from now?"

This show was the thing that really prompted me to come out professionally as a gay man. It's something that's always terrified me because I've been put into those leading-guy parts opposite the woman/girlfriend/wife/whatever. The word has always been that coming out would be a really bad thing for my career. But the sense of freedom that I feel now, the energy that I don't have to put into hiding, has made this such a great choice for me. I really have the show to thank in so many ways. The producers couldn't have been more supportive of me doing things on my own terms in my own time, which was great. The cast members as well were terrific. I think Peter was anxious for me to come out and he couldn't have been better about it. He was very loving about it.

It's interesting how it's had this effect not only externally, but internally. It's hugely life-transforming. This show is going to be really hard to follow up. It's so rare that you get to do work that is of such a sociopolitical nature. It just doesn't really exist that often. It's the birth of a new level of understanding.

"Would you stop looking at me like that? I'm not perfect, you know."

I've gotten emails on my website. I got email from one kid in Israel who said, "I love your character and love the show. It's such a great relief from all the bombing here." How amazing is that? And I got an email yesterday from a guy in Australia who said, "Just wanted to let you know you have a bucketload of fans down here."

I remember signing a picture for somebody who said her girlfriend had come out because of my coming out. This is all because of *Queer as Folk*. I got a letter from a guy who said that this character was the first time that he'd seen a gay character that he could identify with. He's in his mid to late forties and he said that he was from the Midwest and he found out a few years back that three of the guys that he went to high school with had committed suicide because they weren't able to deal with the fact that they were gay. One was the captain of the football team, one was the captain of the basketball team, and one was, he said, "the fiercest debater that I had ever gone up against." He said, "If only there had been this character and you doing what you're doing."

It's a weird thing to find that line between making the choices you know will make you happy and this level of responsibility. It's a strange place to be to notice that I could make the choice to be drunk every night if I want, but people are watching. Not that I want to be a role model, but I'm feeling a sense of responsibility to encourage this group of people—gay folks—who spent so much of their lives feeling like they were to be ashamed of themselves. That's the effect of this show. It is infectious. It is freeing people and it freed me. This show has put me in a place that I didn't really expect to be. I don't know that I would have chosen it, but I wouldn't trade it for the world.

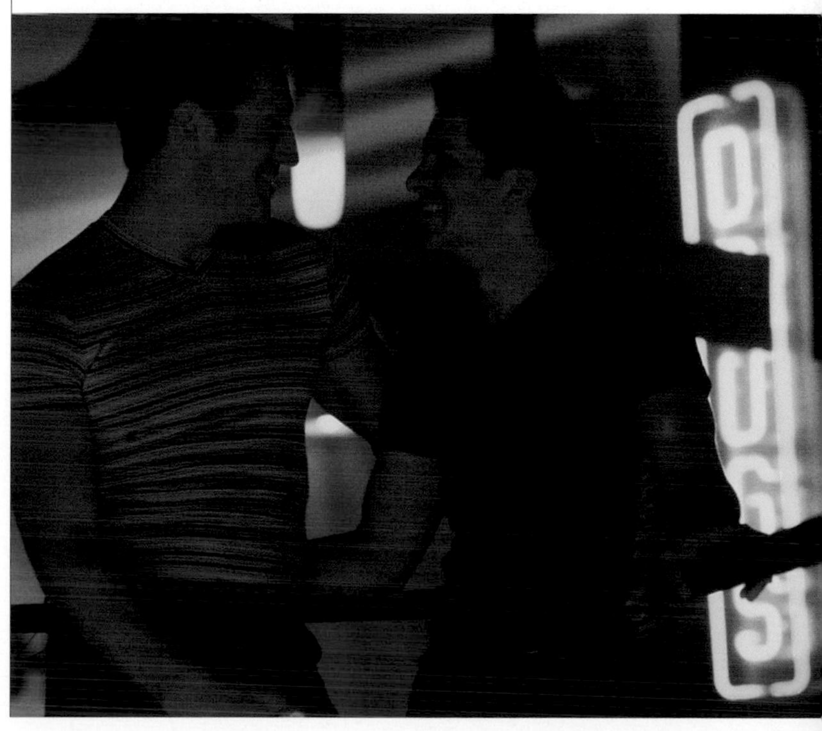

the soundtrack of their lives

The dialogue may have said, "It's all about sex," but the opening images of the *Queer as Folk* pilot also showed that it was about many other things, not the least of which was music. Even before the first scene in Babylon, the viewers were greeted by an orgy of images of gyrating males humping and bumping to the beat in the colorful opening sequence set to the tune "Spunk" by Greek Buck.

Queer as Folk focuses on music far more than most shows on television, and it takes a tremendous amount of work to make sure that the songs always fit, never overwhelm, and always, always rock. "At the very beginning we had a budget—as most shows would—for a composer," producer Sheila Hockin recalls. "We started out trying to do some composed pieces, but we found that even in the course of the first season it wasn't working for us because scored music almost always feels like, as one of our directors calls it, 'emotion lotion.' It's usually trying to tell the audience how to feel. We didn't feel comfortable doing that, because we wanted the audience to feel however they wanted to feel."

Co-producer Bill "Pooch" Goddard is in charge of postproduction, and it's his job to make sure that the show is assembled to maximum effect. An important component is the addition of music. Pooch explains, "I get the music supervisors involved usually with three or four major points in an episode that we're looking to use music for. And we're always trying to play ahead of the curve six months because we shoot so far in advance. But with Ron and Dan, the writing is paramount. So sometimes we will walk away from it and not put music in because we feel that it's too much of a split of focus. We want the story to come through."

Music does help the story come through in many ways, and music supervisors Michael Perlmutter and Scot McFadyen, along with music coordinator Erin Hunt, have the arduous task of hunting through thousands of songs to find the right one. Michael and Scot alternate episodes, and each week they receive about 150 CDs from new and known artists from all around the world. Naturally, they can't listen to every one, but they do try.

"Justin is not one of those young characters you would see on a regular series on network television. He's not the poor little blond seventeen-year-old walking on the beach thinking he should throw himself into the waves," says Daniel Lipman. It's a fitting way to describe one of the central characters on a show that's like nothing else on network television. Justin Taylor is an incredibly self-possessed, mature, and secure soul wrapped in the body of a young man.

Dan goes on to explain the thing that makes both *Queer as Folk* and Justin just so unique. "In the past, we've seen scenarios where a gay character cries and says, 'Oh, God, why did you make me gay?' On our show somebody would drop and say, 'Thank God you made me gay.' I've always seen our show as a celebration of being gay. For me it's very up and triumphant, even with all of the problems the characters go through. And Justin reflects that celebration."

"He's okay with being gay," Ron Cowen adds simply. "I think the world around him might have a problem with it, but in himself I don't think there's a problem." Which brings up the main difference between Justin and Michael,

justin

Song: "The Shining"
Artist: Badly Drawn Boy
Episode 119—Final scene

SCOT McFADYEN: We used Badly Drawn Boy when Brian is bowling in the street after his dad died. That scene was hard because we originally had a Beck song temped in. It was a difficult process looking for an alternative, and everyone was so stuck on the Beck song, but it was a song that was really personal to Beck and he didn't want to license it. When we did put in Badly Drawn Boy, it was actually something that ended up working better. People really responded to it. It's one of the most downloaded songs and the most-asked-about songs when you read the show website. That definitely had an effect.

Song: "The Man I Love"
Artist: John Alcorn (George Gershwin)
Song: "Rapture"
Artist: Lio
Episode 208—Final scenes

SCOT McFADYEN: There was an episode where we had a piano player named John Alcorn from Toronto performing Gershwin. He was a lounge singer and we used that music in and out of the whole episode, ending the episode with "The Man I Love." That was a lot of fun going from Babylon and a song called "Rapture" by Lio and then having it blend into "The Man I Love," which was a nice way to end it.

Song: "Werkin"
Artist: Guido Osario
Song: "Preludio"
Artist: Lance Oullette (J. S. Bach)
Episode 219—About 30 minutes into episode

MICHAEL PERLMUTTER: We used a violin piece and a song called "Werkin" and it was beautifully edited. It was intercut between Brian alone and on his own at Babylon, and Ethan was playing Bach's "Preludio" on the violin. That was really beautifully done. It was beautifully intercut and used by the editors. We provided the song, but the editors really made that happen. They have great taste in music and do such a beautiful job with the editing that the music seems plugged in there effortlessly.

Song: "Crazy Little Thing Called Love"
Artist: Dwight Yoakam
Episode 305—Opening scene

SHEILA HOCKIN: We put Dwight Yoakam's "Crazy Little Thing Called Love" in the scene where Michael's in the clinic with Mel and Lindsay, waiting to donate sperm. Kelly Makin, our director, originally put "Mrs. Robinson" in there, which we loved, but it's a little challenging to get the rights to a Simon and Garfunkel tune. They protect the song very carefully, which is understandable. We went through dozens of other songs and nothing worked for us and we were despairing. Then our music guys phoned and said, "How about Dwight Yoakam?" And we said, "You're obviously crazy." And they came back with, "Well, let's try it. We think you might like this." They put it in the scene and it's hysterical.

"Our music supervisors are probably working at a level that nobody else is in television at the moment," Sheila states with pride. "Just due to the sheer tonnage of music that we go through. In the beginning we were spending eight hours a week working together to pick music and to find what the musical palette of the show would be. We're down to less than that amount of time now."

The process has certainly been streamlined. "In the beginning of the year now we send the editors thirty or forty songs, and then every week we update them with new songs that we've heard," Michael says. "We started to send a lot of music up front so that when the editors were going in there for the first few episodes, they could actually edit the scene to a specific song."

Since music is such an important component to the show, the music supervisors are not the only ones contributing. Oftentimes a director comes in with specific song choices to go with the mood of a scene. Naturally, Ron, Dan, and Sheila contribute when they feel they have something that might work, in addition to having a Toronto DJ serve as a music consultant. Ideas often come from everyone in the production, and Sheila estimates that about twenty people are suggesting music for the music supervisors to work with.

"Sometimes we put in an incredible song and heartbreakingly can't get permission for it," Sheila adds. "That's happened to us a few times, and it takes a lot of getting over because by the time a director has worked with a scene and they've cut it and we've looked at it, the music belongs in that scene, and then they take it away from you. It's really hard. It hasn't happened a huge number of times. Most of the people in the music community have been fantastic."

The production cites David Bowie and Iggy Pop's publishing and record companies among their most supportive agencies. The series also features a lot of independent music from around the world. In fact, Michael and Scot have a bit of a mandate to help promote music. A lot of the artists they've featured on the show admit to receiving more hits because of play on *Queer as Folk* than they get on their own websites.

Between independent music and popular artists, *Queer as Folk* runs the musical gamut. Each character has his or her own musical style, and each episode can reflect many different moods through music. "I love the fact that we have everything from Gershwin to Marilyn Manson," says Scot. "It's a great level of diversity."

"I like dick. I want to
get fucked by dick.
I want to suck dick.
I like sucking dick.
And I'm good at it, too."

the polar opposites rotating on Brian's axis. At seventeen, Justin is already at a place that Michael still hasn't reached by the time he turns thirty.

"I think Justin's a very good role model," says Ron. "He's a teenager who's saying, 'I'm gay, get used to it. If you don't like it, it's your problem, not mine.' I like that about Justin and frankly I wish I could have been that teenager. Who wouldn't? I think there are a lot of young men these days that are that way; for whom being gay is not the end of the world and for whom it's not a reason to think of killing yourself."

That strength allowed Justin to take those first steps onto Liberty Avenue before he was old enough to get a drink at a bar, which led to a difficult path for the writers to walk. "We got a lot of criticism at the beginning of the show about Brian being a predator." admits Dan. "But it was Justin who was the predator. If he left Brian that night and never saw him again, Brian would never think of him again. So he's the one who really motivated the whole series."

But critics of the show refused to acknowledge that aspect of youthful pursuit in the relationship. They saw a twenty-nine-year-old man with a seventeen-year-old boy and wanted to raise an issue where, in reality, there was none either with the characters or even with the legality. As the producers already knew through their research, the age of sexual consent in the state of Pennsylvania is sixteen. To stay true to one of the core relationships established in the British series, they

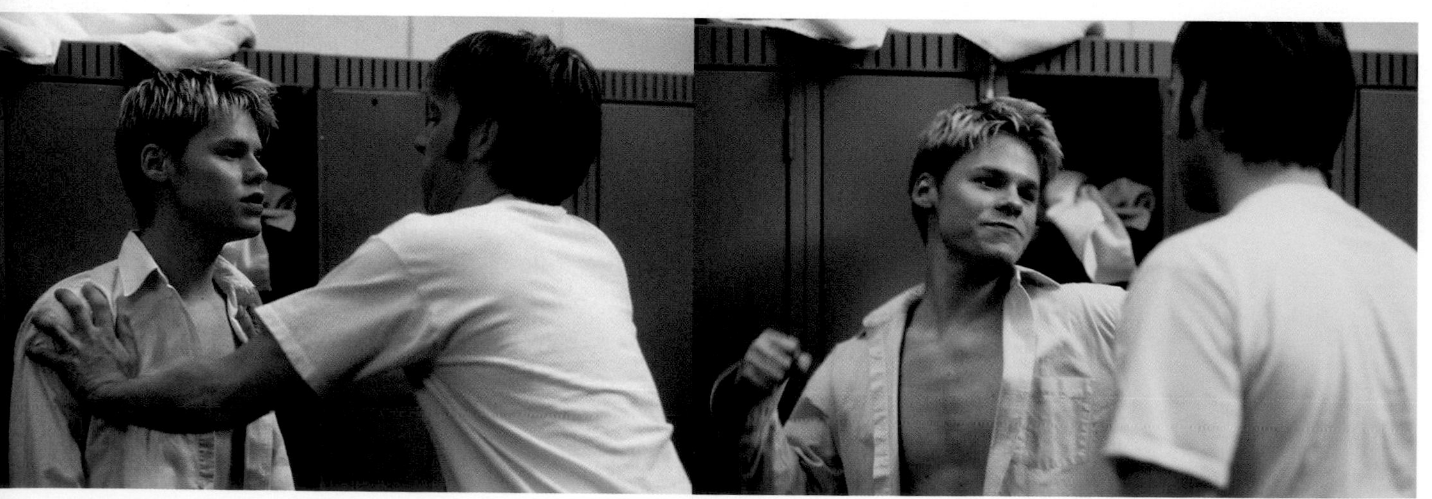

ensured that it was well-balanced and true for the American version because of its importance to the series.

"I always feel that a lot of the show is through Justin's eyes," Dan explains. "Because he becomes involved with characters who are more evolved than he is and older than he is and his life is just beginning as a young gay male. We see how he evolves and how he's turning from a high school boy with sexual desire and yearning into a young gay man who understands the power of sex, the power of his sexuality, and how powerful that is. It's like somebody opening a magic box and there's the light." And part of that light is Brian Kinney.

The relationship with Brian is helping to form the man Justin will ultimately become, for better or for worse. Even when the two formed the covenant for their relationship on the dance floor at Babylon in the second season, it was based on rules that Brian established. According to Dan, "Brian is a man of action. To me, he's Gary Cooper. He doesn't have to say anything, he just does it. A good example was how everyone thought Brian wasn't visiting Justin after he was bashed. The audience knows he was there every single night keeping watch. He's a hero. That's why he became Rage. He's Justin's hero."

Of course, Justin rebelled against Brian's rules almost from the start because his hero couldn't provide all that he needed. Dan continues, "Then because Brian is the antiromantic, Justin meets someone who is romantic. The story of Justin, Brian, and Ethan wasn't just a melodramatic story about 'Oh, I want a boyfriend who loves me.' I always felt that if Justin had met Ethan first and then he met Brian, he would have gone through just the opposite. He had one thing in his

life and then he saw something that he thought he wanted. It was the story of a young gay man torn between the queer life that Brian offered and the imitation straight life that Ethan offered. Here he had someone who offered him a promise of words, which the other one wouldn't give him, so he went off with that."

Naturally, the relationship with Ethan couldn't last because it was entirely based on romance and not reality. More than anything, Justin's life revolves around a forced reality, even though it is a heightened reality for the purpose of dramatic television. No other character on the show has faced the naked hatred and homophobia that Justin has had to cope with. None of the adults in this world have been shown experiencing as much discrimination. But that's also been part of Justin's learning curve and the reason why he becomes so passionate against the Stockwell campaign in the third season. Justin's growth continues to expand into all facets of his character from his art to his politics and, naturally, to his love.

"I've just seen the face of God. His name's Brian Kinney."

justin and randy: face-to-face

"No matter how shitty things get, I always have my art. It's the one place I can go where I'll be safe . . . where no one can get to me."

I read about the British version in some industry magazine or newspaper a few months before I heard about the American version. Then I knew about the American version when my agent pitched the role to me. I hadn't actually seen the British show when I went in to read, so all I had was the pilot script to review. When I read it, I liked how naive Justin was but ballsy at the same time. That drew me to the role.

"I'm the most mature person you know."

I think Justin went through a traditional growth to the kind of maturity that one goes through at that age. I mean it's also a TV show, so he's gone through some horribly traumatic events that I think have aged him as well. But a lot of the maturity that was in the character had to be there for some reason.

I didn't want to keep Brian and Justin together. To make Justin interesting to Brian he needed to have some kind of exceptional qualities and he needed to evolve. I didn't want it to be horribly degrading. I mean, obviously the whole thing with Justin chasing Brian is something that character has to do, but we had to give some obstacles to elevate him out of the destructiveness of that situation.

By the third season I think Justin's older and more mature. I still don't think he has notions of what Brian is capable of doing to him, but he doesn't think their relationship is something it's not. I definitely think that with the quickness with which he went from Ethan back to Brian it sort of demonstrates that a lot of it was sort of rebounding. He's coming from a place of being severely hurt.

"I don't want her to understand me, I want her to leave me alone!"

Justin's relationship with his mom is interesting. I think it's a testament to Sherry because she is just such a great actress. She's added a level of humanity to the part and to the relationship. A lot of the audience tends to be people who are still dealing with how their sexuality affects their relationship with their parents. Therefore I think that relationship is easy to identify with the type of audience we have.

"Sex is part of it. But it's about other things, too. Like how we see each other and ourselves."

There are a lot of people who are empowered by Justin and by the show, but operating under the preconception that a world exactly like this could exist is sort of wrong. It might make people feel like things are more possible than they are in the real world. But the response I get tells me that Justin has inspired them to be a stronger person and to come out means a lot to me. It's funny, though. People often tend to write to me either thinking that I'm Justin, like they don't know I'm the actor, or else they think I'm a prostitute and they want to tell me sexual things that they want.

"It was the best night of my life."

I liked the first season finale. I liked the dancing. I thought it was fun and something really different in the way it was unrealistic. It was this heightened moment that I think worked really well. In a lot of ways more was said in the dance about Brian and Justin's relationship than in any of our sex scenes or anything else. I think that's one of my favorite moments.

"The queer's going. The queer is out the door. The queer's gone!"

Initially there was a lot more fear after Chris Hobbs's attack. Justin was fearless so much in the first season. I think he's back to that now, but right at the beginning of the second season after the attack, the adolescent invincibility that we all once had was really, really shattered. There was a lot more fear. There was a lot more anger. I definitely think Justin is now more like Brian, but I think it comes from a place of a lot of fear and a lot of anger because of that attack.

"A man needs to know when to ask for help."

I like the fact that Justin treats women with respect and has significant relationships with them. Almost all the other characters make these rude vagina jokes from time to time. I think that Justin's respect for women is what allows the relationship with Daphne and Debbie and his own mother and Melanie and Lindsay to have the most legitimacy. He doesn't feel oppressed by women or that he was forced to be a heterosexual by the other gender. Therefore he is able to have meaningful, mutually respectful relationships with the female characters on the show.

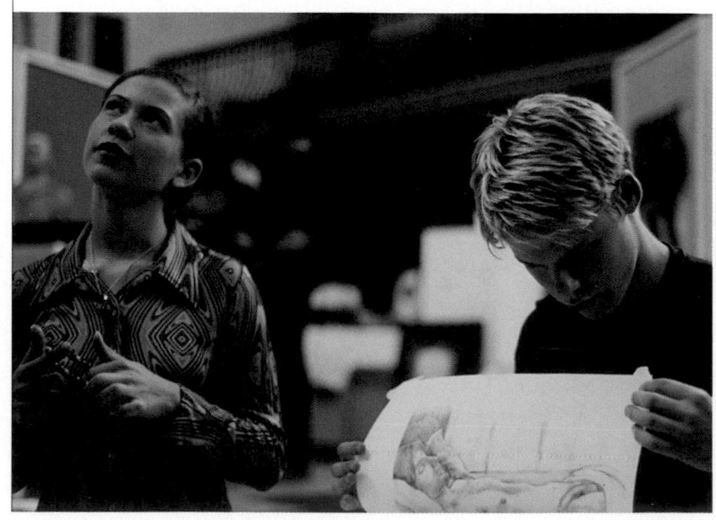

RON COWEN: We were designing all the characters and coming up with their personality profiles trying to think of what they do for a living and their interests. We realized that among the five main guys, Ted, Emmett, Brian, Michael, and Justin, none of them were artists or did anything creative. Dan and I both felt that—being writers and knowing so many gay people—the creative side of a gay person was not represented on the show. There were no artists. We wanted to have an artist in the mix because I think so many gay people are so amazingly creative. I mean if you took away all the gay people in the world who make creative contributions there'd be no music . . . there'd be no theater . . . there'd be no art.

justin's sketch pad

rage

Welcome to Gayopolis! Home of that fabulous superhero Rage! What? You've never heard of Rage? Well, you will after tonight. With powers of mind greater than any known to man, he can bend anyone's will to his, rout the forces of intolerance and injustice, and *still* have the strength to fuck a hundred guys!

DANIEL LIPMAN: There wouldn't be a Rage if we didn't have to be creative out of adversity. We had all the DC Comics characters in the original pilot script because of our relationship with Warner Brothers. We wanted to use likenesses of Superman, Batman, and all those characters on the show. Anyone who has a valuable character is going to be very protective, and DC was protective and they said no. They wouldn't allow us to use their characters. So we had to invent Captain Astro. If they had given us the rights to the characters, there wouldn't have been a Captain Astro and then probably wouldn't have been Rage.

We could do anything we wanted with Captain Astro. So we invented the character, and then, of course, his homophobic publishers decided to kill him. That's how Rage was born. Because the triangle of Brian/Michael/Justin was so important, we wanted to connect Michael and Justin. They had a creative relationship the way that Justin and Brian had a sexual one, and Michael and Brian had an emotional one. So they're all very much connected. Using Justin's ability as an artist, it all seemed to take off from there.

MATURE

READERS

FIRST ISSUE!
COLLECTORS ITEM

sherry miller as **jennifer taylor**

Debbie may be the mom most gay men dream about, but Jennifer Taylor is more likely the mom that most gay men would want to have in reality. In contrast to the most understanding and supportive mom on the planet, Jennifer does make mistakes when it comes to her son coming out of the private-school closet, but she never stops loving him or trying to understand what he's going through. Plus she has the added bonus of not spending all of her time hanging out in gay bars . . . usually.

"Stop running from me, because I'm not running from you. I'm still your mother and you're still my son, and I still love you."

jennifer

jennifer and sherry: face-to-face

"He's only seventeen. He's too young to be having those feelings, to be doing those things. . . . How can you possibly know who you are?"

I don't know if it's partly because I'm in the business so I've been surrounded and had friends who are gay my whole adult life, but I just didn't realize that it was such a big deal. I feel kind of embarrassed about that now, but I suppose when you're straight, you don't really know that some people are so beat down. Let's face it, everybody who's gay has a mother and had to deal with it at some point, and it's either been a positive experience or it's been a horrible experience. But everybody has a mother.

"I am so proud of you."

Justin's difference could have been any difference or any number of—and I put this in quotation marks—"problems" where things aren't just nice and neat and tidy. When you have children, there are lots of things that aren't nice and neat and tidy all the way along. I personally don't have any problems with homosexuality and I don't believe I would have if one of my children were gay. So I had to make it something else for myself to play the part properly. There were some things that I had to do that were just so foreign to me personally.

Probably the toughest thing about the part was feeling like I was losing my baby. *That* I can easily translate to my own children. When your kids start entering a world of sexual activity, it's kind of over. There's no turning back. It's done and they've gone a very independent road. You just worry for their hearts. And you worry about disease and everything else. I don't care if someone has lots of promiscuous sex, at some point they're going to hook into somebody that they care a lot for, and when there's sex involved, it makes everything heightened. You just hold your breath as kids enter the adult world and start getting sexually active.

makyla smith as

daphne chanders

Of all the characters in *Queer as Folk*, Daphne Chanders was the most direct transplant from the British series. Justin's best friend is the one person who is there for him no matter what as he explores this new world. As he grows and evolves, she matures along with him and apart from him from a girl into a woman.

"You've been fucking some twenty-nine-year-old guy all year. So why can't I see someone, too?"

daphne

daphne and makyla: face to face

"That's why I want my first time to be with someone who knows what it feels like . . . like you."

There were a lot of comments about the whole sex thing between Justin and Daphne and it being wrong for my character to be like that. I disagree. She's young and she's scared about doing this for the first time, and who else would you go to but your best friend? That's who I talk to about things, my best girlfriend. And basically that's what Justin was for Daphne. She didn't have a best girlfriend, she had Justin. And he had the right parts so they could, you know.

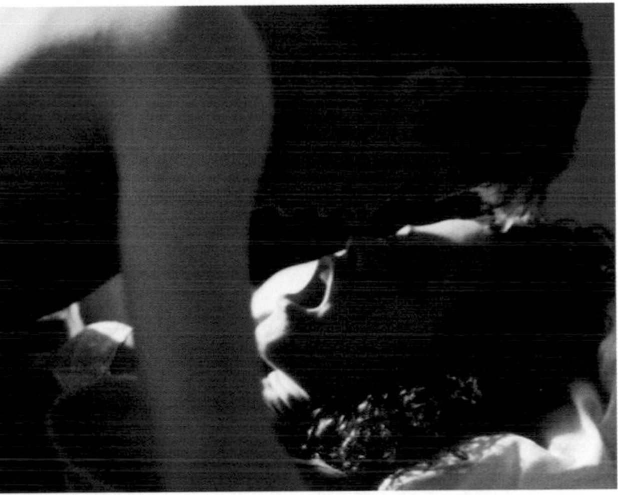

"Hi, I'm not a lesbian, but I'm a big fan."

I think Daphne's a very smart person. She's always interested in looking at things from a different perspective and different viewpoint. She's an outsider. She didn't have very many friends, but I always thought that she was a cheerful person and that she looked at things on the bright side. I think she was excited to get this different way of seeing things. Being so close to Justin, she gets to live kind of through him.

"Justin, you almost died when you came out. How can you go back in . . . for anyone?"

Daphne liked Ethan at first and thought it was a great thing for Justin to be in a relationship with someone his age and going through the things he was going through at the same time. But then she did realize that Ethan was more into himself than Justin. And that's when she started liking Brian again and trying to get Justin to see that Brian never lied to him. He was always honest about the things that he said. He wasn't always nice, but he was honest.

family

Queer as Folk is not filmed on a Hollywood studio lot with over a hundred buildings covering dozens of acres. While part of the production does have offices in Los Angeles, the show itself is largely put together in a lone building in an industrial section of Toronto. The publicist has an office next to the props master and only a few feet away from the producer. For the most part, the cast and crew are on their own. But out of that solitude has grown a sense of friendship and family.

By the very nature of the series, the production staff has to interact with each other in ways unlike most other office coworkers. During any given day, people can be saying things they wouldn't say in front of their mothers, addressing topics even married people will not discuss, and even comparing dildos for size, shape, and overall television presence. It is an odd world in which they work.

"I think that we're awfully lucky," says Sheila Hockin. "I think that the subject matter and the bravery of the cast has allowed us to be like a little renegade production in a way. From the very beginning it was so obvious that we couldn't be mainstream in terms of what we were doing. It's like making a little independent feature film every week, and everybody approaches it with that spirit. We are so lucky in our cast and our crew. They're extraordinarily committed people. Nobody ever phones it in on this show. After three seasons everybody picks up every script and tackles it with the same intensity and desire to make it the best it can be as they did in the beginning."

Much of the credit for the hardworking atmosphere is due to the tone set by the executive producers. Ron Cowen and Daniel Lipman always approach their work with the same credo. "It's just as important for us what happens behind the camera as what happens in front of

it," says Dan. "There are a lot of productions where people don't care and they feel that chaos creates that magical creative energy. We don't believe that. People can put up with jerks if you're doing a movie. You can say, 'Okay, I've got three weeks of this . . . I've got six months of this.' A television show is a family, and if you're fortunate enough to be given the gift of a successful show that goes on for year after year, you have to have people who want to come to work."

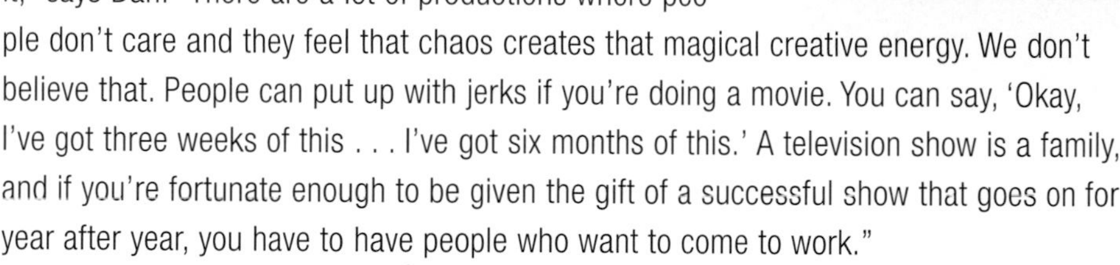

It's not just a sound bite or a press release when the producers or the cast and crew refer to the team as a family. It was clear by how everyone associated with the creation of this book was warmly welcomed into the fold. An excitement and a feeling of camaraderie evident in every department. "I love this show," says key hairstylist Clara Dinunzio, repeating a phrase heard often while the interviews for this book were taking place. "The actors are wonderful. Everyone is wonderful. It's so easy to work on."

To quote all the people who raved about their *Queer as Folk* family would add dozens of pages to this book. Randy Harrison puts it best when describing the relationship between the cast and the crew. "The highlight of the whole experience for me has been the crew. They're just my best friends. They work so hard and they're such fun people. I definitely think when I'm very far away from the show, what I'll look back on most fondly was the relationships I've made and the fun times I've had on the weekends exploring Toronto. I imagine it will never happen again in my career."

SAILOR

acknowledgments

SPECIAL THANKS: To the producers, cast, and crew of *Queer as Folk* who welcomed us into their family and contributed a tremendous amount of their time and effort to create this book.

THANKS: Joel Avirom, Ron Cowen, Amy Cuthbertson, Sallie Fraenkel, Lisa Ghione, Meghan Day Healey, Matt Hilliard-Forde, Sheila Hockin, Tony Jonas, Daniel Lipman, Megan McKeever, Lauren McKenna, Alex Messina, Adam Newman, Jason Snyder, Tom Tobin.

ABOUT THE AUTHOR: Paul Ruditis has written and contributed to various books based on such notable television shows as *Buffy the Vampire Slayer, Charmed, Star Trek: Voyager, Enterprise,* and *The West Wing.* He lives in Burbank, California.

photo credits

All photos by L. Pief Weyman/Showtime except:

page viii: Article by Kristin Hohenadel and Paul Brownfield, photograph by Joss Barratt. Copyright 2003 Los Angeles Times. All rights reserved. Reprinted with permission.
page 4: Laurie Wierzbicki
page 7, top: Keith Munyan
page 7, bottom: Firooz Zahedi
page 8, top: Randall Slaven
page 8, bottom: Greg Tjepkema
page 9, top: Chia Messina
page 9, bottom: Kathy Cooley
page 16: Sean Scoffield
page 17: Mark Seliger/Showtime
page 29, top & bottom: Alex Dukay/Showtime
page 43, top: Rod Kavanagh
page 43, bottom: Adam Newman
page 45: Firooz Zahedi/Showtime
page 47: Mark Seliger/Showtime
page 56, bottom: mm lennan
page 60, bottom: Kelly McDonagh
page 69: Greg Heisler/Showtime
page 70: Sophie Giraud/Showtime
page 90, top: Karen Steyr/Showtime
page 94, bottom: Alex Dukay/Showtime
page 97: Mark Seliger/Showtime
page 111: Mark Seliger/Showtime
page 124, top: Stephen G. Lynch
page 124, center: Karen Steyr/Showtime
page 124, bottom: Stephen G. Lynch
page 125, top: Stephen G. Lynch
page 125, bottom: Patrick Antosh
page 126, top: Patrick Antosh
page 126, bottom: Stephen G. Lynch
page 127, top: Stephen G. Lynch
page 127, center & bottom: Patrick Antosh
page 128, center: Alex Dukay/Showtime
page 131: Greg Heisler/Showtime
page 153: Greg Heisler/Showtime
page 161: Alex Dukay/Showtime
page 167: Mark Seliger/Showtime
page 168: Alex Dukay/Showtime
page 176: Alex Dukay/Showtime
page 179, top row right: Stephen Lynch
page 179, second row left: Sophie Giraud/Showtime
page 179, second row right: Lisa Ghione
page 179, third row left: Sophie Giraud/Showtime
page 179, bottom row left: Sophie Giraud/Showtime
page 179, bottom row right: M. McSweeny